ENCYCLOPEDIA OF
EUROPEAN
BIRDS

ENCYCLOPEDIA OF
EUROPEAN
BIRDS

David Alderton

PaRragon

Bath · New York · Singapore · Hong Kong · Cologne · Delhi · Melbourne

First published by Parragon in 2008

Parragon
Queen Street House
4 Queen Street
Bath BA1 1HE, UK

Created and produced by

13 SOUTHGATE STREET   WINCHESTER   HAMPSHIRE   SO23 9DZ

DESIGN Sharon Cluett, Sharon Rudd, Laura Watson
EDITORIAL Jennifer Close, Jo Weeks

ISBN: 978-1-4075-2441-2

Printed in China

CONTENTS

ABOUT THIS BOOK

The way in which birds are grouped together is based on the same underlying principles that apply in other areas of the natural world. The classificatory system works through a series of ranks, which become increasingly more refined, allowing the individual birds to be recognized within this general framework.

BIRDS AND US

Attempts to evolve a classificatory system not just for birds but for all life forms began with the ancient Greeks, but the modern science of classification, called taxonomy, stems from the pioneering work of Swedish botanist and zoologist Carl Linnaeus in the 1800s. This is not a static field, however, and the scientific names given to birds have changed quite frequently in the past. A major shift in our understanding of bird groups is now starting to occur, thanks to DNA studies, and this will finally establish avian relationships from a genetic rather than an anatomical viewpoint.

DISTRIBUTION MAPS

The maps in this book give an indication of where a particular species is most likely to be seen in Europe. Migrants may occur over a wider area as they fly back and forth between their wintering and breeding grounds.

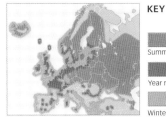

KEY

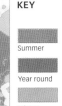

Summer

Year round

Winter

SYMBOLS IN THIS BOOK

The silhouettes give some indication of the profiles of the birds in particular Orders, although there can be marked divergences in a few cases, notably in the Piciformes, which embrace species ranging from woodpeckers to toucans. Each order consists of a number of families. Then below the family rank are the different genera. It is possible to orientate yourself within the classificatory tree by the way in which the names are written. Orders always end with -formes, as in the case of Columbiformes, while at Family level, the ending is -ae, as Columbidae. Genera are the the first rank to be written in an italicized form, as in *Columba*. The species is a binomial name, as in the case of *Columba livia*, and, again, is always written in italics. Where there is a subspecies recognized, there will be a third name, such as *Columba livia livia*, marking the lowest level in the classificatory tree.

SILHOUETTES

GAVIIFORMES   PODICIPEDIFORMES   PROCELLARIIFORMES   PELECANIFORMES   CICONIIFORMES

ANSERIFORMES   FALCONIFORMES   GALLIFORMES   GRUIFORMES   CHARADRIIFORMES

COLUMBIFORMES   PSITTACIFORMES   CUCULIFORMES   STRIGIFORMES   CAPRIMULGIFORMES

APODIFORMES   CORACIIFORMES   PICIFORMES   PASSERIFORMES

THE WORLD OF BIRDS

Birds are hard to overlook. Their ability to fly makes them conspicuous at times, and certainly even in cities, birds are much in evidence. It is easy to appreciate the beauty of birds and their aerial abilities. They can be attracted readily to gardens by providing food and nesting opportunities, helping in some cases to control pests. Even a passing acquaintance with birds reveals the underlying fascination surrounding their lifestyles. There are about 8,800 different species of birds occurring worldwide, and over 500 of these can be seen in Europe on a regular basis. Sadly, however, some of the more spectacular species have died out in former parts of their habitats, but now with greater understanding of their needs, reintroduction schemes are being carried out in various areas. In spite of the rather depressing coverage of conservation topics as far as birds are concerned, with oil spills and pollution threatening their numbers, projects of this type offer hope for the future.

CONSERVATION CHALLENGE Birds of prey such as the Golden Eagle (*Aquila chrysaetos*) have suffered particularly from human persecution, and because such birds are relatively scarce, having large territories, they are vulnerable compared with more adaptable, free-breeding species that live in large flocks.

WHAT ARE BIRDS?

Perhaps the most obvious characteristic associated with birds – an ability to fly – is actually not one of the features that separate them from other vertebrate groups. In fact, a number of birds such as penguins, kiwis, and ostriches cannot fly, while on the other hand, mammals such as bats have mastered the power of flight. A distinguishing characteristic of birds is, however, their body covering. Feathers, which help to protect the body and insulate it as well as providing an ability to fly, are only seen in birds. Another trait of birds is the way in which they reproduce: all species lay eggs with a hard calcareous ('chalk-like') shell.

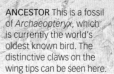

ANCESTOR This is a fossil of *Archaeopteryx*, which is currently the world's oldest known bird. The distinctive claws on the wing tips can be seen here.

BIG BEGINNINGS *Quetzalcoatlus* had a wingspan approaching 12 m (40 ft). This pterosaur is therefore the largest creature yet discovered that possessed the power of flight. It fed on small sea creatures, lacking any teeth in its narrow jaws.

THE ORIGINS OF BIRDS

Over the past decade, the origins of birds have become clearer, and many zoologists believe that they are descended from small dinosaurs, which evolved the ability to fly. They survived the mass extinction of their larger relatives that took place at the end of the Cretaceous era, some 65 million years ago, and soon became the dominant group of vertebrates possessing the power of flight. Birds rapidly diversified and spread round the world, replacing the pterosaurs, a reptilian group that had first taken to the skies about 130 million years previously.

Fossilized evidence of the early birds which would reveal the history of their development is sparse, compared with many dinosaurs. This is partly due to their much smaller size. Their bodies were more likely to be eaten by larger scavengers rather than being preserved in such a way that their remains would ultimately be fossilized. Nevertheless, a growing number of avian fossils have been unearthed over recent years, particularly in the area of present-day China, revealing more about how the group developed.

The earliest recognizable bird is still *Archaeopteryx*, whose remains were unearthed in a Bavarian slate quarry in Germany during 1861. Based on the age of the layer of rock in which the fossil was found, this bird died about 145 million years ago. *Archaeopteryx* had a similar appearance to modern birds, with recognizable feathers, and was able to fly rather than just glide from tree to tree.

It would appear that these early birds were far less agile on the wing than their descendants today. They were equipped with claws on their wing tips, which allowed them to clamber around on branches. This characteristic is still evident in one species today – the South American Hoatzin (*Opisthocomus hoatzin* – see box).

Hoatzin chicks

Like early bird ancestors, Hoatzin chicks hatch with claws on the tips of their wings. The nest is often built above water, but, thanks partly to their claws, if they fall in they can anchor onto vegetation and then climb back up to the nest site. These claws are soon shed as the chicks grow older and are able to start flying.

OSTRICH The bulk of the Ostrich (*Struthio camelus*) means that these avian giants cannot fly, relying instead on their powerful legs to outrun potential predators.

Early birds such as *Archaeopteryx* also had sharp teeth in their jaws. These gradually disappeared as the bird's skeleton lightened, enhancing its flying abilities. Seabirds hunting fish were seemingly the last group to lose their teeth, reflecting the difficulties of grasping their slippery prey. Gradually, however, the shape of their bills became modified to undertake this task efficiently.

Many of the avian families that are now in existence had already evolved around 38 million years ago. Fossils cannot show the colours of these early birds, but it is likely that seabirds were relatively dull, with black-and-white coloration predominating, while forest species were probably more brightly coloured.

EXTINCT GIANTS

The African Ostrich is the biggest bird on earth today, but there used to be other, even larger and far more ferocious species. These birds were all too large to fly, but they made up for this by their long-legged gait, which enabled them to move fast on land. The most fearsome group were the phororhacids that roamed from the southern United States down across South America and lived and hunted in flocks. They could grow to about 3 m (10 ft) tall and had powerful bills as well as sharp talons on their feet, which allowed them to overpower their quarry easily.

AVIAN MOVEMENTS

Birds are present today throughout the world, with their ability to fly having made it possible for them to reach and colonize even very remote and far-flung islands. Yet on the other hand, they can adapt, so that some species prove very localized in terms of their distribution, remaining resident in what can be a small area throughout the year.

MOBILE POPULATIONS

One of the characteristic features of European birds is that many species do not stay in a particular region throughout the year. Typically, species move from their Arctic breeding grounds to overwinter further south, where the climate is more favourable and food is easier to find at this time of year. Waders will breed on the flat, treeless plains in the far north, thanks to the presence of permafrost here, which creates ideal feeding conditions for them. During the brief Arctic summer, the sun melts the upper layer of soil, but the water cannot drain away because of the frozen soil beneath. Pools then form, and these soon team with insect life, which makes an ideal nursery environment for the young waders. Before long, they will be strong enough to fly with their parents to wintering grounds along the Norfolk coast of England for example, where winter conditions are less harsh than in the Arctic.

STAYING PUT

Some birds adapt to stay in a harsh environment. Snowy Owls (*Nyctea scandiaca*) for example have feathering on their feet to protect against the extreme cold, being forced to live largely on the ground in the Arctic region, where it is too cold for trees to grow. They moult into whiter plumage in winter, so that they can remain camouflaged to aid with catching prey where there is little cover

Migration

When heading from Europe to Africa, virtually all birds cross the Mediterranean at the shortest point, flying via the Straits of Gibraltar. Birds coming from further east will fly down across Italy or over Greece. Migration means birds face numerous hazards: shooting, for example, is widespread in parts of the Mediterranean, threatening migrating birds' numbers as they fly through this region.

SUMMER VISITORS Swallows (*Hirundo rustica*) come to Europe each year from their African wintering grounds, and rear their chicks here. Their navigational skills are such that pairs actually return to the same nest sites, assuming they survive the hazards of flying back and forth.

available. Those species likely to fall victim to predators, such as the Rock Ptarmigan (*Lagopus mutus*), also acquire white winter plumage that is shed in the spring.

SUMMER VISITORS

Some birds, such as swallows and swifts, are only summertime visitors to Europe, with their arrival being regarded as a traditional sign of spring. They come here from their African wintering grounds to breed and feast on a wide range of flying insects. In bad summers, however, the number of chicks reared will be adversely affected, and over a period of time, this can result in an overall population decline.

Virtually all birds, ranging from small passerines to large storks, share set flight paths when migrating (*see* box). These may not be the shortest, most direct route, but just like aircraft, birds avoid crossing over large expanses of sea.

VISITORS FROM FURTHER AFIELD

Migrants come to Europe not just from Africa, but also further east, from Asia. They may stay here for the

summer months, or visit during the winter, as is the case for many waterfowl in search of favourable wintering grounds. There may even be species from North America seen in Europe. These are usually gulls or other sea birds, which are not migrants as such, but occasional visitors.

Other birds may reach Europe having been effectively blown across the Atlantic, and they are less well equipped to survive for any period of time in this alien environment. The Scilly Isles, off England's southwest coast, are a common area where these so-called 'vagrants' are observed, because this is the first area where such birds can land.

GLOBAL WARMING

There are signs that global warming could be playing a part in influencing the innate desire of birds to migrate. With a series of milder winters in parts of Europe over recent years, some warblers are remaining resident here, rather than returning to their southerly wintering grounds. The risk is that if faced with a harsh winter, these birds would then be very vulnerable to starvation.

Other more sinister effects could become significant in the future. A continuing rise in the world's temperature could affect the Arctic permafrost, causing it to thaw. If the water drains away, there will be no feeding grounds for waders breeding here in the future, leading to a potentially catastrophic population crash.

COLOUR CHANGE Rock Ptarmigan (*Lagopus mutus*) in summer plumage (*below*) and transformed to blend into the winter landscape (*left*). This colour change is particularly vital in an area where there is little natural cover for the birds.

MIGRATION MOVEMENTS A flock of Golden Plovers (*Pluvialis apricaria*) seen on their wintering grounds in Kent, England. In the early spring, these plovers will once again head northwards to their breeding grounds within the Arctic Circle.

ESCAPEE A number of avian species are now found in Europe that have become established here for various reasons in the recent past. One of these is the Indian Ring-necked Parakeet (*Psittacula krameri*), the only member of the parrot family living wild in Europe.

Threats

The major threats facing birds today include:
■ Loss of habitat, including nesting sites
■ Declining food sources often linked with human activity, such as overfishing
■ Oil and other forms of environmental pollution
■ Hunting pressures
In most cases, it is a combination of these factors which brings a species to the verge of extinction.

AVIAN ENVIRONMENTS

A number of different factors influence the distribution of birds. They include the availability of food, which is perhaps the most significant consideration, but suitable breeding sites are very important, too. In addition, habitat loss and other environmental changes are very likely to have an adverse impact on the range of a species.

CHANGING ENVIRONMENTS

Birds can spread into new areas thanks to human intervention. Within Europe, there are a number of different birds that have been introduced for a variety of reasons from elsewhere, and are now thriving. During Victorian times, there was a vogue for translocating birds to new areas of the world. A number of the waterfowl with free-ranging populations in Europe today, such as the Mandarin Duck (*Aix galericulata*) from Asia or the Carolina Duck (*Aix sponsa*) from the United States, are the result of ancestors who escaped from ornamental wildfowl collections and started breeding successfully in the wild.

One of the most spectacular introductions of this type is the Indian Ring-necked Parakeet (*Psittacula krameri*). It is thought that today's flocks may be descended from aviary escapees from the 1960s or possibly earlier. There are now groups established around London and elsewhere in the United Kingdom, as well as a number of other major cities in Europe. These parakeets remain largely dependent on bird table fare to keep them sustained over the winter, however, when other food is in short supply, but the climate is no barrier to their survival. This is a species that in its native habitat roams up into the Himalayan region where winters can be bitterly cold.

A number of game birds, including the Common Pheasant (*Phasianus colchicus*), now resident in Europe owe their origins here to having been imported for shooting purposes. Again, some survived and started breeding in the wild. Today, however, the perceived risks of introducing so-called invasive species means that there is much tighter legislation in most countries relating to the release of non-native birds, so that it is unlikely that these deliberate introductions will continue in the future.

Avian species may also extend their range naturally. This is most commonly triggered by adverse conditions within their normal area of distribution, which force them to move further afield or face starvation. Movements of this type, known to ornithologists as irruptions, have been well documented in the case of a number of species such as sandgrouse (*Pterocles* species), although today they are often less common than in the past.

Just occasionally, birds may move for no evident reason into a new area, expanding their range, as in the case of the Collared Dove (*Streptopelia collaria*). It used to be a species confined largely to Asia, but then during the 1930s, these doves were recorded first in Hungary, and continued to expand their range westwards across Europe. Early sightings occurred in the United Kingdom in the 1950s, and within little more than a decade, Collared Doves had colonized most of the country. They also crossed to Ireland, being seen there for the first time in 1959. What triggered this rapid expansion of their range, however, remains a mystery.

Birds are adaptable, as can be seen by walking down virtually any city street. Pigeons will be one of the most common sights in this type of environment, but they have evolved from Rock Dove (*Columba livia*) ancestors. This particular species can still be seen along some stretches of the European coastline. From mediaeval times through until the 1700s, Rock Doves and their descendants were being bred well away from their native haunts in

FERAL PIGEONS These descendants of the Rock Dove (*Columba livia*) are widely found throughout European cities today, having adapted to living and breeding in this type of environment. They frequently scavenge on the streets rather than being regular bird-table visitors in the suburbs.

dovecotes, as a source of food. Inevitably, some strayed, and so a feral population evolved. The term 'feral' is used to describe a wild species that is domesticated and then reverts to living wild again.

City centres, with their tall buildings, are not at all dissimilar from the Rock Dove's original habitat. Pigeons can build nests successfully on window ledges, and they do not need insects or any special food for rearing their chicks as they produce a protein-rich secretion in their digestive tract, known as crop milk. It is hardly surprising that they have moved into this type of neighbourhood so successfully, especially when there are often parks in the vicinity as well, offering additional feeding possibilities.

More remarkable, perhaps, is the way in which the Peregrine Falcon (*Falco peregrinus*), the traditional predator of the Rock Dove, has followed suit, taking advantage of the relative abundance of its natural prey in cities. There are now pairs of Peregrines to be seen in various localities in city habitats, both living and nesting successfully there.

HABITAT IMPROVEMENT

Environmental studies have shown how being more aware of the breeding cycle of birds can help to increase their numbers, with just slight adjustments in habitat management bringing big results. Simply cutting a field of hay later in the year may mean that ground-nesting birds can complete their breeding cycle successfully. Improving the environment also helps. Cleaning up waterways and rivers usually enhances the bird life too, by bringing back insects and other creatures that form part of their diet.

SPORTING CHANCE? The Common or Ring-necked Pheasant (*Phasianus colchicus*) is a native of Asia, but it has been introduced to Europe as a game bird. Each year, the wild population is supplemented with others that are deliberately released. These birds therefore have a mixed ancestry.

AVIAN ANATOMY

The factor that has shaped the form of the bird's body more than any other is its ability to fly. Even in the case of today's flightless species, evidence suggests that they actually evolved from ancestors possessing the power of flight. The key element has been to lighten the body weight, enabling the bird to fly with less effort and energy. Birds have lost the teeth and jaw muscles seen in mammals in favour of a lightweight bill, and the skeleton too is lightened, with many of the bones being hollow.

BEATING WINGS The long feathers running along the back of the wing of this Bewick Swan (*Cygnus columbianus*) are the flight feathers, which provide the thrust that a bird needs to be able to become airborne.

Parts of a bird

Specific terms are used to describe the various areas of a bird's body, and assist in the identification of individual species by enabling differences in coloration or markings to be highlighted easily. These features can also help in terms of determining an individual's gender. More general descriptions may also be used, such as the underparts, which relates to the underside of the body, or the upperparts, running down over the back to the rump.

Crown
Forehead
Eye ring
Nape
Back
Throat
Wing bar
Rump
(under wings)
Breast
Upper tail
coverts
Side
Belly
Tail
Under tail coverts

ADAPTATIONS FOR FLIGHT

The muscles needed for flight require large quantities of oxygen. The lungs of birds do not expand and contract on the scale of those in mammals, but connect instead to a series of air sacs in the body, which effectively draw air through the respiratory system rather like bellows.

Even the way in which the waste products of the body's metabolism are processed reflects the bird's fundamental need to keep its weight to a minimum. Instead of having a bladder that fills with urine, birds have evolved to produce a very concentrated form of urine called uric acid. This is voided with faecal matter from the body.

The transformation of the front limbs into wings for flight has affected the bird's overall centre of gravity. As a result, the actual position of the bird's legs has effectively moved further forwards, compared with a mammal, in order to enable it to walk rather than toppling over.

The aerofoil principle that allows aeroplanes to fly mimics that of a bird's wings. The upper surface is curved, and the rate at which air passes over the top of the wing compared with the area below differs. It is this shift in air pressure, which is lower above the wing, that makes flight possible. Heavy birds such as albatrosses, swans, and pelicans cannot take off as easily as a small finch, but need to build up momentum by running over the surface of the water in order to lift off, propelling themselves with strong downward wingbeats. This calls into play powerful breast muscles on each side of the chest.

Once in flight, flapping the wings provides propulsive power. There are specialist flight feathers running along the back of each wing, whose position alters during the flight cycle. The primary flight feathers, located towards the tips, are the longest, and provide thrust. They move independently to adjust air resistance. The secondary flight feathers, closest to the body, are shorter, and help to give the bird lift in flight. With each downward thrust, the flight feathers are held together, helping the bird to climb. When the bird wants to slow down to approach a perch, it glides, ceasing to flap its wings but adjusting their position to help to reach the branch. Although birds fly instinctively, this skill needs to be mastered, and young birds sometimes misjudge a landing and slide off their intended perch. To slow down more quickly, a bird spreads its tail feathers, increasing air resistance and exerting a greater drag effect.

Once airborne, even large birds can stay there quite easily. Vultures seek out ascending columns of hot air known as thermals, which serve to keep them airborne. They rarely need to flap their wings, gliding instead in the rising column of heated air. Some birds, including albatrosses, spend most of their lives in the air, even feeding on the wing, scooping up fish from the surface of the ocean. Swifts, too, are poorly adapted to perch, let alone walk on the ground. They may find it very difficult to become airborne if grounded, due to the length and shape of their wings. Studies suggest they even sleep in flight.

SWIMMING All birds that spend large amounts of time in or on the water have webbed feet for more efficient paddling. This allows them to swim faster and with less effort. Birds that often dive and swim underwater, such as auks and guillemots, use front limbs as flippers. Propulsive power underwater is generated by their legs rather than their wings.

Flight

While the basic structure of the wing remains broadly identical, birds display a range of wing shapes, and these can give important clues as to their lifestyles. Birds such as swifts that spend much of their time in flight have angular wings and can fly with relatively little effort, often gliding as well as soaring, and flying fast on occasions, particularly when they are migrating. Other long-distance migrants such as curlews may have a similar wing structure, while the wing shape of kestrels enables them to hover, while they scan the ground below for prey. The wings of bee-eaters allow these birds to manoeuvre themselves in flight, to the extent that they can fly directly into horizontal nesting tunnels in cliff faces, as well as seizing flying insects. Pheasants, in contrast, are heavy birds, and not well adapted to flight. It takes considerable muscular effort for them to become airborne. Nevertheless, the rounded shape of their wings enables them to glide down smoothly when they spot a suitable area of cover. Vultures have long wings so they can remain airborne for long periods with minimal effort, gliding on thermals.

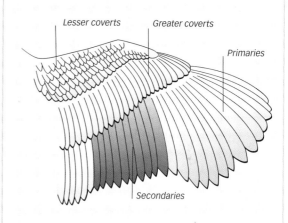

AN EXTENDED VIEW OF A BIRD'S WING, SEEN FROM ABOVE.

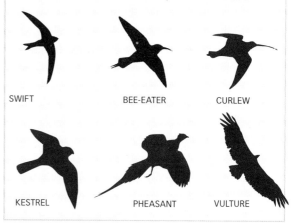

FEEDING

Birds exploit a wide range of different foods, depending partly on the species concerned, and in many cases, for those living in temperate areas, their diet varies through the year, reflecting the way in which the availability of food alters according to the season.

The shape of a bird's bill gives clear insights not just into its feeding habit, but also its lifestyle. Finches for example have short, conical bills that allow them to crack open the outer casing of a seed to reach the edible kernel inside. The crossbills (*Loxia* species) have the most specialized bills of this type, which are twisted as their name suggests, enabling them to prize out the seeds from fir cones in the coniferous forests where they live.

Birds that need to prise food out from hiding places, such as woodpeckers seeking grubs in the bark of trees, or waders probing in the sand, tend to have long, pointed bills for this reason. Birds of prey, on the other hand, have sharp, curved bills, often combined with sharp, modified claws called talons on their toes. These enable them to grasp their quarry and dismember it easily, compensating for a lack of teeth.

In contrast, species that feed largely on insects have small bills, which are often narrow in shape, as seen in swifts and warblers. Such an arrangement allows them to catch their food with relative ease.

SPECIALIZED HUNTERS Birds of prey have hooked bills, enabling them to rip their prey apart with relative ease. They also have strong feet, equipped with sharp, curved talons. This enables them to catch and carry heavy prey, such as the fish caught by this Osprey (*Pandion haliaetus*).

FIT FOR PURPOSE The bird's bill serves as a specialist tool, having evolved primarily to obtain food, but also being used for other purposes. These include preening the feathers and helping to build the nest as appropriate, reflecting the lifestyle of the individual species.

INTERNAL ANATOMY

The initial part of the bird's digestive system is quite different from that of a mammal. Food usually passes down into the crop, which acts as a storage organ, although if the bird is hungry, it will bypass here, going directly into the glandular section behind, which is called the proventriculus. From here, the food enters the gizzard, where it is broken down. The structure of the gizzard is directly influenced by the bird's diet. In the case of finches, it is a thick-walled, muscular organ, as the

GRANIVORE

RAPTOR

SPECIALIST SEED EATER

FISHING

FILTER FEEDER

NECTAR FEEDER

PROBING

INSECTIVORE

NETTING

SURFACE SKIMMING

seed needs to be ground away into small pieces. It is worn down by a combination of the muscular movements of the gizzard wall, along with the grit which the bird also eats for this purpose.

After leaving the gizzard, the nutrients in the food are then absorbed into the body through the wall of the small intestine. Birds such as grouse which feed largely on shoots and other vegetation rely on a beneficial population of micro-organisms further down the digestive tract in order to be able to digest their food. This is because they do not have the enzymes necessary to break down the cellulose in the cell walls of the vegetation. They therefore have a pair of large blind-ending sacs, called caeca, at the junction of the small and large intestines, where this breakdown of cellulose can take place.

THE SENSES

Birds rely very heavily on their sense of sight for information about the world around them. They have keen eyesight, and are able to detect movements in their vicinity that could indicate the approach of a predator, enabling them to fly off. A recent study has also confirmed that birds possess the ability to see in the ultraviolet part of the spectrum, which means that an individual which may appear black to us could resonate with colour to another member of its own species.

Keen vision can also have advantages in terms of locating prey, as in the case of vultures for example. They spend long periods airborne, effectively cruising the skies for signs of a carcass on the ground below, which will provide them with a source of food. Vultures are also one of the few groups of birds that possess a sense of smell,

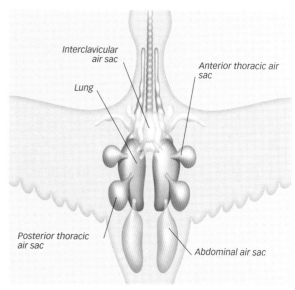

AIR SACS Birds have a different breathing system to mammals. Although they do have lungs, they also have air sacs. Very efficient gaseous uptake in the bird's body is essential, to give sufficient oxygen for the flight muscles.

Interclavicular air sac
Anterior thoracic air sac
Lung
Posterior thoracic air sac
Abdominal air sac

and this helps to draw them towards a meal as well, explaining how when one bird locates a carcass, others will then turn up in very rapid succession.

Hearing is significant in the case of some birds, typically those such as owls which hunt after dark. They are able to hear ultrasonic sound waves, which means they can detect the calls of rodents such as mice, inaudible to our ears. When pinpointing the source of a sound before launching a strike, the owl will move its head silently, remaining still so as not to give any warning of its presence.

The ears of birds are not conspicuous in most instances, except in the case of vultures where the plumage on the head is very sparse. Birds do not have external ear flaps, with the ear openings simply being apparent as holes in the skin, normally located under the feathers behind the eyes.

HEART BEAT

The activity of flying means that birds require oxygenated blood to be pumped to their flight muscles. The basic structure of a bird's heart is similar to that of a mammal, consisting of four distinct chambers. Where it differs, however, is in terms of the heart rate itself. Even when a bird is resting, its heart may be beating a thousand times a minute, and this rate will increase considerably once it starts flying.

ON DISPLAY Birds' ears are usually hidden, but one is visible as an opening behind the eye in this Egyptian Vulture (*Neophron percnopterus*), thanks to the lack of plumage on its head.

PINPOINT ACCURACY As a hunter, the Barn Owl (*Tyto alba*) depends not just on its acute hearing, aided by its rotating head, but also on its sense of sight to pinpoint the position of its prey accurately.

THE AVIAN LIFECYCLE

Most birds in Europe nest in the spring and summer, when conditions are most favourable for the survival of their eggs and offspring too. Breeding usually starts with a period of display, often being accompanied by nest-building. Cock birds tend to become more aggressive and territorial. Some birds display at communal sites called leks, and bird song is used to define territories.

MATING GAME Some birds such as the Black Grouse (*Tetrao tetrix*) have communal display grounds, with individuals mating randomly, whereas in other cases, especially waterfowl such as swans, pairs form a lifelong bond.

BREEDING AND EGG DEVELOPMENT

Hormonal changes, often linked closely with the increase in day length that marks the onset of spring, trigger the development of ova in the hen's ovary. Unlike mammals, hens only retain their right ovary. The ovum released from here passes down into the funnel-shaped infundibulum, marking the start of its journey down the oviduct. It usually takes about 30 hours from this point until the egg will be laid. Fertilization needs to occur relatively high up in the oviduct, before the ovum becomes encased in its shell, as this will otherwise form an impenetrable barrier.

Following fertilization, what is effectively the egg's yolk then moves down into the magnum, where the so-called white of the egg, or albumen, is added. After this, the egg is wrapped in shell

membranes in the part of the oviduct called the isthmus. Finally, it passes into the shell gland, where the hard, calcareous covering that forms the shell is applied.

NESTING BEHAVIOUR

Birds that nest in tree holes generally lay white eggs, whereas those that breed in more open situations produce eggs of variable coloration. This helps to conceal them against the background where they are laid. This variation in coloration is achieved by means of colour pigments from the shell gland. The shape of the egg can also vary somewhat. They tend to be relatively oval, with one end being slightly narrower. In the case of cliff-nesting sea

FIGHT FOR THE NEST
Birds become far more territorial at the start of the breeding season, and skirmishes at this stage, as shown by these Ospreys, are not uncommon. Even in the case of birds that breed communally, there are often disputes over nest sites at the outset.

birds however, their eggs are almost pear shaped. This helps to restrict the egg's mobility, making it less likely that it will be dislodged and roll off the rock.

Sea birds tend to lay in a crevice, using little if any nesting material. At the other extreme, some birds such as the Long-tailed Tit (*Aegithalos caudatus*) build ornate nests. In contrast, the female Cuckoo (*Cuculus canorus*) builds no nest, but instead parasitizes those of other species, producing eggs to mimic those already in the chosen nest.

One or both parents may be responsible for incubating the eggs, depending on the species concerned. The incubation period is variable, but for small passerines, it typically lasts between 12 and 14 days. The birds will not begin incubating until their clutch is nearly complete. This ensures that all the chicks then hatch close together, thereby improving their chances of survival.

The nesting period tends to be short, particularly for garden birds such as sparrows and tits, with their young often leaving the nest when they are just two weeks old. This often occurs before the flight feathers have unfurled fully from their protective casing in which they emerged through the skin. As a result, the young birds will not be able to fly well at this stage and many fall prey to predators such as cats, but since there may be four or more fledging, enough young birds from a nest usually survive to ensure the overall population is maintained. The adults often start building another nest nearby before their first brood are fully independent. This high

Egg shapes and sizes

Birds' eggs vary quite widely, both in terms of their size and coloration, as shown by this selection of eggs from around the world. Birds which lay in the open, on the ground or in nests usually lay speckled eggs, as this random patterning helps to disguise their presence.

ODD COLOUR (WILLOW PTARMIGAN)   ODD SHAPE (COMMON MURRE)   TINY SIZE (RUFOUS HUMMINGBIRD)   LARGE SIZE (ANDEAN CONDOR)

reproductive potential reflects the uncertain and usually relatively brief lives of such birds, which often only survive for perhaps two years in the wild.

The situation tends to be different in many birds of prey, however, as they face fewer threats to their survival, except human persecution. They generally only nest once a year, and may produce just a single chick, and their life expectancy can be measured in decades. The same applies to sea birds, which also are often long-lived.

NEWLY HATCHED FERAL PIGEON Such chicks are totally helpless at first, and entirely dependent on their parents to brood them, keeping them warm and providing their food. In due course, their eyes open and their feathers grow.

A BROOD OF YOUNG CANADA GEESE Waterfowl as a group have chicks that hatch in a more advanced state of development, able to see, feed and even swim soon after hatching, although they still have down plumage and cannot fly.

WATCHING BIRDS

Birdwatching is a particularly popular hobby, partly because it can be carried out anywhere, even while sitting in your home. Also, it does not require a large investment of any kind, although if you want to become a dedicated 'twitcher', heading off in search of rarities and vagrants, this will prove to be potentially expensive. Specialist ornithological holidays are an increasingly popular option as well.

BASIC EQUIPMENT

Many people interested in birds like to watch those in their gardens. Carefully siting a bird table or feeder will allow you to observe the birds here conveniently and comfortably from inside your home. It helps to have a pair of binoculars available, so you can see the birds in more detail and see their behaviour at closer quarters.

You can often acquire suitable binoculars from camera shops, or buy them on the Internet, but one of the advantages of obtaining your binoculars on the high street is that you will be able to try them out, and find a pair that is most suited to your needs. It is important to consider what you require, as additional features add to the cost of a pair. Should you be spending time outside birdwatching

MUTUAL BENEFIT
Bird tables and feeders provide a great opportunity to observe birds from the comfort of your armchair. A large number of species may be drawn here, particularly when the weather is bad, and providing food aids their survival.

for example, then waterproofing can be significant. Equally, anti-fogging is a useful feature to prevent the lenses misting over, which would stop you from seeing birds clearly. Another aspect to bear in mind is how far you are likely to be away from the birds, as you need to consider the focussing distance. This is normally in the region of 3–4 m (10–13 ft), but for watching waterfowl, for example, this distance may not be adequate.

Binoculars offer flexibility, and are easy to carry, but they are not the only option for birdwatching these days. Especially for home use, or if you regularly visit a birdwatching site such as an estuary, then a fieldscope is worth considering. This is rather like a telescope in design, having just a single eye-piece, and it can be mounted on a tripod. Fieldscopes are therefore ideal for observing birds over a period of time in one locality, rather than when you are on the move. It is also relatively easy to fix a digital camera to this type of unit, enabling you to take close-up images of the birds. If you want to try this type of photography, it is worth spending some time experimenting in the controlled surroundings of a garden.

LOCATION

When you venture further afield birdwatching, you may need to do some research in advance. If you are intending to visit a coastal area, check the tide times in advance on the Internet, so that there will be no risk of turning up when the sea is in, making it unlikely that you will see the

Safety tips

Going birdwatching should be a safe pursuit, but you need to take sensible precautions, bearing in mind that you are likely to be heading off into areas where there will be few if any other people around. Take a mobile phone therefore, so that you can seek help in any emergency. Always wear suitable clothing and footwear, and pack a map and compass plus adequate drinking water if you are trekking off any distance.

Be very careful in boggy grounds, and also near cliff edges: these can crumble easily and unexpectedly, so do not venture too close to the edge. When birdwatching along the coast, be sure to check tide times, because the sea usually comes in very quickly over mud flats and you could end up being trapped. If you actually venture out to sea, then it will be advisable to wear a life-jacket. Always check the weather forecast too, before setting off any distance – if only because birdwatching in heavy rain is not necessarily great fun!

birds as you had hoped. The best time to visit will be when the tide is going out, as this is the stage that the birds will start feeding as the mud flats become exposed.

Bear in mind that sometimes these areas can be treacherous to walk on, so take care and heed local advice. Do not allow yourself to become trapped in your enthusiasm by the incoming tide and always have a mobile phone with you in case of any accident so that you can summon help quickly.

The same applies in tidal estuaries, where currents can be particularly strong. Try to stay on dry land in such cases, rather than wading across the area. It is also very important not to disturb the birds that you are trying to watch. In most birdwatching areas, there are hides available, which allow you to have a good view of the birds in relative comfort. Even so, facilities are often very limited, so do not forget to take a drink with you, and something to eat if you intend to be out for long.

When you are going out birdwatching, it is also important to dress carefully. In cold weather, be sure that you will be warm enough, especially as you will sitting around quietly for most of the time, rather than being able to move and keep warm. Choose clothing which helps you to blend in with the background as far as possible, with a green camouflage jacket being useful in woodland. Always move quietly, pausing frequently to listen for sounds such as the drumming notes of a woodpecker banging on the trunk of a tree, because this can be very significant in helping you to locate where birds are within the area at that moment.

NATURE RESERVES There are a number of reserves in most countries today where it is possible to observe flocks of migrant and resident birds in special buildings known as hides. This allows the birds to be watched in relative comfort without disturbing them.

NOVELTY ACT On occasion, a bird may be sighted well away from its usual haunts, and once word of its presence spreads, many birdwatchers, often called 'twitchers', will descend on the area in the hope of making a sighting of this so-called vagrant.

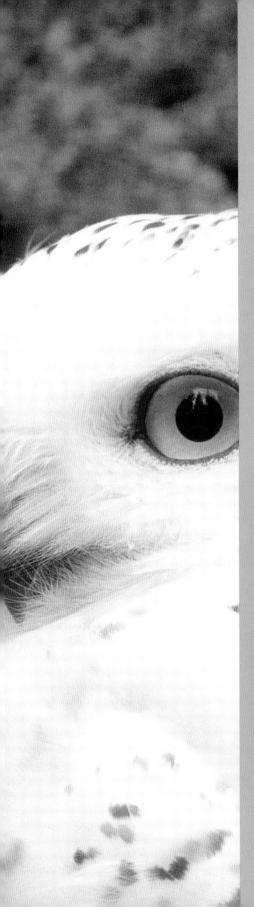

GALLERY OF BIRDS

The following pages reflect the wide diversity of birds found within Europe. Some are just summertime visitors, heading back to warmer climes in Africa or elsewhere after the end of the breeding season, whereas others are resident in parts of the continent throughout the year. Certain birds undertake seasonal movements across the region itself, notably those breeding in the far north. A few species have, however, adapted to thrive even under the most severe climatic conditions, remaining within the Arctic Circle throughout the year. Much depends on their diet – even these hardy birds may be forced to move elsewhere if food is in short supply. There are also birds that turn up unexpectedly, sometimes blown across the Atlantic, and other American species that regularly but unpredictably visit Europe in small numbers. Distributions only provide a general guide to where birds may be seen at any stage. Migratory birds are likely to be observed well away from their usual haunts when flying to and from their breeding grounds, depending on their flight paths.

HABITAT ADAPTATION Snowy Owls (*Nyctea scandiaca*) are birds that occur in the far north of Europe. They are well protected against the bitter cold by their plumage, which extends down over their legs and toes.

GAVIIFORMES

Divers

A primitive Order of water birds comprising a single family of only five species. They are uncomfortable on land but supremely adapted for their aquatic environment, with buoyant, insulating plumage, legs set far back on the body, and elliptical tarsi for greater streamlining. They can be recognized by their attitude of swimming low in the water with their back almost submerged, diving and reappearing in an entirely different place. Their calls, wild and eerie, are evocative of their remote breeding haunts in the freshwater lagoons of the far north, although all species tend to winter at sea.

White-billed Diver

FAMILY Gaviidae

SPECIES *Gavia adamsii*

LENGTH 75–100 cm (29½–39½ in)/wingspan 150 cm (59 in)

HABITAT Lakes/sea

CLUTCH SIZE 1–3

DISTRIBUTION Occurs in eastern high Arctic, northern Eurasia, Alaska, and northwest Canada to North Pacific down to Japan.

A RARE VAGRANT from the High Arctic, this hefty diver resembles the Great Northern, but can be distinguished by its angled lower mandible, giving the bill an upturned appearance, and by its slightly swollen forehead. In all other respects it is very similar and is easily confused when seen at a distance at sea.

PLUMAGE Richly patterned during the breeding season, all divers moult into drab brownish grey plumage during the winter months. They do not breed in Europe

Black-throated Diver

FAMILY Gaviidae

SPECIES *Gavia arctica*

LENGTH 58–73 cm (23–28¾ in)/wingspan 120 cm (47¼ in)

HABITAT Lakes/open sea

CLUTCH SIZE 1–3

DISTRIBUTION Two races are currently recognized, breeding in northern Eurasia, northeast Siberia, and western Alaska.

AMONGST THE MOST visually stunning of all European water birds with its boldly chequered upperparts, this diver resembles a smaller version of the Great Northern. Slightly larger and bulkier than the Red-throated Diver, it is recognizable in all plumages by its stouter, more dagger-like bill. Its song is a desolate and mournful wailing.

PICTURE PERFECT This handsome bird is best seen when its harlequin pattern of black, white, and grey is reflected in the still water of its favourite breeding haunts.

Great Northern Diver

FAMILY Gaviidae

SPECIES *Gavia immer*

LENGTH 68–91 cm (27–36 in)/ wingspan 135 cm (53 in)

HABITAT Lakes/coasts/ open sea

CLUTCH SIZE 1–3

DISTRIBUTION Breeds in Iceland, overwintering here and also in other coastal areas of Europe including Scandinavia, around the British Isles, and down to the Iberian Peninsula.

THE GREAT NORTHERN DIVER is best known for its wailing, bubbling call that epitomizes the atmosphere and landscape of the North American lakes. It is usually encountered in Europe in its subtle grey-and-white winter dress when it can pose identification challenges with the similar White-billed Diver.

BLENDING IN The boldly chequered pattern of this remarkable bird renders it surprisingly well camouflaged in its aquatic habitat.

Red-throated Diver

FAMILY Gaviidae

SPECIES *Gavia stellata*

LENGTH 53–69 cm (21–27 in)/ wingspan 110 cm (43¼ in)

HABITAT Lakes/open sea

CLUTCH SIZE 1–3

DISTRIBUTION Summer visitor to Iceland, Scotland, Scandinavia, and northeast Europe. Winters in coastal areas of Europe, the Mediterranean, and further east.

THIS IS MORE subtly plumaged than the other diver species, with its pale grey head, deep red throat patch, and narrowly striped crown and nape. In its drab winter plumage it can be distinguished by the more slender build and narrow, slightly upturned bill. Its song is a mournful wailing, and its flight call is a goose-like cackling.

IDENTIFICATION Both sexes wear the dark red throat patch, which can appear black from a distance. Pairs engage in elaborate courtship 'dances' together.

PODICIPEDIFORMES   Grebes

This Order contains a single family represented globally throughout the northern and southern hemisphere by 22 species divided into six genera. Superficially similar to divers, grebes share their aquatic lifestyle but bear slight structural differences: for example, in having lobed rather than webbed feet. Pairs engage in highly ritualized and very beautiful courtship 'dances', in which their elaborate head plumes or markings are shown off to full effect. The nest is an island of floating vegetation and the chicks are brooded on the backs of their parents and will frequently hitch a ride in this way when the adults are swimming.

Little Grebe

FAMILY Podicipedidae
SPECIES *Tachybaptus ruficollis*
LENGTH 25–29 cm (10–11½ in)/ wingspan 40–44 cm (15¾–17¼ in)
HABITAT Rivers/ponds
CLUTCH SIZE 4–6

DISTRIBUTION Eight races are recognized ranging throughout the Old World from Europe, Asia, and Africa to Indonesia and New Guinea.

THE SMALLEST European grebe, this species has a dumpy, tailless appearance accentuated by its habit of 'fluffing up' its rear end. Close examination in summer plumage reveals rich burgundy-chestnut cheeks and throat. The pale yellow gape patch makes a distinctive white spot on an otherwise dark head. Its habits are more skulking than other grebes.

SAFE SEAT The Little Grebe's newly hatched chick nestles safely on the back of its parent who will catch tiny prey items and feed it until it can catch its own.

Slavonian Grebe

FAMILY Podicipedidae
SPECIES *Podiceps auritus*
LENGTH 31–38 cm (12–15 in)/ wingspan 60–65 cm (23½–25½ in)
HABITAT Lakes/ponds/coasts
CLUTCH SIZE 4

DISTRIBUTION Two races occur spanning western Europe, Asia, Iceland, Canada, and northern North America.

KNOWN IN the United States as the Horned Grebe, the bright orange raised head plumes of breeding birds earns this species that appropriate name. It may be easily mistaken for the similar Black-necked Grebe (*see* p 30), especially in the drab winter plumage, but has a flatter-headed, less alert appearance. These birds winter on estuaries and sheltered coastlines.

WARY Slavonian Grebes always nest close to the edge of a pool, being ready to slip into the water at the first sign of danger.

Great Crested Grebe

FAMILY Podicipedidae

SPECIES *Podiceps cristatus*

LENGTH 46–51 cm (18–20 in)/ wingspan 85–89 cm (33½–35 in)

HABITAT Lakes/sea bays

CLUTCH SIZE 4

DISTRIBUTION Three races range through the Old World from Europe, Asia, and Africa south to Australia and New Zealand.

THIS IS A DISTINCTIVE and elegant bird in the breeding season, especially when the characteristic head plumes are raised in intricate pair-bonding displays. These exotic-looking plumes were also very fashionable adornments for 19th-century ladies' hats, and the species was hunted almost to extinction as a result. Opposition from largely female pressure groups led to the establishment of the Royal Society for the Protection of Birds in the United Kingdom. Legal protection, and an increase in suitable breeding habitats through the creation of gravel pits, has allowed this species to increase its range and numbers. Although primarily a freshwater bird of large rivers, lakes, and gravel pits, Great Crested Grebes are frequently seen on shallow coastal waters during the winter diving for fish alongside more marine species. Large nests of aquatic vegetation are built close to the water, sometimes on partially submerged tree trunks.

SHARED PARENTING A pair of tiny Great Crested Grebe chicks eagerly await food; one parent takes them for a ride around their territory while the other seeks small fish and invertebrates.

Red-necked Grebe

FAMILY Podicipedidae
SPECIES *Podiceps grisegena*
LENGTH 40–50cm (15¾–19¾ in)
/wingspan 81 cm (32 in)
HABITAT Lakes/coasts
CLUTCH SIZE 4–5

DISTRIBUTION Two races occur, spanning northern Europe, Asia, and North America.

SMALLER THAN THE Great Crested (*see* p 29), this grebe has a shorter-necked and more compact appearance. In breeding plumage, the white face patch and yellow base of its bill, contrasting with the deep chestnut neck, are conspicuous. It is more secretive, but also more vocal than its larger relative.

NESTING A floating nest of tangled waterweeds provides a safe site for the Red-necked Grebe to incubate its eggs.

Black-necked Grebe

FAMILY Podicipedidae
SPECIES *Podiceps nigricollis*
LENGTH 28–34cm (11–13½ in)/
wingspan 58 cm (23 in)
HABITAT Lakes/sea bays
CLUTCH SIZE 3–4

DISTRIBUTION Three races occur, spanning Europe to central Asia, Africa, and Canada and the United States.

THIS SPECIES CLOSELY resembles the Slavonian Grebe (*see* p 28) in both summer and winter plumages, but holds the neck more upright and is shorter bodied, with the rear end more 'fluffed up'. The forehead is much steeper and the lower mandible sharply angled, giving the bill an upturned appearance. These grebes often nest in small colonies at the margins of lakes, but they need access to deep, open water.

APPEARANCE In common with other grebes, the sexes are identical and both parents help with incubation and care of the young.

Pied-billed Grebe

FAMILY Podicipedidae

SPECIES *Podilymbus podiceps*

LENGTH 31–38 cm (12–15 in)/ wingspan 58–62 cm (23–24½ in)

HABITAT Pools/open water

CLUTCH SIZE 4–7

DISTRIBUTION Three races, spanning the New World from Canada, south to Argentina. Most often seen in Europe as a winter vagrant.

THE PIED-BILLED GREBE IS an occasional rare vagrant from North America. Distinguishing features are the dumpy, short-bodied appearance reminiscent of the Little Grebe (*see* p 28) though somewhat larger, and the short, pale, thick bill. As the name suggests, this is conspicuously marked with a central black band in summer. This species does not breed in Europe.

HARD TO IDENTIFY In winter plumage, the Pied-billed Grebe loses all distinctive colourings; it is at this time of year that it is more likely to turn up as a vagrant species in Europe.

PROCELLARIIFORMES

Petrels and shearwaters

The shearwaters and petrels are long-winged seabirds noted for their tube-noses; their nostrils form two short tubes on top of the bill. They also have a strong, musky smell that is very apparent around their nesting colonies. Superbly well adapted to life at sea, they come to land only to breed, usually favouring wild and remote stretches of coastline and rocky islands. The long wings aid their gliding flight and they spend many hours skimming over the waves in search of food. Most of them are remarkably long-lived birds, with some, like the Northern Fulmar, attaining ages of over 50 years.

Northern Fulmar

FAMILY Procellariidae
SPECIES *Fulmarus glacialis*
LENGTH 47 cm (18½ in)/
wingspan 102–112 cm (40–44 in)
HABITAT Coasts/open sea
CLUTCH SIZE 1

DISTRIBUTION Fairly common breeding species around rocky coasts of northwestern Europe, dispersing in winter to open seas, often following fishing fleets and mingling with other seabirds.

THE NORTHERN FULMAR resembles a small gull, but flies on stiffly held wings and glides frequently. The wings and back are mostly pale grey and the head and remainder of the body pure white. The black eye has a dark smudge behind it making it appear very large. Smelly oil is spat at intruders to its nest site.

MARINE SPECIALIZATIONS Good eyesight enables the Northern Fulmar to spot its food as it glides over the sea on outstretched wings, and the hooked bill is used to pluck food from the surface.

Cory's Shearwater

FAMILY Procellariidae
SPECIES *Calonectris diomedea*
LENGTH 46 cm (18 in)/ wingspan 100–125 cm (39–49 in)
HABITAT Islands
CLUTCH SIZE 1

DISTRIBUTION Breeds colonially on secluded rocky islands and cliffs in Mediterranean and east Atlantic, travelling to the south Atlantic to spend the winter, but occasionally wandering elsewhere.

THIS IS A LARGE shearwater with mainly brown plumage above, a slightly paler head, and white underparts. At close range, the yellow bill may be visible. This species is usually seen in soaring flight far out to sea. Many harsh wailing and croaking calls are made at the breeding colonies and during feeding frenzies.

DIVING Cory's Shearwaters splash-dive for small fish near the surface, attracted to the scene by the feeding activities of other birds.

European Storm-petrel

FAMILY Hydrobatidae
SPECIES *Hydrobates pelagicus*
LENGTH 15 cm (6 in)/ wingspan 36–39 cm (14¼–15½ in)
HABITAT Open sea/islands
CLUTCH SIZE 1

DISTRIBUTION Breeds in colonies on rocky islands around coasts of western Europe and Mediterranean, dispersing over wide area of sea for rest of year.

THE SMALLEST PETREL resembles a House Martin when seen in flight; black plumage with a white rump, and a fluttering flight pattern on long wings are unlike other seabirds. The feet sometimes 'patter' over the water, and at other times are held up as the bird glides like a shearwater. At their nesting colonies, they produce a quiet purring sound.

NESTING Storm-petrels are burrow nesters on rocky islands and return to the same site year after year. A musky smell can be detected near occupied burrows.

Little Shearwater

FAMILY Procellariidae
SPECIES *Puffinus assimilis*
LENGTH 27 cm (10½ in)/
wingspan 60–65 cm (23½–25½ in)
HABITAT Islands
CLUTCH SIZE 1

DISTRIBUTION Breeds on rocky islands in the Atlantic, including Canaries and Azores, and is rarely seen north of the breeding grounds, wandering mainly south in winter.

THE SMALLEST OF the shearwaters is very similar to the much commoner and larger Manx Shearwater, but is best identified at sea by its more fluttering flight lower over the water on more rounded wings. At very close range, the blue feet and shorter bill may be visible; the face also looks whiter due to the smaller black crown. In strong gales, a hovering flight is sometimes adopted, hanging with dangling feet, pecking at food on the water surface. At the nesting colonies on rocky islands, they will only come ashore on dark moonless nights to avoid predators; high-pitched cackling calls communicate with partners in nesting burrows.

VARIATIONS The Little Shearwater's black cap varies in size depending on the origin of the bird, with some having very white faces, and others from the Cape Verde islands having much more black.

Great Shearwater

FAMILY Procellariidae
SPECIES *Puffinus gravis*
LENGTH 46 cm (18 in)/
wingspan 100–115 cm (39–45 in)
HABITAT Islands/open sea
CLUTCH SIZE 1

DISTRIBUTION Breeds on islands in the south Atlantic, but migrates north during the European summer to the east coast of North America.

AT A DISTANCE, the dark cap is the most obvious feature of this large shearwater, and if seen in a mixed flock with other shearwaters, its size, brown upperparts, and narrow white rump patch are also useful identification features. It closely resembles Cory's Shearwater, but the cap and darker bill separate them. Fishing boats are an attraction and if a flock gathers near one, loud clamouring calls can be heard as birds squabble over food. The typical shearwater gliding flight is interspersed with high soaring.

PLUMAGE The white throat and neck of the Great Shearwater help to give it the strikingly 'capped' appearance typical of this species.

Sooty Shearwater

FAMILY Procellariidae

SPECIES *Puffinus griseus*

LENGTH 41 cm (16 in)/ wingspan 94–109 cm (37–43 in)

HABITAT Open sea

CLUTCH SIZE 1

DISTRIBUTION A long-distance migrant from the southern seas, seen off the coast of western Europe from August to October.

THIS IS A MEDIUM-SIZED shearwater with mostly dark plumage. The upperparts are very dark brown, looking black at long range, but the long narrow wings are silvery on the underside. When battling against very strong winds, the wings are swept back giving a skua-like profile. There may be confusion with the Mediterranean Shearwater, which is also dark, but the Sooty is much larger and darker. Usually seen in flocks in late summer, off western European coasts, very large gatherings can sometimes be found near fishing fleets off the continental shelf where there are concentrations of bait fish. Autumn storms in the Atlantic sometimes drive them close to the shore.

FEEDING FLOCK A large flock of Sooty Shearwaters home in on a shoal of bait fish, dipping over the water to catch small fish at the surface.

Manx Shearwater

FAMILY Procellariidae

SPECIES *Puffinus puffinus*

LENGTH 35 cm (14 in)/ wingspan 76–89 cm (30–35 in)

HABITAT Islands/open sea

CLUTCH SIZE 1

DISTRIBUTION Breeds on cliffs and islands in north Atlantic with bulk of population in Britain and Ireland. Wanders far into Atlantic in winter.

TAKING OFF A Manx Shearwater runs across the surface before taking off to start its typical gliding flight on outstretched wings.

THIS MEDIUM-SIZED, long-winged shearwater appears uniformly black above and white below. At close range, the black bill and pink legs can be detected. When seen at sea, the shearwaters change from black to white as they perform their typical shearwater flight, just clipping the surface from time to time with a wing tip. Occasionally they will make a more fluttering flight to change direction or catch their food. Nesting colonies often support many thousands of birds, which visit on very dark nights making hoarse, four-note calls while circling in the darkness. A single chick is raised in a burrow, and then abandoned, being left to find its own way to sea.

Mediterranean Shearwater

FAMILY Procellariidae

SPECIES *Puffinus yelkouan*

LENGTH 34–39 cm (13–15½ in)/ wingspan 80–89 cm (31½–35 in)

HABITAT Islands

CLUTCH SIZE 1

DISTRIBUTION Nests colonially on isolated cliffs and islands in Mediterranean and overwinters at sea in Mediterranean, sometimes wandering into the Atlantic.

THIS BIRD IS very similar to the slightly smaller Manx Shearwater, and difficult to separate in some lights, but the plumage is browner above, rather than black, and the underparts are a dirty white; those from the western Mediterranean are darkest below. At certain angles, the toes project a short way beyond the tail.

WANDERER The Mediterranean Shearwater spends most of its life in the Mediterranean, but occasionally travels further afield.

Wilson's Storm-petrel

FAMILY Hydrobatidae

SPECIES *Oceanites oceanicus*

LENGTH 18 cm (7 in)/wingspan 40–42 cm (15¾–16½ in)

HABITAT Islands/open sea

CLUTCH SIZE 1

DISTRIBUTION A very scarce summer visitor to deep waters off southwest Britain and Biscay from the Antarctic, rarely seen close to the shore.

THIS SMALL, square-tailed petrel has a white rump and toes projecting beyond the tail in flight. When observed pattering over the water, it is long-legged by comparison with other small petrels. If seen with the more common European Storm-petrel (*see* p 33), it looks longer winged and in good light, short pale wing panels may be detected. It is usually only seen from ships sailing over very deep water in late summer.

SCARCE The very rare Wilson's Storm-petrel is infrequently seen close to land in the northern hemisphere unless driven ashore by storms.

Madeiran Storm-petrel

FAMILY Hydrobatidae

SPECIES *Oceanodroma castro*

LENGTH 19 cm (7½ in)/ wingspan 45 cm (17¾ in)

HABITAT Islands/open sea

CLUTCH SIZE 1

DISTRIBUTION Breeds colonially on rocky Atlantic islands off Portugal, including Madeira and Azores, and feeds far out to sea, rarely coming near land in winter.

THIS BIRD IS A TYPICAL small storm-petrel and a very difficult one to separate from the other similar species unless seen really well, when the slightly larger white rump patch and heavier bill may be more obvious. The tail may appear square-ended or very slightly notched, and the flight pattern is less fluttery than the other petrels. The Madeiran Storm-petrel is a very elusive bird, and difficult to see as it feeds far out to sea and does not follow ships. At the nesting colonies, visited in summer and late autumn, quiet purring calls and a squeaky contact note may be heard and the typical musky odour will be detected.

HOUSE HUNTING A Madeiran Storm-petrel investigates a possible nesting site in a rock crevice during a very rare visit to land on a remote Atlantic island.

Leach's Storm-petrel

FAMILY Hydrobatidae

SPECIES *Oceanodroma leucorhoa*

LENGTH 20 cm (8 in)/wingspan 45–48 cm (17¾–19 in)

HABITAT Islands/open sea

CLUTCH SIZE 1

DISTRIBUTION Breeds on north Atlantic Islands, sometimes in very large colonies, dispersing over vast area of ocean in winter.

LEACH'S STORM-PETREL is best identified at sea by its forked tail. If seen with the more common European Storm-petrel (*see* p 33), Leach's appears larger and longer winged, and the pale wing panels are more obvious, contrasting with the browner plumage. The flight pattern is quite strong: the wings are held at a sharp angle and the bird flies on a zig-zag course without pattering on the water. It is also very unlikely to follow ships. Mainly seen at sea, birds are occasionally storm-wrecked near the coast. At the remote island breeding colonies, strange chuckling calls are heard as birds reach their burrows.

IDENTIFICATION Pale wing panels and a forked tail, and powerful flight are key features for identifying Leach's Storm-petrel.

PELECANIFORMES

Gannets, cormorants, and pelicans

This group of large water birds, all fish-eaters, are extremely well adapted to life in open water, but all tied to land for nesting. Many of them are long-lived, tough, and resilient birds, able to withstand harsh conditions at sea and make long migrations. They often nest colonially, sometimes in staggeringly high numbers. Gannets are open ocean birds, wandering on vast migrations every year, and only coming near land in the breeding season. Cormorants and shags are more likely to be seen close to the shore, and they generally fish in shallow water. Pelicans are usually found in warmer regions and often fish in rivers and lakes.

Northern Gannet

FAMILY Sulidae
SPECIES *Morus bassanus*
LENGTH 87–100 cm (33–39½ in)/ wingspan 165–180 cm (65–71 in)
HABITAT Open sea/islands
CLUTCH SIZE 1

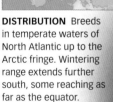

THIS IS A large seabird with dazzling white plumage and contrasting black primary feathers. Close inspection reveals the subtle yellow head and toes striped with blue-green. Immatures are dark, speckled with white. They can be identified in flight by their long, pointed bill and tail. Breeding colonies reverberate with their hoarse croaking calls.

DISTRIBUTION Breeds in temperate waters of North Atlantic up to the Arctic fringe. Wintering range extends further south, some reaching as far as the equator.

CLOSE PAIRS Each nest is a carefully measured distance from aggressive neighbours. Returning partners are greeted by elaborate posturing.

European Shag

FAMILY Phalacrocoracidae
SPECIES *Phalacrocorax aristotelis*
LENGTH 65–80 cm (25½–31½ in)/ wingspan 90–105 cm (35½–41¼ in)
HABITAT Sea/inland waters/ rocky coasts
CLUTCH SIZE 1–6

THE EUROPEAN SHAG is smaller than the Cormorant, without white patches, and with a distinctly rounded forehead accentuated by the crest worn by breeding adults. It shares its relative's glossy plumage, upright posture, and habit of holding its wings outstretched. It breeds on or at the base of sea cliffs and stacks, often among boulders.

DISTRIBUTION Occurs from Iceland and northern Scandinavia south to Iberian Peninsula, and central Mediterranean east to Black Sea.

HANDSOME This is a beautiful bird when examined at close quarters, with its glossy green head and neck, vivid yellow gape, and blue-green eye.

Common Cormorant

FAMILY Phalacrocoracidae

SPECIES *Phalacrocorax carbo*

LENGTH 80–100 cm (31½–39½ in)
/wingspan 130–160 cm (51–63 in)

HABITAT Sea/inland waters

CLUTCH SIZE 3–4

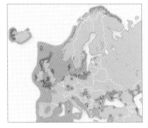

DISTRIBUTION Occurs from central and south Europe east to India and China.

THIS IS A familiar bird of open water, both coastal and inland lakes and reservoirs where it is often very tolerant of human activity. The superficially black plumage bears a green-purple gloss visible at close quarters. Breeding adults can be distinguished by the yellow gape and white throat and flank patches. It perches upright, often with wings spread.

NESTING BEHAVIOUR At coastal sites, Cormorants prefer flatter ground on inshore islands, cliff-tops, and stacks.

Pygmy Cormorant

FAMILY Phalacrocoracidae

SPECIES *Phalacrocorax pygmaeus*

LENGTH 45–55 cm (17¾–21½ in)/wingspan 80–90 cm (31½–36 in)

HABITAT Freshwater rivers and lakes/reedbeds

CLUTCH SIZE 4–6

DISTRIBUTION Occurs discontinuously from south-eastern Europe and Turkey to the region of the Aral Sea.

THE PYGMY CORMORANT is small and compact, but compared with the larger species its tail looks longer and its head looks smaller, and in good light the dark chocolate-brown head contrasts with the more glossy black plumage that is all flecked with white in the breeding season. In winter, adults have a very pale throat. Large groups often swim and hunt together and then perch on waterside trees.

SUNBATHING A Pygmy Cormorant spreads its wings after a fishing expedition, not as was once thought, to dry them, but to raise its body temperature and speed up digestion.

FLOCK OF WHITE PELICANS White Pelicans (*see* p 44) spend the colder winter months on large shallow lakes in northeast Africa, migrating overland in large flocks. They congregate in the shallows at dusk to roost for the night.

Dalmatian Pelican

FAMILY Pelicanidae

SPECIES *Pelecanus crispus*

LENGTH 160–180 cm (63–70 in)/
wingspan 310–345 cm (122–136 in)

HABITAT Rivers/lakes/deltas/
estuaries

CLUTCH SIZE 2–3

DISTRIBUTION Breeds from Yugoslavia to China. Winters from Greece to China, typically in the Balkans and in the southern Caspian Sea.

THE DALMATIAN PELICAN is easily confused with the White Pelican with which it is sometimes found, but is slightly larger with a greyish tinge to the plumage, grey rather than yellow legs and a throat pouch of deep orange. It lacks the conspicuous black-and-white underwing pattern of the White Pelican in flight.

DISTINCTIVE The Dalmatian Pelican's crown feathers are raised in all plumages but form a distinct curly crest in breeding adults.

White Pelican

FAMILY Pelicanidae

SPECIES *Pelecanus onocrotalus*

LENGTH 140–175 cm (55–69 in)/
wingspan 270–360 cm (106–142 in)

HABITAT Lakes/deltas/lagoons/
marshland

CLUTCH SIZE 1–3

DISTRIBUTION Breeds from eastern Europe to western Mongolia.

THE WHITE PELICAN is a bulky bird, the size of a swan. The white plumage is often suffused with a pinkish-orange tinge. Juveniles are grey-brown. In flight, the black flight feathers of the wings are conspicuous and flocks circling in thermals can resemble White Storks (*see* p 50). They nest colonially on islands or in reedbeds in shallow lakes and river deltas.

SPECIALIZED FEEDER Pelicans feed by scooping up fish in the skin beneath bill, known as the gular sac, before ejecting the water and swallowing the fish.

CICONIIFORMES

Herons, storks, and ibises

A group of medium–sized, and some very large, wading birds, with pointed toes rather than webbed feet. Most have very long legs and long necks to enable them to wade in water and stab at their prey. Bitterns, herons, and egrets are elegant, streamlined birds that retract their necks in flight. Storks are larger and hold their necks out in flight, and are also capable of soaring to great height to aid long-distance migration. Ibises have down-curved bills, ideal for probing into waterweeds and soft mud, and spoonbills have strange flattened bill tips that sift through mud for food.

Eurasian Bittern

FAMILY Ardeidae

SPECIES *Botaurus stellaris*

LENGTH 65–80 cm (26–31½ in)/ wingspan 100 –130 cm (39–51 in)

HABITAT Marshland/reedbeds

CLUTCH SIZE 4–6

DISTRIBUTION Occurs across Palearctic and oriental regions.

MORE OFTEN HEARD than seen, this cryptically camouflaged and secretive bird is best known for its 'booming' call, one of the most remarkable of all bird vocalizations, which can be heard at distances of up to 5 km (3 miles). Bitterns adopt a 'camouflage posture' when disturbed, remaining motionless with bill pointing skywards, virtually disappearing against the vegetation.

APPEARANCE Bitterns are shorter-necked and more squat than the herons. At close range, the Bittern's plumage is a varied pattern of rich chestnut, black, and cream.

Little Bittern

FAMILY Ardeidae

SPECIES *Ixobrychus minutus*

LENGTH 30–36 cm (12–14 in)/ wingspan 49–58 cm (19¼–23 in)

HABITAT Freshwater swamps/ marshland

CLUTCH SIZE 5–6

DISTRIBUTION West, central, and southern Europe and North Africa eastwards to western Siberia and to northeast India.

A SECRETIVE summer visitor from Africa to reed beds and overgrown ditches across most of Britain, the Little Bittern is the smallest of the herons, spending most of its time concealed in dense cover. Strange, nocturnal croaking calls, repeated endlessly through the night, may be the only clue to its presence. Creamy-white wing patches show clearly in flight.

RARE SIGHT The Little Bittern sometimes emerges from the reedbeds to feed at the margins, when it can be quite fearless.

Great White Egret

FAMILY Ardeidae

SPECIES *Egretta alba*

LENGTH 85–104 cm (33½–41 in)/
wingspan 145–170 cm (57–67 in)

HABITAT Inland and coastal
wetland/farmland

CLUTCH SIZE 3–5

DISTRIBUTION Occurs across
western and central Europe to
central Asia, especially in the
vicinity of the Black and Caspian
seas. Overwinters in the
Mediterranean and further
south in Africa.

THE GREAT WHITE EGRET is
unmistakeable with its gleaming white
plumage and large dagger-like yellow bill;
approaching the size of a Grey Heron (*see*
p 48), it stands out conspicuously when
wading in the shallows of a lake. It is much
larger than the more common Little Egret
and flies on slower, more powerful
wingbeats. Long, dark legs and feet trail
behind the body in flight, but the neck is
held hunched up. The bill becomes much
darker in the breeding season, and the
long 'aigrettes' or white plumes develop,
but there are no colour changes to the
plumage as in the Cattle Egret. Normally
silent, dry croaking sounds are made at
the breeding colonies.

FEEDING GROUNDS Great White Egrets often gather in
shallow water to hunt for frogs, fish, and invertebrates,
but they are equally at home in drier marshes.

Cattle Egret

FAMILY Ardeidae

SPECIES *Bubulcus ibis*

LENGTH 48–53 cm (19–21 in)/ wingspan 90–96 cm (35½–38 in)

HABITAT Grassland

CLUTCH SIZE 4–5

DISTRIBUTION Resident in southwest Iberia, coastal Mediterranean regions, and north Africa, with some dispersal in winter.

THE CATTLE EGRET often adopts a rather hunched posture with its neck retracted as it waits for a beetle or small lizard to move; it then pounces with great agility to seize its prey. Its normal habit is to follow grazing animals and wait for them to drive food out of the vegetation. Cattle Egrets nest colonially in trees, nearly always by water, but spend most of their time foraging in drier habitats. They will follow grazing animals into marshy areas, however. Gleaming white plumage becomes orange-tinged in places in the breeding season and the yellow bill also develops a darker tone. Normally silent, harsh croaking calls are sometimes uttered at the breeding colonies.

SYMBIOTIC RELATIONSHIP A Cattle Egret will wait for a cow to disturb invertebrates from the long grass, following closely as it grazes.

Little Egret

FAMILY Ardeidae

SPECIES *Egretta garzetta*

LENGTH 55–65 cm (21½–25½ in)/ wingspan 88–95 cm (34½–37½ in)

HABITAT Open wetland

CLUTCH SIZE 3–6

DISTRIBUTION Palearctic distribution, from France, Spain, and northwest Africa east to Korea and Japan

NOW AN INCREASINGLY familiar sight in western Europe, the elegant Little Egret frequents coastal marshes and lowland lakes over a wide area, sometimes occurring in large numbers in good feeding areas. Many birds migrate south in winter to southern Spain and North Africa, but the coastline of Britain also supports a large population. Little Egrets have bright yellow feet and can be observed wading in shallow water, agitating the mud with their feet to disturb small fish and shrimps. They nest in trees in noisy and rather smelly colonies.

DISTINCTIVE A slender black bill, long black legs, and yellow feet are key features for identifying the Little Egret.

Grey Heron

FAMILY Ardeidae
SPECIES *Ardea cinerea*
LENGTH 90–98 cm (35½–38½ in)
/wingspan 155–175 cm (61–69 in)
HABITAT Shallow water
CLUTCH SIZE 3–5

DISTRIBUTION Resident in the British Isles and parts of western Europe, north to southern Scandinavia. Summer visitor further east and north, overwintering in the Mediterranean region.

STANDING PATIENTLY at the water's edge, completely immobile, the Grey Heron shows remarkable skill in hunting fish; one stab from the powerful bill is usually enough to secure its prey, which could be a large eel or flatfish. Grey Herons have also been observed to catch water birds, small mammals, and frogs, and will sometimes move slowly through shallow water pushing their long feet in front of them in order to drive prey out into the open. At rest, they often stand on one leg with the neck hunched up, and they also fly with the neck retracted, unlike cranes. Usually solitary and quite territorial, Grey Herons occasionally nest in loose colonies high up in large trees.

COLOUR CHANGE The Grey Heron's powerful bill develops an orange tint in the breeding season.

Purple Heron

FAMILY Ardeidae

SPECIES *Ardea purpurea*

LENGTH 78–90 cm (30¾–35½ in) /wingspan 110–145 cm (43–57 in)

HABITAT Open, shallow freshwater swamps

CLUTCH SIZE 4–5

DISTRIBUTION Summer visitor across most of southern Europe in areas of suitable habitat, especially between the Caspian and Black Seas. Overwinters in tropical parts of Africa.

THE SINUOUS, almost snake-like appearance of this shy inhabitant of reedbeds and swamps is accentuated by the dark stripes running longitudinally along the head and neck. Wonderfully camouflaged against the dense, aquatic vegetation of its favoured habitats, it is seldom seen in the open unless flushed. Richly coloured – warm buff to golden chestnut, chocolate brown to deep burgundy – it is a beautiful bird for those fortunate enough to get a close-up view in good light. Juveniles are a warm russet-brown and cream.

CAMOUFLAGED The Purple Heron usually hunts its prey at the edge of reedbeds and in shallow channels where its superb camouflage is used to best advantage.

Squacco Heron

FAMILY Ardeidae

SPECIES *Ardeola ralloides*

LENGTH 44–47 cm (17¼–18½ in) /wingspan 80–92 cm (31½–36 in)

HABITAT Reedbeds

CLUTCH SIZE 4–6

DISTRIBUTION A summer visitor from Africa to most of the Mediterranean region, and an occasional vagrant further north.

WHEN STANDING STILL amongst reed stems, the Squacco Heron is very difficult to spot, as its warm buff-coloured plumage blends in perfectly with the surroundings. In flight, however, it becomes much more conspicuous, as the broad wings are almost all white. Immature birds and adults in winter have much more streaking on the plumage. Squacco Herons nest in colonies and are often found alongside other species of herons, although when feeding they are usually more solitary and skulking. On migration, they often turn up on stretches of open water.

IN WAIT Squacco Herons hunt their food among reed stems and in very shallow water, usually remaining camouflaged in dense cover.

Black-crowned Night Heron

FAMILY Ardeidae

SPECIES *Nycticorax nycticorax*

LENGTH 56–65 cm (22–25½ in)/ wingspan 90–100 cm (35½–39½ in)

HABITAT Fresh, brackish, or salt water

CLUTCH SIZE 3–6

DISTRIBUTION Found across western, central, and southern Europe eastwards to central and southern Asia.

THE NIGHT HERON gains its name from its habit of feeding primarily at night. During the day, these herons tend to roost communally in trees, often at some distance from the water. As dusk falls, small flocks will fly together to a favourite feeding area such as the margin of a reedbed or a shallow lake. When roosting during the day, Night Herons can often be approached quite closely, but at night they are likely to fly off making harsh frog-like calls if they are disturbed. Untidy platforms of twigs are constructed in trees or reed beds during the nesting season, often in small colonies and in association with other heron species.

STILL The Night Heron can remain motionless for long periods, even while perching in the open, and usually adopts a hunched position. The yellow legs turn red briefly during courtship.

European White Stork

FAMILY Ciconiidae

SPECIES *Ciconia ciconia*

LENGTH 100–115 cm (39½–45 in) /wingspan 155–165 cm (61–65 in)

HABITAT Open areas/wetland/ farmland

CLUTCH SIZE 3–5

DISTRIBUTION Populations found throughout Europe in the summer months.

THE WHITE STORK seems to seek the company of humans both for nesting and feeding. Huge platforms of sticks are constructed on roof tops and telegraph poles in inhabited areas, and storks regularly follow people working in fields to look for prey items disturbed by their activity. Storks spend the winter in Africa and migrate north in spring to traditional nesting sites; on arrival, they start a magnificent bill-clapping display to establish their territories. They readily take to artificial nesting platforms, such as cartwheels, placed on poles to encourage them.

OPPORTUNIST A White Stork wades in shallow water looking for frogs, but it is equally at home on dry land seeking snakes, lizards, and beetles.

Black Stork

FAMILY Ciconiidae

SPECIES *Ciconia niger*

LENGTH 95–100 cm (37½–39½ in)
/wingspan 145–155 cm (57–61 in)

HABITAT Woodland/marshland/
grassland

CLUTCH SIZE 3–5

DISTRIBUTION Summer visitor
to central and eastern Europe;
resident in Spain/Portugal.

BLACK STORKS ARE most at home in large, waterlogged forests with plenty of large trees to nest in and shallow, overgrown waterways to feed in. Although it is a large and conspicuous bird, the Black Stork is very shy at the nesting site and easily disturbed. They spend the winter in Africa and migrate north to Europe late in the spring, stopping off at various shallow lakes and rivers on the way to feed. In flight, when silhouetted against the sky it can be surprisingly difficult to distinguish between Black and White Storks, despite the obvious differences in their body colouring. Black Storks are fairly quiet birds, but they sometimes perform a bill-clapping display.

DIET Black Storks usually feed on amphibians, hunting them in shallow water, but they will also attempt larger prey like eels.

NESTING STORKS White Storks (*see* p 50) construct massive nests of sticks on traditional nesting sites, and are often found on buildings. Each year new material is added to the nest, so that it grows and grows.

Glossy Ibis

FAMILY Threskiornithidae

SPECIES *Plegadis falcinellus*

LENGTH 50–66 cm (19¾–26 in)/
wingspan 88–105 cm (34½–41¼ in)

HABITAT Shallow lakes/ponds/
rivers

CLUTCH SIZE 3–5

DISTRIBUTION Wide
discontinuous breeding
distribution in southern Europe.

ALTHOUGH IT APPEARS all dark at a distance, the Glossy Ibis has shiny purple-brown plumage with a green gloss on the wings. The long, down-curved bill is used for probing into marshy ground and searching amongst vegetation for frogs and invertebrates. Glossy Ibises often fly in long straggling lines to go to roost in trees at night. Nests are built in trees; at the breeding sites ibises will produce strange grunting and croaking calls.

FORAGING Glossy Ibises often feed in small groups on marshy ground, searching for frogs and beetles.

White Spoonbill

FAMILY Threskiornithidae

SPECIES *Platalea leucorodia*

LENGTH 75–95 cm (29½–37½ in)
/wingspan 120–135 cm (47–53 in)

HABITAT Shallow, usually
extensive wetland

CLUTCH SIZE 3–4

DISTRIBUTION Occurs from
southern Spain, the Netherlands,
and southeastern Europe to
central and east Asia.

THE EXTRAORDINARY SHAPE of the long, spatulate-tipped bill of the Spoonbill makes it instantly recognizable, but at long range, when the bill shape can not be seen, it can easily be confused with an egret. Spoonbills tend to roost with their bodies held in a horizontal, rather than vertical, posture and often stand on one leg. The bill is swept from side to side through soft mud and silt to filter out tiny invertebrates. The sexes are very similar, but males are larger with longer bills and legs. Spoonbills nest in colonies in large trees, usually apart from other birds.

PLUMAGE CHANGE In the breeding season,
the adult Spoonbill develops a long head crest
and a yellowish band across the chest.

Greater Flamingo

FAMILY Phoenicopteridae

SPECIES *Phoenicopterus ruber*

LENGTH 120–145 cm (47¼–57 in) /wingspan 140–170 cm (55–67 in)

HABITAT Open, shallow, saline lagoons and deltas

CLUTCH SIZE 1

DISTRIBUTION Found from southern Spain and southern France eastwards to Kazakhstan.

THE STRANGE SHAPE of the Greater Flamingo, with its long neck, long legs, and peculiarly bulbous bill, is the perfect adaptation to feeding on tiny shrimps and plankton in shallow lakes and soft mud. Flamingos can wade in quite deep water if required, but need to reach the bottom with their bills so that they can sweep through the silt to dislodge tiny creatures. Although rather ungainly in appearance on the ground, and clumsy when trying to take off, Flamingos are elegant and powerful in flight; the legs and neck are fully extended and the wings look long and broad as they fly. Nests take the form of strange mud turrets constructed at lake margins.

HABITAT Greater Flamingos seek out shallow, muddy lakes and salt pans where they can wade safely in search of food.

Northern Bald Ibis

FAMILY Threskiornithidae

SPECIES *Geronticus eremita*

LENGTH 55–65 cm (21½–25½ in) /wingspan 80–95 cm (31½–37½ in)

HABITAT Barren country

CLUTCH SIZE 3–4

DISTRIBUTION A very scarce breeding bird, declining rapidly, with a few scattered breeding sites in Morocco and possibly Turkey.

ALTHOUGH VERY SIMILAR to the more common species, the Northern Bald Ibis is more likely to be found in dry terrain seeking food on land rather than at water margins. The plumage is dark glossy black and green and there is a rather scruffy crest at the back of the bald head. Nests are constructed on cliffs and the sites chosen are usually within range of water, which they visit from time to time. In winter, they tend to move to shorelines and remote lakes.

RARE SIGHT The Bald Ibis is most likely to be encountered in remote and arid regions, and is now a very scarce bird.

ANSERIFORMES

Swans, geese, and ducks

A large group of web-footed water birds ranging in size from large swans to small dabbling ducks. Long necks facilitate feeding in various depths of water and there are many other adaptations, enabling some to dive, some to dabble, and others to feed on land. Bill shapes and sizes reflect the various methods of feeding, from grazing to prising up submerged molluscs and catching fish. A wide range of habitats have been exploited, from the high Arctic tundra to lowland marshes and swamps, and many of the ducks, geese, and swans are powerful flyers, making long annual migrations.

Tundra (Bewick's) Swan

FAMILY Anatidae

SPECIES *Cygnus columbianus bewickii*

LENGTH 115–140 cm (45½–55 in)/ wingspan 170–195 cm (69–76¾ in)

HABITAT Tundra/grassland

CLUTCH SIZE 3–5

DISTRIBUTION Breeds in north Siberia; winters in western Europe.

THIS IS A medium-sized, all-white swan that carries its neck straight and erect. The rounded yellow patch at the base of the black bill differs subtly between individuals, but never extends beyond the nostril. Juveniles have grey feathers and a mostly pinkish bill. The voice is a loud honking or crooning, while resting flocks make a musical murmuring sound.

BEWICK'S SWAN Once recognized as a separate species, this race of the Tundra Swan was named after a Northumbrian wood engraver called Thomas Bewick.

Whooper Swan

FAMILY Anatidae

SPECIES *Cygnus cygnus*

LENGTH 145–160 cm (57–63 in)/ wingspan 205–235 cm (81–92½ in)

HABITAT Non-tundra/fields

CLUTCH SIZE 3–7

DISTRIBUTION Occurs in Iceland and Arctic Europe. Winters in western and central Europe.

THE WHOOPER IS a large all-white swan with a long neck that is usually carried straight and erect. The yellow base to the black bill typically extends to a point beyond the nostril, distinguishing it from the smaller but otherwise similar Bewick's Swan. Juveniles have grey feathers and a primarily pinkish bill.

LOUD CALLS Like its close relative in North America, the Trumpeter Swan, the Whooper is named after its distinctive loud call heard from flocks on water or in flight.

Mute Swan

FAMILY Anatidae

SPECIES *Cygnus olor*

LENGTH 145–160 cm (57–63 in)/ wingspan 200–240 cm (79–94½ in)

HABITAT Freshwater/quiet saltwater areas

CLUTCH SIZE 5–8

DISTRIBUTION Occurs in the British Isles, north, west, and central Europe.

THIS IS A LARGE AND HEAVY swan with a rounded head and distinctive orange bill that has a black knob at the base. The neck is usually carried gracefully curved and the wings are often arched. Juveniles are normally brown with a greyish bill but sometimes occur in white plumage. This white morph is often called 'Polish swan'. The Mute is less vocal than the Whooper and Bewick's, usually making a hoarse, snoring, or grunting call; it hisses when threatened. In flight, the wingbeats produce a loud, rhythmic singing sound. It flies with its neck extended. The Mute Swan was introduced into many western and central European countries. West European birds prefer even, regulated canals, ditches, and park lakes.

HUMAN CONTACT Unlike other European swans, the Mute Swan is resident throughout its range, often breeding close to human habitation.

White-fronted Goose

FAMILY Anserinae
SPECIES *Anser albifrons*
LENGTH 66–76 cm (26–30 in)
HABITAT Tundra/grassland
CLUTCH SIZE 5–6

DISTRIBUTION Breeds in the far north of Russia and Siberia, and also in Greenland. The two populations overwinter in separate areas further south.

A WHITE FOREHEAD and barred underparts are key identification features of this large species, which has orange legs, and generally a pink bill. Birds from Greenland have a yellowish bill, but all have the strongly barred underside.

Greenland birds overwinter in Ireland and Scotland, while the Russian birds move south and west to mild coastal areas.

FLOCKING IN White-fronted Geese feed in large flocks on marshes, flying in with a chorus of excited calls.

Greylag Goose

FAMILY Anserinae
SPECIES *Anser anser*
LENGTH 76–89 cm (30–35 in)
HABITAT Moorland/marshland
CLUTCH SIZE 4–6

DISTRIBUTION Resident in lowland Britain, Scandinavia, Balkans, and Turkey; summer visitor to Europe and Iceland; moves southwest for winter.

THE GREYLAG, the largest grey goose, feeds in the open in summer on grasses, roots, and shoots. The orange bill, pink legs, and plain underside are sometimes difficult to distinguish at a distance or in poor light, but the pale forewing panels seen in flight are a useful identification feature. Ringing flight calls are heard when large flocks take to the air, and birds on the ground often make a loud hissing sound when angry. Now increasingly common in a wide range of lowland habitats, this is the ancestor of domesticated farmyard geese, which may be all white with orange bills.

LARGE VISITOR The stocky greylag goose is the only large grey goose likely to be seen breeding in Europe in summer, the others being residents of the far north.

Pink-footed Goose

FAMILY Anserinae
SPECIES *Anser brachyrhynchus*
LENGTH 61–76 cm (24–30 in)
HABITAT Mountains/lowland
CLUTCH SIZE 4–5

DISTRIBUTION Breeds in Iceland, Greenland, and Svalbard. Overwinters in northwest Europe, especially abundant in Britain.

A COMBINATION OF the relatively small size, compared with other grey geese, the black-and-pink bill, and pink legs help distinguish the Pink-footed Goose, which may overwinter in mixed flocks with other species of geese in some areas. In summer, they migrate north to traditional breeding sites, where they nest in scattered colonies on the ground on the arctic tundra, often choosing river islands or cliff ledges for safety. The whole population moves south in the autumn to feed in open grassy areas, usually on agricultural land. Shy and nervous birds, they rapidly take to the air with a clamour of loud calls if disturbed. In any case, they are very vocal with a variety of shrill calls. Large flocks of these geese, sometimes numbering many thousands, fly to safe roosting sites at dusk, often in a V-shaped formation.

TRACKED Many Pink-footed Geese carry numbered rings on their legs, which help to track their movements between breeding sites and overwintering areas.

Lesser White-fronted Goose

FAMILY Anserinae

SPECIES *Anser erythropus*

LENGTH 53–66 cm (21–26 in)

HABITAT Tundra/coats

CLUTCH SIZE 4–5

DISTRIBUTION A summer visitor to extreme northern Scandinavia and Russia, migrating south to overwinter in low-lying coastal areas.

THIS, THE SMALLEST of the grey geese, is a scarce visitor to western Europe, but occasionally turns up in a flock of larger geese when it can often be picked out by its faster rate of feeding. A close view will reveal a golden-yellow eye ring, and a large area of white on the head, extending further back on the crown than in the White-fronted Goose (*see* p 58); also, the pink bill is smaller, and the wing tips extend beyond the tail. The calls are similar to the White-fronted Goose, but higher pitched. This is now a very rare bird in Europe and it is under threat from shooting and habitat destruction in the eastern part of its range.

DISTINGUISHING FEATURES The yellow eye ring and short pink bill help to identify this diminutive goose.

Bean Goose

FAMILY Anserinae
SPECIES *Anser fabalis*
LENGTH 71–89 cm (28–35 in)
HABITAT Taiga/tundra
CLUTCH SIZE 4–6

DISTRIBUTION Summer visitor to wet open forests and taiga in north Scandinavia and Russia. Migrates south and west to freshwater marshes for winter.

THIS LARGE GREY GOOSE stands out among others in mixed flocks by its greater size and rather darker head and neck. The legs are orange, and the orange bill is sometimes marked with black patches: the extent of this varies with populations from different breeding grounds. Always shy and alert, Bean Geese readily take to the air with loud trumpeting flight calls if disturbed. Juveniles resemble adults, with dull orange legs; families migrate together in autumn.

LOOKOUT Always on the alert for predators, one vigilant Bean Goose keeps a keen look out for danger while the others are feeding.

Brent Goose

FAMILY Branta
SPECIES *Branta bernicla*
LENGTH 56–61 cm (22–24 in)
HABITAT Tundra/coasts
CLUTCH SIZE 3–5

DISTRIBUTION Breeds in the extreme north on Arctic islands and coastal tundra. Over winters along muddy coasts and estuaries in western Europe.

THIS IS A SMALL, dark goose, similar in size to a Mallard (*see* p 71), and the only one with an all-black head. Adults have white patches on the side of the neck and mostly dark grey-brown plumage. Brent Geese from Greenland have pale undersides and all tend to migrate and overwinter together in Ireland. The Black Brant, breeding in Canada and Alaska, has much darker underparts with a white flash along the flanks. Croaking calls are heard from birds in flight and on the water, where they tend to roost in large flocks after feeding.

WHITE NECK An adult Brent Goose can be identified by the white patches on the sides of the neck, which are absent in juveniles.

Canada Goose

FAMILY Branta
SPECIES *Branta canadensis*
LENGTH 92–102 cm (36¼–40 in)
HABITAT Lakes/marshland
CLUTCH SIZE 5–6

DISTRIBUTION Introduced from North America and now resident in Britain and southern Scandinavia, and a partial migrant to other areas of western Europe.

THE CANADA GOOSE is very large with an all-black neck and white cheeks and throat. The plumage is predominantly brown, becoming much paler underneath, and the large bill and strong legs are black. It is a far less nervous bird than the other large geese, and now very common in parks and inland lakes, often forming large flocks. This is the goose most likely to be seen inland in western Europe at all

LANDING An adult Canada Goose flexes its powerful wings before settling on the water, safe from predators.

times of the year. In flight, Canada Geese communicate with a loud honking call, and during the mating season birds are especially noisy. Flocks tend to roost together at night, flying in noisy V-formation from their feeding areas to a safe overnight area. Canada Geese were introduced into Britain from North America as an ornamental bird for wildfowl collections. Many birds escaped, and this species is now reaching pest proportions in some areas.

Barnacle Goose

FAMILY Branta
SPECIES *Branta leucopsis*
LENGTH 58–69 cm (22–24 in)
HABITAT Arctic coasts
CLUTCH SIZE 3–5

DISTRIBUTION Breeds in Greenland and Svalbard and overwinters in coastal western Europe, rarely occurring inland.

THIS IS A COMPACT, medium-sized goose with a black neck and bill and a white face. There is a distinct contrast between the black neck and silvery-white underside. The legs are short and black and the bill is relatively small. The rest of the plumage is in shades of grey with black bars. Barnacle Geese feed on tundra vegetation in summer and then coastal grassland plants in the winter, where they form huge flocks in traditional overwintering areas. In flight, they travel in an irregular U-formation, calling with a shrill, bark-like 'kaw'. They return to exactly the same Arctic nesting sites each year.

RICH FOOD The Barnacle Goose favours coastal grasslands in winter, which provide richer feeding than the sparse tundra vegetation of its summer breeding grounds.

Red-breasted Goose

FAMILY Branta
SPECIES *Branta ruficollis*
LENGTH 53–56 cm (21–22 in)
HABITAT Tundra/marshland
CLUTCH SIZE 3–5

DISTRIBUTION Breeds along Arctic coast of Russia and Siberia; overwinters in the south in steppe areas around Caspian and Black Seas.

THIS VERY SMALL, compact goose has a short, stubby bill and thick neck. Its deep chestnut-red throat, breast, and cheeks are very obvious features at close range, but at a distance, and among other 'black' geese, the black flanks with a large white horizontal stripe are more striking; this also shows up well in flight, when the red colour is not easily seen. Most of the population overwinters in the east of the region, but a few wander further west, where they mingle with winter flocks of Brent Geese (*see* p 61).

RICH COLOURS The colours of this goose are unmistakeable. The sexes are identical; juveniles have about five pale wing bars.

Ruddy Shelduck

FAMILY Anatinae
SPECIES *Tadorna ferruginea*
LENGTH 64 cm (25 in)
HABITAT Lakes/rivers
CLUTCH SIZE 8–12

DISTRIBUTION Resident in Turkey and Middle East; some move north to drier habitats in summer. Some migrate south to Africa in winter.

THIS IS A LARGE DUCK, goose-like in profile, with rich orange-brown plumage and a paler head. In flight, the wings show bold black tips and large white patches. The flight calls mimic those of the Greylag Goose (*see* p 58). They may nest far from water in a tree hollow or rock face, and then lead the young a considerable distance to safety. In autumn, they migrate to feeding areas, often flying at a great height.

COLLARED During the breeding season the male has a black collar, but he loses this feature in winter.

Shelduck

FAMILY Anatinae
SPECIES *Tadorna tadorna*
LENGTH 61 cm (24 in)
HABITAT Coastal marshland
CLUTCH SIZE 8–15

DISTRIBUTION Widespread resident around the coasts of Europe, Scandinavia, and North Africa; sometimes also on large lakes. Some fly south for winter.

THIS IS A LARGE, colourful duck with boldly marked plumage, a red bill, and pink legs and feet. The head and neck look long in proportion to the body. The red bill is larger in the male; it also has a large lump in front of the forehead. The glossy green head contrasts with the white neck and chestnut-coloured chest band. Shelducks feed on tiny molluscs in estuarine mud, sifting them out with their specially adapted bill. Females nest in burrows close to water, taking their chicks to the water soon after hatching. In summer, huge flocks of Shelducks, including almost all the British population, migrate to the mouth of the Elbe in Germany to moult.

BILL DISTINCTION Although the sexes are very similar, the male Shelduck can be identified by the prominent lump on top of his bill.

Egyptian Goose

FAMILY Anatinae

SPECIES *Alopochen aegyptiacus*

LENGTH 70 cm (27½ in)

HABITAT Freshwater

CLUTCH SIZE 5–8

DISTRIBUTION Introduced into England in the 18th century and now resident in small numbers in the wild here and in neighbouring regions.

THIS IS A LARGE, GREYISH-BROWN duck with goose-like proportions, hence the confusing name. The black-and-white wing pattern and similar size mean that it may be confused with the Ruddy Shelduck in flight. At close range, however, the dark eye patches, paler plumage, dark-edged pink bill, and long, reddish-pink legs distinguish it. The sexes are very similar, but juveniles are browner and lack the dark face patch. When feeding on land, Egyptian Geese often stand with an upright, goose-like posture, and in silhouette do not look at all like ducks. Small flocks may be found on inland marshes and river banks, although they nest separately, often in tree holes, ruined buildings, or under deep shrub cover. Both sexes help with incubation, and when newly hatched, the chicks are quickly taken to the safety of water. They feed on grasses and water plants and are usually most common on freshwater marshes and in winter floods. Males make a loud, hoarse quack, and there are also some quiet whistling calls.

NATURALIZED ALIEN The Egyptian Goose, originally from Africa, seems quite at home in the wetlands of western Europe, having been established here for over 200 years.

Harlequin Duck

FAMILY Anatinae

SPECIES *Histrionicus histrionicus*

LENGTH 43 cm (17 in)

HABITAT Rivers/coasts

CLUTCH SIZE 6–8

DISTRIBUTION Restricted to Iceland, breeding on large fast-flowing rivers and wintering on the coast. Very occasionally found elsewhere in Europe.

FROM A DISTANCE, the drake Harlequin Duck looks dark, but at close range the unique combination of blue, white, chestnut, and black becomes clearer. The females are a uniform brown above with three pale patches on the face. At sea they can be distinguished from scoters (*see* p 82) by their more compact shape and smaller bills. Harlequins thrive in fast-flowing rivers and by stony lake margins where they dive in the roughest water for

WATERSIDE PERCH A colourful male Harlequin Duck stand on a riverside boulder before diving into the torrent.

blackfly larvae. Only the female sits on the eggs; the males tend to form flocks of their own prior to moulting. A thin, nasal 'vee-ahh vee-ahh' call is given by males, but it is rarely heard above the rushing water.

Pintail

FAMILY Anatinae

SPECIES *Anas acuta*

LENGTH 56–66 cm (22–26 in)

HABITAT Tundra/coast

CLUTCH SIZE 7–9

DISTRIBUTION Widespread and common across Europe, spending the winter in southern Europe, and migrating north for the breeding season.

THE DRAKE PINTAIL is striking in appearance with very elongated central tail feathers, and a brown head and throat with a bold vertical white stripe at the side. The female is very plain in comparison, with a pale brown head and finely patterned brown breast and flanks; however, the tail is more pointed than in other ducks. Pintails breed in scattered colonies on freshwater lakes and marshes and overwinter in similar habitats further south, often in large mixed flocks with other species. Quiet calls include a short whistling 'krruu' rather like the Teal (*see* p 68), and a deep crowing call from the female during courtship.

LONG TAIL The male Pintail has one of the longest tails of any duck, but the bold brown-and-white pattern on the head and neck is a more striking feature.

Northern Shoveler

FAMILY Anatinae

SPECIES *Anas clypeata*

LENGTH 51 cm (20 in)

HABITAT Marshland/lakes

CLUTCH SIZE 8–12

DISTRIBUTION Resident in western Europe; many migrate to eastern Europe and Iceland for the summer, overwintering in south and west Europe.

BOTH SEXES of the Northern Shoveler can be recognized by the strange shape of the bill: its shovel shape gives the birds' profile a drooped appearance around the head when they are on the water or at rest on land. The large, flattened bill is used for sifting through mud and weed to find food. The drake has a dark glossy green head, white breast, and chestnut flanks, but the female is almost all plain brown with a green wing patch. When in flight, both sexes show pale blue wing panels.

YELLOW EYE The drake is the only dabbling duck to have a yellow eye. The shovel-shaped bill is an important adaptation for feeding.

Teal

FAMILY Anatinae
SPECIES *Anas crecca*
LENGTH 35 cm (13¾ in)
HABITAT Ponds/lakes
CLUTCH SIZE 8–12

DISTRIBUTION Widespread resident across western and central Europe and Iceland; large numbers migrate north to breed, returning for winter.

THE SMALLEST DUCK in Europe, Teals are often found in large noisy flocks. When disturbed, they fly off in tight formation, resembling plump waders. Drakes have a chestnut head with a broad green stripe. At rest, the horizontal white stripe along the flanks and yellow patch below the tail are very visible. Females are very plain with a small green wing patch.

GREEN PATTERN The green facial stripe of the drake Teal has a fine yellow border surrounding it.

Blue-winged Teal

FAMILY Anatinae
SPECIES *Anas discors*
LENGTH 38 cm (15 in)
HABITAT Marshland/lakes
CLUTCH SIZE 8–12

DISTRIBUTION A resident of North America and a very scarce visitor to western Europe, occurring mostly in Britain and Ireland.

THIS VERY RARE VISITOR to Europe sometimes occurs on western coasts after severe Atlantic gales when it may have been blown off course and found shelter with other ducks. At rest, the bold white crescent on the side of the face of the adult drake is a very noticeable feature, and if seen in flight the blue wing panels help identification. As this is a popular bird in wildfowl collections, some of the birds seen on the coast may be escapees.

BLUE WING PANEL A drake stretches its wing and reveals one of the key features for identifying this rare transatlantic vagrant. Females also have the blue wing panel.

Mandarin Duck

FAMILY Anatinae
SPECIES *Aix galericulata*
LENGTH 43 cm (17 in)
HABITAT Wooded lakes
CLUTCH SIZE 9–12

DISTRIBUTION Introduced into Britain and now naturalized in small numbers in many parts of the south and midlands with a few colonies further north. Also breeds in parts of Western Europe.

THIS MOST EXOTIC LOOKING duck is a native of China and was originally introduced into Britain for ornamental wildfowl collections. Many have escaped and established themselves in the wild in Britain and other areas of western Europe. The extraordinary plumage of the male is not matched by that of the female who is mottled brown and grey, with a very slight crest, and a large pale ring around the eye. Males perform elaborate courtship displays, showing off their plumage to advantage. Calls are not often heard, but males make a sharp, brief whistle, and females a very brief quack. Females nest in hollow trees near water, often over 5 m (16½ ft) high. The newly hatched chicks leap to the ground and follow their mother to the water.

IMPRESSIVE CREST When displaying, the drake Mandarin fluffs out his neck feathers and raises the crest in order to impress nearby females.

Wigeon

FAMILY Anatinae
SPECIES *Anas penelope*
LENGTH 46 cm (18 in)
HABITAT Lakes/marshland
CLUTCH SIZE 7–8

DISTRIBUTION Resident in northwest Europe and Iceland and a summer visitor to breeding grounds in northern Europe and Scandinavia.

THIS IS A SMALL, NEAT dabbling duck that feeds on vegetation on marshes and arable land, and is rarely found far from fresh water. The typical whistling 'whee-oo' call, given by the drakes, is frequently heard from feeding and roosting flocks; the ducks produce a quieter purring call. The male Wigeon is a very colourful bird with a chestnut head and creamy crown, and a conspicuous white line along the grey wings; in flight this shows as a large white patch. The female Wigeon is far less colourful with mainly brown mottled plumage and a green patch on the wing. Females can be separated from other similar ducks by their more rounded heads, short bills, and short pointed tails. In flight, both ducks and drakes show white on the underside. In summer, moulting males have brownish flanks and they lack the buff crown. Wigeons usually live in large flocks, and migrate to southern Europe and North Africa for the winter.

MALE WIGEON A short bill, peaked head, and chestnut plumage on the sides of the face identify the drake. These wigeons often occur in mixed flocks with other similar ducks.

Mallard

FAMILY Anatinae

SPECIES *Anas platyrhynchos*

LENGTH 58 cm (23 in)

HABITAT Lakes/marshland

CLUTCH SIZE 10–12

DISTRIBUTION Common and widespread resident across almost all of Europe and Scandinavia, but a summer visitor to the extreme north. Some head south to North Africa in winter.

THE MALLARD is the most familiar of all ducks, occurring in almost every type of watery environment. The drake's colouring – a glossy green head with a white collar, yellow bill, and deep chestnut breast – is a combination not found in other wildfowl. The female is a much plainer mottled brown colour, but both have a green patch on the wing. Mallards become very secretive in the nesting season when the female seeks out a tree hollow or other concealed site for her nest. The Mallard is the ancestor of all farmyard ducks.

PARK DUCKS Mallards are almost always found in pairs and are very common birds in urban parks, becoming quite tame, especially when food is offered.

Garganey

FAMILY Anatinae

SPECIES *Anas querquedula*

LENGTH 38 cm (15 in)

HABITAT Freshwater marshland

CLUTCH SIZE 8–11

DISTRIBUTION A summer visitor to Europe, but absent from the far west and north. Overwinters in the Iberian Peninsula and North Africa.

THE CURIOUS RATTLING CALL of the drake Garganey is often the only clue to the presence of this very secretive small duck which rarely occurs in large numbers like the similar-sized Teal (*see* p 68). If seen well, the drake's white stripe above the eye is a good feature for identification, and in flight, the wings show grey-blue panels. The female is a very plain mottled brown colour, but shows a faint white spot at the base of the bill and a pale stripe over the eye. Small groups of Garganeys may be seen together in spring, but they disperse to separate breeding sites in summer.

DISTINCTIVE Although one of the smallest ducks, the drake Garganey has very distinctive summer plumage.

Black Duck

FAMILY Anatinae

SPECIES *Anas rubripes*

LENGTH 53–61 cm (21–24 in)

HABITAT Marshland/lakes

CLUTCH SIZE 1–12

DISTRIBUTION A North American vagrant or escapee from a collection, which turns up in areas of western Europe.

BLACK DUCK IS NOT really an appropriate name for this North American species, but at a distance the overall effect is of a very dark-plumaged bird. The true colour of both males and females is a very dark brown-grey, rather like a dark female Mallard (*see* p 71). However, if a single Black Duck is seen among female Mallards, the contrast is quite striking. The head is a pale yellow-brown and the bill of the male is similar to the yellowish-green bill of the drake Mallard. The head of the female is greyer than that of the male and the bill is dull by comparison. In flight, the adult male shows strikingly white underwings and a very dark belly. The feet and legs are a rich red-orange. The turquoise wing patch is not very easy to see as it lacks the white edges that occur in the Mallard. The female has a green wing patch, which also lacks the white edging. This is a very rare species in Europe, but it may turn up having been blown off course by severe Atlantic gales and then settle with other similar species, usually Mallards. It is known to hybridize with Mallards, on both sides of the Atlantic, leading to some very confusing plumages and making identification very difficult. The calls are very similar to the Mallard, but deeper in tone.

STRETCHING ITS WINGS A Black Duck in flight, clearly showing its white underwings.

Wood Duck

FAMILY Anatinae
SPECIES *Aix sponsa*
LENGTH 43–51 cm (17–20 in)
HABITAT Wooded lakes
CLUTCH SIZE 9–12

DISTRIBUTION A North American species, often kept in collections, from which it may escape and establish small populations in the wild.

CLOSELY RELATED to the Mandarin Duck (*see* p 69), but slightly larger, the colourful Wood Duck is likely to be encountered in similar habitats, although it is a very rare species in the wild in Europe, and outside of wildfowl collections is most likely to be seen on wooded urban lakes with other escapees. Males have a metallic blue-green head, marked with fine white lines, and buff-coloured flanks. The bill is red and black and the eye is strikingly red. The female is very similar to the female Mandarin but has rather more white around the eye and is generally darker. This species is also known as the Carolina Duck.

PATTERNING The unmistakeable head markings of the male Wood Duck make this rare visitor easy to identify. Wood Ducks find perching out of water very easy.

Gadwall

FAMILY Anatinae
SPECIES *Anas strepera*
LENGTH 51 cm (20 in)
HABITAT Marshland
CLUTCH SIZE 8–12

DISTRIBUTION Widespread across most of western Europe and Iceland, spreading east in summer; moves to milder southern and western areas for the winter, often near coasts.

THE BLACK UNDERTAIL area of the male Gadwall is its most noticeable feature, relieving the grey-brown plumage. At close range, fine worm-like patterns can be seen on the breast and wings. In flight, the small white wing patch shows clearly on males and females. The duck resembles a very slim female Mallard (*see* p 71) but with a paler belly and an orange stripe along the side of the bill. Gadwalls prefer freshwater lakes with reedy margins and shallow muddy areas. Only the females tend the young, which are taken to water soon after hatching.

PLAIN DUCK The drake Gadwall is the least colourful of all the dabbling ducks, but the wings do have a square white patch.

Marbled Teal

FAMILY Anatinae

SPECIES *Marmaronetta angustirostris*

LENGTH 41 cm (16 in)

HABITAT Marshland/pools

CLUTCH SIZE 9–13

DISTRIBUTION A very scarce and declining summer visitor to southwest Europe with small populations elsewhere in the Middle East and North Africa.

THIS SECRETIVE, SMALL dabbling duck is becoming increasingly difficult to find in its traditional haunts in southwest Europe. Favouring small, shallow, and well-vegetated pools, Marbled Teal arrive on their breeding grounds in spring and establish a territory, keeping fairly quiet and rarely making a call, although during courtship the males make a high-pitched squeaky whistle. Nests are constructed in deep vegetation, sometimes a long way from the water and occasionally in old thatched roofs of boat houses. The sexes are very alike and there is no coloured patch on the wing. The pale mottled plumage blends in well with the dappled light of thick reed beds. In flight, the greyish-brown wings show a pale spot on the forewing and dark wingtips. The underwing is white and there is a dark patch surrounding the eye, contrasting strongly with the paler face and chin. The dark bill is long and slender, resembling that of the rather larger Pintail (*see* p 67). There is no crest but the head has a fairly scruffy look about it. Juveniles are very similar to the adults but lack the scruffy head and are barred rather than spotted on the flanks. After the breeding season, the Marbled Teal leaves the reedbeds and marshes and heads for more open waters, including larger lakes, and may even spend time on ephemeral desert pools.

MOTTLED PLUMAGE The Marbled Teal is best identified by the soft brown-and-white mottled plumage and the dark eye patch.

Red-crested Pochard

FAMILY Anatinae

SPECIES *Netta rufina*

LENGTH 56 cm (22 in)

HABITAT Reedy lakes

CLUTCH SIZE 6–12

DISTRIBUTION Scattered across central Europe with most migrating to the south and west coasts in winter. Some are collection escapees.

THIS IS A LARGE, long-bodied duck with conspicuous broad white wing bars clearly visible in flight. Males have a large orange-red head and a contrasting long coral-red bill. The rest of the body is black with paler flanks. The female is similar in proportions, but has more subdued fawn and brown coloration with a dark-grey, pink-tipped bill. Moulting males look more like females but retain the red eye and red bill, while juveniles look very similar to females. Red-crested Pochards prefer shallow, reedy lakes where they can upend and dabble for food in the margins; they will also dive for food in deeper water, taking mainly plant material.

DUCK AND DRAKE A pair of Red-crested Pochards show the marked contrast in plumage between the brightly coloured male and the more drab female.

Pochard

FAMILY Anatinae

SPECIES *Aythya farina*

LENGTH 46 cm (18 in)

HABITAT Lakes/marshland

CLUTCH SIZE 6–11

DISTRIBUTION Widespread resident across parts of western Europe, with many migrating east to breed and then south and west in winter.

THE DRAKE POCHARD has a very clearly defined chestnut head and neck, black breast, and grey upperparts, which are distinguishable from a long distance. Females have similar proportions, but paler grey-brown plumage. In profile, the male's peaked head is distinctive. Juveniles are browner versions of the female. Pochards are usually seen bobbing about far out on a lake, but they will also dabble in shallow water in secluded lake margins.

RED EYE The drake Pochard's bright red eye contrasts with its chestnut head; these features remain even when the bird is moulting.

Tufted Duck

FAMILY Anatinae
SPECIES *Aythya fuligula*
LENGTH 43 cm (17 in)
HABITAT Lakes/large rivers
CLUTCH SIZE 5–12

DISTRIBUTION Resident across western Europe, with a large population migrating to northern Europe, Scandinavia, and Iceland in summer.

THE TUFTED DUCK is very striking: it is a small diving duck with bold glossy black-and-white plumage and a bright yellow eye. Males have a long drooping crest in the breeding season, and the dark brown females, who also have the yellow eye, have a very short tuft at the back of the head. Females sometimes have a pale area around the bill. Juveniles are similar to females but with an even shorter tuft on the head. In flight, both sexes show broad white wing bars, although the male looks much darker overall. Tufted Ducks are usually seen in small flocks out in the middle of large lakes where they will dive for food on the bed of the lake. In the breeding season, they are fairly secretive and solitary, but on migration they often form very large flocks, usually on freshwater lakes but occasionally along sheltered stretches of coastline.

DISTINCTIVE LOOKS A drake in breeding plumage, with the long tuft of feathering evident at the back of the head. These waterfowl are not an uncommon sight on lakes in public parks.

Greater Scaup

FAMILY Anatinae
SPECIES *Aythya marila*
LENGTH 48 cm (19 in)
HABITAT Lakes/marshland
CLUTCH SIZE 6–15

DISTRIBUTION A summer visitor to Iceland, Scandinavia, and northern Russia, migrating south and west to sheltered coasts for the winter.

AT FIRST GLANCE, and at a distance, the Scaup may be mistaken for the slightly smaller Tufted Duck, but the back is pale grey, the head is dark glossy green, and there is no crest. Female Scaups resemble female Tufted Ducks but they always have a large area of white around the base of the bill and a dark grey back with a pattern of fine worm-like lines. Scaup prefer to live on very large upland lakes or sheltered fjords and bays where they can dive for small molluscs. In winter they gather in large flocks, which may be far out from the shore over quite deep water.

GREEN HEAD Bright sunlight brings out the glossy green plumage of the male Scaup's rounded head; at a distance it always appears to be dull black.

Ferruginous Duck

FAMILY Anatinae
SPECIES *Aythya nyroca*
LENGTH 41 cm (16 in)
HABITAT Lakes/marshland
CLUTCH SIZE 7–11

DISTRIBUTION Resident and partial migrant across central and eastern Europe, the Middle East, and North Africa. Rare in western Europe.

A VERY DISTINCTIVE small duck with almost uniform deep chestnut plumage and a contrasting white eye in the male. In both sexes the upperparts are darker than the flanks and head; juveniles are brown rather than chestnut. Both sexes show a large white patch under the tail. In profile the head has a peaked appearance. The strong white wing bars and white belly are very obvious in flight. More solitary and far less common than the similar Pochard (*see* p 75), the Ferruginous Duck is usually found in small numbers in large shallow lakes and marshes.

CHESTNUT COLOUR The Ferruginous Duck is shy and usually lurks in reedbeds, but will occasionally swim into the open, revealing its deep chestnut colouring.

Eider

FAMILY Somateria
SPECIES *Somateria mollissima*
LENGTH 58 cm (23 in)
HABITAT Rocky coasts
CLUTCH SIZE 4–6

DISTRIBUTION Resident around the coasts of northwest Europe; some migrate south to North Sea coasts in winter.

THE EIDER IS A LARGE, stocky duck with a massive wedge-shaped bill used for wrenching large molluscs off the sea bed, which it reaches by diving. Females have mottled, soft brown plumage at all times; in the breeding season, males have mostly white upperparts, black flanks and crown, and a green neck. When moulting later in the summer, males show mostly dark plumage with areas of white on the wings. Full-grown juveniles resemble the females with brown, finely patterned plumage. When breeding male Eiders are very vocal, making a loud, fluty 'ah-oooh-ee' call, while females chatter away with a quiet cackling call. Outside the breeding season, moulting males form large flocks on open water over the mussel beds where they feed. Mothers gather in large crèches with other females and their ducklings, keeping away from the males. The soft down from the female is used to insulate the nest and is collected by Eider farmers for fillings for pillows and so on.

BREEDING PLUMAGE This male Eider shows the species' distinctive head profile. The female is brown.

King Eider

FAMILY Somateria
SPECIES *Somateria spectabilis*
LENGTH 56 cm (22 in)
HABITAT Arctic coasts
CLUTCH SIZE 4–7

DISTRIBUTION A rare winter visitor from the high Arctic to sheltered northern coasts of Scandinavia, Iceland, and very rarely south in harsh winters.

THE STRIKING MALE KING EIDER is the only waterfowl that, from a distance, appears light in front and dark behind. With a close view, the very colourful head markings are more obvious, and if seen in mixed flocks with common Eider, the red bill and forehead make a good contrast.

HEAD DRESS The drake King Eider's colourful head appears rather bulbous in profile and helps to identify it in poor light and in all plumages.

Breeding males show short black wing tufts, and these are still present during the summer moult, when the bird is rather drab. Females have a more rounded head and mottled brown plumage; at certain angles their very short wing tufts can be seen. Drakes make a three-note cooing call in the breeding season.

Steller's Eider

FAMILY Somateria
SPECIES *Polysticta stelleri*
LENGTH 46 cm (18 in)
HABITAT Arctic tundra/coasts
CLUTCH SIZE 6–8

DISTRIBUTION A very rare visitor to northern coasts in winter; more common in northern Norway. Breeds in the coastal High Arctic.

THIS IS A FAR SMALLER BIRD than the other eiders, resembling a dabbling duck. The blue-grey bill is shorter and less wedge-shaped. Rather than diving, Steller's Eider is more likely to upend itself in shallow water to feed. Males have a white head with two green patches, black-and-white upperparts, and rufous flanks. Females are dark brown with a white-bordered purple wing patch. Away from their breeding grounds they are mostly silent, but they make a whistling flight call. Although largely coastal, Steller's Eiders often nest by freshwater pools, taking the young to the coast soon after hatching.

DRAKE A colourful drake Steller's Eider moves up onto the seashore to feed in the seaweed. Although good divers, they prefer to feed close to land.

EIDER DUCKS ON SNOW (*see* p 78) A group of Eiders
roost on an ice floe in the Arctic, their thick downy
plumage providing excellent insulation against the
extreme cold. Only the males have colourful plumage.

Velvet Scoter

FAMILY Mergini
SPECIES *Melanitta fusca*
LENGTH 56 cm (22 in)
HABITAT Taiga lakes/coasts
CLUTCH SIZE 7–10

DISTRIBUTION Resident along north coasts of Scandinavia and around the Baltic; moves to Taiga lakes in summer, and overwinters on rocky coasts.

THE VELVET SCOTER is a plump, dark sea duck with white wing bars and red feet in both sexes, features that are easily seen in flight. The drake is very dark, but has a white spot behind the eye and orange sides to the large wedge-shaped bill. The similar-sized females and the juveniles are much browner and have two pale patches on the face. Small flocks gather with other sea ducks off the coast in winter.

WHITE EYE A colourful wedge-shaped bill, red legs, and white eye patch separate the Velvet Scoter from other species. Relaxed birds appear to have thick necks.

Common Scoter

FAMILY Mergini
SPECIES *Melanitta nigra*
LENGTH 48 cm (19 in)
HABITAT Coasts/moorland
CLUTCH SIZE 6–9

DISTRIBUTION A summer visitor to Scandinavia, northern Britain, Iceland, and northern Russia; overwinters on coasts of northwest Europe.

THE DRAKE SCOTER is the only completely black waterfowl to be seen in this region, the black relieved by the orange patch on top of the bill. In flight the wings show slightly paler primaries, and juveniles have pale undersides. Females and juveniles are very dark brown with pale sides to the face and neck. On the water the raised pointed tail and thinner neck distinguish them from Velvet Scoters. Large flocks may gather to feed in winter, but they are more solitary when nesting.

SWIMMERS Scoters are very buoyant ducks, usually found in large flocks just off the coast in winter. Wedge-shaped bills help them take molluscs from the sea bed.

Goldeneye

FAMILY Mergini
SPECIES *Bucephala clangula*
LENGTH 46 cm (18 in)
HABITAT Lakes/coasts
CLUTCH SIZE 6–11

DISTRIBUTION Widespread summer visitor to Scandinavia, northern Europe, and Russia; moves south and west in winter to ice-free lakes and coasts.

THIS IS A COMPACT DIVING DUCK with a markedly triangular-shaped head. Drakes have mostly black-and-white plumage with a dark glossy green head and white cheek spot, and females are browner with a dark brown head and no white spot. Adults have bright yellow eyes. Juveniles resemble females, but have brown eyes. In flight, the white wing bars are striking and the head looks large and rounded. Goldeneyes dive frequently and for long periods.

WATERBORNE The Goldeneye spends most of its life on the water, diving to find tiny molluscs for food.

Barrow's Goldeneye

FAMILY Mergini
SPECIES *Bucephala islandica*
LENGTH 53 cm (21 in)
HABITAT Lakes/rivers/coasts
CLUTCH SIZE 8–14

DISTRIBUTION Rarely seen outside of Iceland, where it lives on large lakes and rivers, moving to sheltered coastal areas in the winter.

AT FIRST GLANCE similar to the Goldeneye, Barrow's Goldeneye is larger, and the drake's head is purple with a white patch between the bill and eye. The head has a more rounded appearance and the bill is very slightly shorter. Females and juveniles, and moulting males, have mostly grey-brown plumage, but at all stages there is a large white wing bar. Barrow's Goldeneye is common in Iceland, forming large flocks on shallow lakes and sheltered coasts. They nest on rocky cliffs or ruined buildings.

GLOSSY HEAD
The drake Barrow's Goldeneye is easily identified by its rounded, glossy purple head and the white crescent-shaped patch on the face.

Smew

FAMILY Mergini
SPECIES *Mergus albellus*
LENGTH 41 cm (16 in)
HABITAT Lakes/rivers/coasts
CLUTCH SIZE 6–9

DISTRIBUTION A rare summer visitor to northern Europe and Scandinavia, migrating to the southwest to ice-free lakes and coasts for winter.

THE DRAKE SMEW looks almost all white when on the water, but in flight has a much more black-and-white appearance. The white head has a large black eye patch and there are thin black lines along the wings and flanks; the lower flanks are grey. Females are known as 'redheads' because of their chestnut-red head; their overall colouring is much greyer than the male, and they have white cheeks. Both sexes dive constantly and are easily disturbed if encountered close to the shore, usually flying off in different directions. Moulting males and juveniles resemble females, having much greyer plumage and reddish heads. Small flocks sometimes gather together near reedbeds in winter if the feeding is good.

SMALL SAWBILL The Smew is the smallest of the Sawbills: diving ducks with serrated bills specially adapted for catching fish.

Goosander

FAMILY Mergini
SPECIES *Mergus merganser*
LENGTH 58–66 cm (23–26 in)
HABITAT Lakes/rivers
CLUTCH SIZE 7–14

DISTRIBUTION Resident in western Europe, migrating north to breed in Scandinavia and Russia, and moving south to ice-free waters in winter.

THE GOOSANDER IS long-bodied and streamlined with a slender red bill terminating in a hooked tip; the bill is serrated to help catch fish caught by diving in lakes and rivers. The drake has a dark glossy green head, black upperparts, and pale salmon-pink flanks. Females and juveniles are much greyer and have orange-brown heads. Goosanders nest in hollow trees or rock crevices and are then solitary, but they may form flocks of thousands in winter.

CRESTED HEAD Females have orange-brown heads and mostly grey plumage; the crest can be raised during courtship or when alarmed.

Red-breasted Merganser

FAMILY Mergini
SPECIES *Mergus serrator*
LENGTH 53–58 cm (21–23 in)
HABITAT Lakes/coasts
CLUTCH SIZE 7–12

DISTRIBUTION Widespread resident around coasts of western Europe, Iceland, and Scandinavia; some go north to breed, then south for winter.

SMALLER THAN THE GOOSANDER and with greyer flanks, the Red-breasted Merganser has a more conspicuous and rather scruffy crest on its glossy green head, and a light chestnut breast, making it look darker overall. Females are also very similar to Goosanders but have a smaller crest and less clearly defined neck markings. They are likely to be found on coasts in the breeding season and in winter and usually in smaller flocks, favouring sheltered bays and estuaries.

UNTIDY CREST The drake Red-breasted Merganser has an easily recognized profile, with a long, slender bill and an untidy crest.

Ruddy Duck

FAMILY Oxyurini

SPECIES *Oxyura jamaicensis*

LENGTH 41 cm (16 in)

HABITAT Shallow lakes

CLUTCH SIZE 6–10

DISTRIBUTION Introduced into Britain from North America; established widely in the south from where it is spreading to other parts of western Europe.

THE RUDDY DUCK is one of the 'stiff-tails', a family of small diving ducks that keep their long pointed tails raised when on the water. The male makes an elaborate 'bubbling' display during which the tail is held erect and the bill is tapped against the chest. Drakes have a white face, bright blue bill, and chestnut plumage, while females and juveniles are mottled grey brown with paler bills and buff-coloured faces. Ruddy Ducks dive frequently and are unable to walk on land. The Ruddy Duck is hybridizing with the White-headed Duck and causing a serious decline in the latter species.

STIFF TAIL The drake Ruddy Duck uses his fanned-out tail in an elaborate courtship display that is designed to impress the female.

White-headed Duck

FAMILY Oxyurini

SPECIES *Oxyura leucocephala*

LENGTH 46 cm (18 in)

HABITAT Shallow reedy pools

CLUTCH SIZE 5–12

DISTRIBUTION A very scarce, scattered resident in southwest Europe, eastern Mediterranean, Turkey, and the Balkans. Found further east in summer.

THE WHITE-HEADED DUCK is now a very scarce species, partly due to hybridizing with the Ruddy Duck, but also because of habitat loss. Males have a mostly white head with a pale blue bill, but young birds may have a black head. Females and juveniles have darker heads and bills and more mottled brown plumage. White-headed Ducks spend much time diving for food and are very reluctant to fly.

BULGING PROFILE The plain-plumaged female White-headed Duck shows the characteristically swollen profile to the base of the bill.

Long-tailed Duck

FAMILY Mergini
SPECIES *Clangula hyemalis*
LENGTH 41–53 cm (16–21 in)
HABITAT Coasts/lakes/tundra
CLUTCH SIZE 5–9

DISTRIBUTION Resident in Iceland and Scandinavia; moves to tundra in summer and retreats to ice-free coasts of western Europe in winter.

THIS IS A SMALL, COMPACT, diving sea duck with a rounded head and very short bill. In winter, the drakes have mostly white plumage with a black chest and wing bars, and a chestnut back, but in summer, they have much darker heads and necks with a large white cheek patch. Females and juveniles are browner with a pale area around the eye. Long-tailed Ducks are familiar winter visitors to many stretches of coastline, especially in the North Sea and Baltic, where they sometimes gather in large flocks offshore. They are constantly on the move, diving for molluscs on the sea bed or pursuing each other on the surface. Sometimes a whole flock takes off and flies rapidly to another area where they settle in great excitement. On migration to their breeding grounds, vast flocks gather in the Baltic before heading north in vast numbers, usually in late May. When breeding, they may be more scattered. They make strange yodelling calls on the nest sites.

PINK BILL The drake Long-tailed Duck in winter is unmistakeable with its very long tail and pink-tipped bill.

FALCONIFORMES

Birds of prey

Although some members of this Order are large in size, others are surprisingly small, reflecting the adaptability of the group as a whole. All members of this Order are predatory birds, but they may not be active hunters. A number of species, notably vultures, scavenge on carcasses, while others will avail themselves of carrion when it is available.

All species have hooked bills and powerful feet, equipped with curved nails often described as talons. These serve to catch and hold their prey more effectively. As they are at the top of the food chain, birds of prey are generally not very numerous.

Black Kite

FAMILY Accipitridae
SPECIES *Milvus migrans*
LENGTH 55 cm (21¾ in)/ wingspan 170 cm (67 in)
HABITAT Open country
CLUTCH SIZE 2–3

DISTRIBUTION Summer visitor extending from the Iberian Peninsula across much of Europe; widespread in eastern areas.

BLACK KITES occur in a wide range of habitats, and are the world's most common bird of prey. They may even be seen near city areas, where they will scavenge on garbage, although rodents and rabbits are their more usual prey.

NOT BLACK Despite its name, this kite's plumage is not in fact black. Its underparts are brownish.

Red Kite

FAMILY Accipitridae
SPECIES *Milvus milvus*
LENGTH 70 cm (27½ in)/ wingspan 185 cm (73 cm)
HABITAT Woodland
CLUTCH SIZE 1–3

DISTRIBUTION Resident in the Iberian Peninsula and to the northeast. Reintroduced in parts of the United Kingdom.

THESE KITES USED to be very common in towns and cities in the United Kingdom, including London, but by the early 1900s they had been almost totally wiped out due to human persecution; the remaining birds were confined to Wales. A successful reintroduction scheme has since seen their numbers increase significantly again.

FISH EATERS These kites are often found near water and fish feature in their diet, but they are adaptable, and may steal from other birds.

Black-winged Kite

FAMILY Accipitridae
SPECIES *Elanus caeruleus*
LENGTH 35 cm (13¾ in)/
wingspan 95 cm (37½ in)
HABITAT Open country
CLUTCH SIZE 3–4

DISTRIBUTION A rare species, confined to southwest France, north and western Spain, and southern Portugal. Also occurs in North Africa.

A PALE WHITE HEAD and underparts, with pale grey colouring over the back and wings, helps to identify adult birds of this species. Black wing patches are present on the shoulders. They feed mainly on rodents, preferring to hunt in grassland areas, although they may also prey on small birds.

YOUNG BIRD This is a young Black-winged Kite, recognizable by the rusty suffusion on the chest and underparts.

Osprey

FAMILY Pandionidae

SPECIES *Pandion haliaetus*

LENGTH 60 cm (23¾ in)/
wingspan 158 cm (62¼ in)

HABITAT Near lakes and coasts

CLUTCH SIZE 2–3

DISTRIBUTION Summer visitor
to parts of Scandinavia and
eastern Europe, also Scotland.
Resident in western Spain and
in the Mediterranean.

ALSO KNOWN AS the Fish Hawk because
of its specialized feeding habits, the
Osprey hunts over the sea as well as
freshwater, hovering to look for fish in the
water below. It then dives down feet first,
aiming to grab its quarry in its powerful
talons. Pairs nest high up, building a large
platform of twigs and other items such as
driftwood and seaweed. This can measure
over 100 cm (40 in) in diameter, and is
often reused annually.

FEEDING YOUNGSTERS Young Ospreys spend up to
two months in the nest before flying for the first time.

Short-toed Eagle

FAMILY Accipitridae

SPECIES *Circaetus gallicus*

LENGTH 69 cm (27 in)/
wingspan 190 cm (75 in)

HABITAT Open country

CLUTCH SIZE 1

DISTRIBUTION Summer visitor
to the Iberian Peninsula and
France and to eastern Europe.
Overwinters in the Middle East
and northwest Africa.

THESE EAGLES are found in arid
areas, where they hunt reptiles,
particularly snakes, although they
also prey on lizards. Mammals and
birds form a relatively insignificant
part of their diet. Short-toed Eagles
rely on their very keen eyesight to
detect their quarry beneath them
while in flight, although they may
also hunt from a convenient perch.
These eagles can tackle large
snakes, over 150 cm (59 in) in
length, including venomous species,
holding them down with their feet
and killing them with their powerful
beak. They have also been observed
catching amphibians in water.

DISTINCTIVE Adult Short-toed Eagles of both
sexes have darker brown upperparts, and
distinctive barring on their underparts.

Spanish Imperial Eagle

FAMILY Accipitridae

SPECIES *Aquila adalberti*

LENGTH 85 cm (33½ in)/ wingspan 132 cm (52 in)

HABITAT Open country

CLUTCH SIZE 2–3

DISTRIBUTION Restricted to central and southwestern parts of Spain, much further to the west than the range of the closely related Imperial Eagle.

PREYING FROM ABOVE These eagles often hunt by swooping down on their prey from a perch. Many young birds are killed in flight by colliding with power lines.

THE RANGE OF this species has contracted significantly over the course of the past century. It used to be seen over virtually the entire Iberian Peninsula, and also occurred in Morocco, but hunting pressures have taken a severe toll on its numbers. Furthermore, the introduction of the rabbit disease myxomatosis to Europe in the 1950s decimated the numbers of rabbits, which form the mainstay of its diet. By the end of the 1970s its population had dropped to just 30 pairs, but current estimates suggest there are now in the region of 130 pairs. This means that the Spanish Imperial Eagle is still one of the most critically endangered birds of prey in the world.

OSPREY (*see* p 90) The power of the osprey is such that it can seize and lift fish weighing up to 2 kg (4.4 lb) from the water's surface. Once airborne, the osprey carries its prey in both feet, keeping the fish horizontal, the head forwards.

Golden Eagle

FAMILY Accipitridae

SPECIES *Aquila chrysaetos*

LENGTH 91 cm (36 in)/
wingspan 210 cm (82¾ in)

HABITAT Upland mountain
areas

CLUTCH SIZE 1–3

DISTRIBUTION Found in the
Iberian Peninsula, Scotland,
and sporadically in southern
and eastern Europe. Resident
in northern Scandinavia.

THE COLOUR OF the Golden Eagle is predominantly dark brown; a paler, golden-brown area of plumage evident in the vicinity of the neck accounts for its name. These eagles tend to inhabit remote areas, such as the Scottish moors, where they display a variety of hunting techniques. They may fly high, swooping down on their quarry, or can travel low over the ground, attempting to flush their prey from cover. Alternatively, a Golden Eagle may choose a perch, from where it can scan the surrounding area for hunting opportunities. Although they are sometimes blamed for taking lambs, the reality is that they tend only to scavenge on the carcasses. Rodents, rabbits, and birds, including grouse, feature prominently in their diet in Europe. However, Golden Eagles are adaptable hunters: as an example, the population on the Swedish island of Gotland prey largely on hedgehogs, in the absence of other larger prey. When breeding, pairs construct a large eyrie, which is often at least 150 cm (59 in) in diameter. They add to this each year, so eventually a nest can be up to 200 cm (79 in) across. Young birds may stay with their parents for months after fledging.

IMPOSING PREDATOR Golden Eagles roam over a wide expanse of countryside, with a single pair typically occupying an area of 100 sq km (38 sq miles).

Great Spotted Eagle

FAMILY Accipitridae

SPECIES *Aquila clanga*

LENGTH 69 cm (27 in)/
wingspan 168 cm (66 in)

HABITAT Woodland/wetland

CLUTCH SIZE 1–3

DISTRIBUTION Summer visitor
from southern Scandinavia
south to the Ukraine. Resident
around north Italy. Overwinters
in the Middle East and Africa.

THESE EAGLES ARE great wanderers, sometimes travelling enormous distances from their traditional range, which is reflected by a few confirmed sightings in Spain. Pairs occupy very large territories, even where prey is plentiful, so they are not easily observed. The female is significantly larger in size than her mate. Their eggs are laid in a large nest made of sticks and vegetation, built high in a tree. Hatching should occur after six weeks, with fledging taking place about two months later.

WHITE FLECKS
This youngster has the typically juvenile white markings on its back and wings. It will finally acquire adult plumage at five years old.

Imperial Eagle

FAMILY Accipitridae

SPECIES *Aquila heliaca*

LENGTH 83 cm (32¾ in)/
wingspan 132 cm (52 in)

HABITAT Open country

CLUTCH SIZE 2–3

DISTRIBUTION Occurs in
southeast and east Europe, to
the west of the Caspian Sea.
Resident in areas in the south
as far as the Mediterranean.

SEPARATED BY a considerable distance from their Spanish relatives (*see* p 91), Imperial Eagles also range over a much wider area. Their feeding preferences are influenced by their location, although these eagles will generally take their quarry on the ground rather than in flight. In wetland areas, they will feed on water birds too, even hunting flamingos, and they have been known to kill smaller birds of prey such as Marsh Harriers. Imperial Eagles also eat carrion, particularly during the breeding season when there are chicks to feed in the nest.

WARM WINTERS Imperial Eagles breed in
eastern Europe but may fly as far south as the
Nile Valley in Tanzania to overwinter.

Steppe Eagle

FAMILY Accipitridae

SPECIES *Aquila nipalensis*

LENGTH 74 cm (29 in)/ wingspan 190 cm (75 in)

HABITAT Open country

CLUTCH SIZE 1–3

DISTRIBUTION Breeding range includes the very southeast of Europe; otherwise restricted to Russia and extinct in Ukraine. Overwinters in eastern Africa.

THESE EAGLES MAY BE SEEN more widely in Europe when they are migrating across the southeastern part of the continent. Their main area of distribution extends eastwards, across Asia. Those found in western parts feed almost entirely on susliks (ground squirrels), rather than other rodents or other prey. Although they may drop down on their quarry, Steppe Eagles also wait patiently by the susliks' burrows, seizing individuals as they emerge from underground. They may even chase prey on foot, particularly in the case of invertebrates. Occurring in relatively open country, these birds of prey tend to nest in among rocks or may use an abandoned building for this purpose. A wide variety of material, ranging from old clothing to bones, may be used to build their nest. The incubation period will last approximately 45 days, with the young eagles fledging once they are about two months of age.

SOLITARY Only when they are migrating are Steppe Eagles likely to be seen in flocks.

Lesser Spotted Eagle

FAMILY Accipitridae

SPECIES *Aquila pomarina*

LENGTH 65 cm (25½ in)/
wingspan 150 cm (59 in)

HABITAT Grassland

CLUTCH SIZE 1–3

DISTRIBUTION Summer visitor
from northeastern Germany
and Poland, south to Turkey.
Winters in southeastern and
central areas of southern Africa.

ITS SLIGHTLY SMALLER SIZE can help to distinguish the Lesser Spotted Eagle from its larger relative (*see* p 95). Juveniles can be distinguished easily, as they have a distinctive red-golden patch on the nape of the neck. They are also not as heavily spotted with white over their wings. Adults are less easily identified, but the Lesser Spotted Eagle has a smaller bill, and shorter feathering on the upper part of the legs. In some parts of their range, amphibians make up a significant proportion of the Lesser Spotted Eagle's diet. They favour small quarry, ranging from frogs to voles, sometimes hunting on the ground. A pair will build their nest in woodland, high up in a tree. The same site may be used repeatedly, for up to a decade.

NESTING SITES While these eagles hunt in open country, pairs will seek out nearby wooded areas where they can breed in trees. They prefer remote areas.

Tawny Eagle

FAMILY Accipitridae

SPECIES *Aquila rapax*

LENGTH 72 cm (28¼ in)/
wingspan 185 cm (73 in)

HABITAT Wooded areas

CLUTCH SIZE 1–3

DISTRIBUTION Ranges up to
North Africa and may be seen
in Europe, but it is not resident,
nor does it breed here. Present
also in Asia.

ALTHOUGH TAWNY EAGLES are not seen with any regularity in Europe, they are nomadic by nature and some North African birds may cross the Straits of Gibraltar and be seen in southern parts of Spain. This species is often relatively pale in colour, as befits a bird which lives in semi-desert countryside, with pairs being forced to nest in the open. Young birds are even paler than adults; their plumage is beige overall. Inhabiting areas where hunting opportunities are limited, these eagles will frequently eat carrion, and they are also adept at stealing food from other predators.

GROUND FEEDER Tawny
Eagles will hunt insects on
the ground, as well as
frequently feeding on carrion,
often roadkill.

White-tailed Sea Eagle

FAMILY Accipitridae

SPECIES *Haliaeetus albicilla*

LENGTH 91 cm (36 in)/
wingspan 274 cm (108 in)

HABITAT Coasts/rivers

CLUTCH SIZE 2

DISTRIBUTION Occurs from
northern Norway south to
Turkey in suitable habitats.
Successfully reintroduced to
some areas, including Scotland.

THESE LARGE EAGLES occurred over a much wider area of western Europe, but their numbers fell dramatically during the 20th century. These eagles have also been reintroduced to parts of their range where they had become extinct, as in Scotland, using young birds brought from other areas where the species occurs, and their numbers are increasing again in some regions. They feed not just on fish, but also water birds and carrion.

FISHING SKILLS A White-tailed Sea Eagle grabs a fish from the water in its powerful talons.

Bonelli's Eagle

FAMILY Accipitridae

SPECIES *Hieraaetus fasciatus*

LENGTH 65 cm (25½ in)/
wingspan 180 cm (71 in)

HABITAT Wooded areas

CLUTCH SIZE 1–3

DISTRIBUTION Confined to
southern Europe. Most common
on the Iberian Peninsula;
resident throughout its range.

RED AND WHITE Adult Bonelli's Eagles have streaked, whitish underparts, while those of juveniles are a reddish-buff shade, with markings restricted to the vicinity of the throat.

BONELLI'S EAGLE RANKS as one of the rarer eagles of Europe, with its total population believed to be comprised of fewer than 1,000 pairs. Even in its Spanish heartland, its numbers have undergone a significant decline over recent decades. While it is heavily hunted, partly because it is thought to catch racing pigeons, habitat changes affecting the availability of other prey such as partridges have had an adverse impact on its numbers as well. Birds feature prominently in its diet, along with rabbits. Pairs have sometimes been recorded as hunting in tandem, one eagle driving quarry towards its waiting mate.

Booted Eagle

FAMILY Accipitridae

SPECIES *Hieraaetus pennatus*

LENGTH 51 cm (20 in)/
wingspan 120 cm (47¼ in)

HABITAT Open country

CLUTCH SIZE 1–3

DISTRIBUTION Summer visitor
in the Iberian Peninsula and
France. Present in areas of
eastern and northern Europe.

DIMINUTIVE EAGLE The Booted
Eagle is one of the smallest species
of eagles, and is variable in
coloration. The paler version is
often more numerous.

THE COLORATION of Booted Eagles
can vary quite markedly within
individual populations, with two
distinctive colour morphs being
recognized. The more common of
these is the so-called dark or rufous
morph, which is reddish-brown in
colour, as its name suggests. There is
also a pale morph, identifiable by its
pale grey coloration, although it still
has a slight rufous tinge to its body.
The majority of Booted Eagles also
have a white area on each side of the
wing which is most apparent from the
front. This feature, when present,
allows them to be distinguished
easily from other birds of prey.
In addition, Booted Eagles
have dense white feathering
resembling boots extending
down the legs to the
feet, which gives
them their name.

Egyptian Vulture

FAMILY Accipitridae

SPECIES *Neophron percnopterus*

LENGTH 65 cm (25½ in)/ wingspan 168 cm (66 in)

HABITAT Montane areas

CLUTCH SIZE 1–3

DISTRIBUTION Summer resident in the Iberian Peninsula, the Balearics, Sicily, southern Italy, and the eastern Mediterranean, via Greece to Turkey. Overwinters in Africa.

THESE BIRDS OF PREY will seek edible items at rubbish dumps through their range, although they will also catch various invertebrates such as locusts. In some areas, they have learnt to smash the eggs of other birds, such as pelicans, by hitting them with stones.

SLENDER BILL The bill of the Egyptian Vulture is long and slender, very suited to scavenging.

Lammergeier

FAMILY Accipitridae

SPECIES *Gypaetus barbatus*

LENGTH 125 cm (49¼ in)/ wingspan 280 cm (110¼ in)

HABITAT Montane areas

CLUTCH SIZE 1–2

DISTRIBUTION Resident in the Pyrenees between France and Spain. Also occurs around the Mediterranean, being found on Corsica, and in eastern Greece and Turkey.

THESE VULTURES will frequently consume bones, in addition to carrion. They sometimes pick up large bones weighing nearly 4 kg (9 lb), and drop these from some height in order to smash them into smaller pieces which they can eat. They also treat tortoises in this way, picking them up from the ground.

BONE BREAKER The Lammergeier needs patience: it may take a bird 20 or so attempts to break a bone by dropping it onto rocks.

Griffon Vulture

FAMILY Accipitridae

SPECIES *Gyps fulvus*

LENGTH 110 cm (43½ in)/ wingspan 265 cm (104½ in)

HABITAT Montane areas

CLUTCH SIZE 1

DISTRIBUTION Resident across the Iberian Peninsula, in the eastern Mediterranean area, east through Turkey.

THE HUGE SIZE of these vultures means they are hard to overlook. Although they do not associate in flocks, groups of up to 40 soon form around a fresh carcass. They feed on the body organs of larger mammals such as goats, using their powerful bills to open the body cavity.

STRONG SENSES Griffon Vultures can locate carcasses on the ground by their keen eyesight and their acute sense of smell.

Eurasian Black Vulture

FAMILY Accipitridae

SPECIES *Aegypius monachus*

LENGTH 115 cm (45¼ in)/ wingspan 295 cm (116 in)

HABITAT Montane areas

CLUTCH SIZE 1–2

ALSO SOMETIMES known as the Monk Vulture, this species is the largest of the vultures seen outside the Americas. It is not easy to distinguish the sexes because, unlike many other birds of prey, the females are not significantly larger than their mates. Incubation lasts about two months, and the young vultures spend nearly four months in the nest.

DARK COLOURS These vultures are dark brownish-black in colour overall, with a pale pinkish area of skin evident on the head of the adults.

DISTRIBUTION Occurs in central Spain and the Balearics. Also present in the eastern Mediterranean from Greece to Turkey, and to the north and northeast of the Black Sea.

VULTURES AT A FEAST A group of Griffon Vultures around a carcass. Individuals may gorge themselves to such an extent that they are unable to fly without regurgitating some food first. Large groups prevent other animals feeding.

Northern Marsh Harrier

FAMILY Accipitridae

SPECIES *Circus aeruginosus*

LENGTH 55 cm (21¾ in)/
wingspan 122 cm (48 in)

HABITAT Wetland areas

CLUTCH SIZE 4–5

DISTRIBUTION Ranges from
Spain north through western
Europe and is a summer visitor
in northern Europe. Mainly
overwinters in Africa.

AS THEIR NAME SUGGESTS, the
distribution of this harrier is closely allied
to wetland areas, where there are large
areas of reeds, providing them with
nesting cover. They seek prey further
afield, however, even venturing over
farmland. They catch a wide variety of
quarry, with rodents featuring prominently
in their diet. Northern Marsh Harriers also
take water birds, and are quite capable of
overpowering species as big as the
Common Pheasant (*see* p 127). They hunt
mainly on the wing, plunging down onto
their quarry as soon as it is sighted.

HUNTING TRIP
Northern Marsh
Harriers may hunt as
far as 8 km (5 miles)
from their nest site.
Sometimes, they may
not catch their own
prey, but will steal it
from Hen Harriers.

Hen Harrier

FAMILY Accipitridae

SPECIES *Circus cyaneus*

LENGTH 55 cm (21¾ in)/
wingspan 110 cm (43¼ in)

HABITAT Open country

CLUTCH SIZE 4–6

DISTRIBUTION Resident in
parts of Spain, France, Ireland,
Scotland, and parts of northern
Europe. Summer visitor further
north. Overwinters in the south.

THE HEN HARRIER is an
adaptable species that can be
seen in all types of open country
through its wide range, which
includes moorland and dunes.
When hunting, the larger
females are able to catch bigger
prey than males. Pairs generally
nest on the ground, choosing a
well-concealed location,
although in Ireland, they may
nest in trees. Their young
develop quite rapidly, to the
extent that they are able to leave
the nest from just two weeks of
age if danger threatens.

BROWN HEN Sexing of this species is
possible not just on the basis of size, but
also coloration: hens are brown.

Pallid Harrier

FAMILY Accipitridae

SPECIES *Circus macrourus*

LENGTH 50 cm (19¾ in)/
wingspan 110 cm (43¼ in)

HABITAT Open country

CLUTCH SIZE 4–5

DISTRIBUTION In the summer occurs in the northeast, above the Black Sea, extending via the Caspian Sea into Asia. Overwinters in Africa.

THESE HARRIERS WANDER across a much wider area of Europe than their distribution suggests, being recorded as far west as Britain every two or three years. Small mammals such as voles form the basis of their diet, but they also prey on birds and insects.

PALE COLORATION The cock Pallid Harrier is grey with white underparts; hens are brown with a pale collar.

Montagu's Harrier

FAMILY Accipitridae

SPECIES *Circus pygargus*

LENGTH 50 cm (19¾ in)/
wingspan 112 cm (44 in)

HABITAT Open country

CLUTCH SIZE 4–5

DISTRIBUTION Summer visitor to the Iberian Peninsula, France, and sporadically across Europe; more widespread in the east. Overwinters in Africa.

THIS SPECIES is decidedly rare in some areas, with typically fewer than ten pairs being recorded as breeding in Britain each year. Even so, Montagu's Harrier does breed regularly in some 18 European countries, and may do so on a more limited basis in about a dozen others, so that it is relatively widespread. Pairs usually nest on the ground, on a suitable pad of vegetation. The chicks hatch after approximately a month, and will be able to fly about five weeks later.

COCK BIRD The black wing patch evident in the cock bird distinguishes Montagu's Harrier from a male Hen Harrier.

Levant Sparrowhawk

FAMILY Accipitridae
SPECIES *Accipter brevipes*
LENGTH 37 cm (14½ in)/ wingspan 76 cm (30 in)
HABITAT Wooded areas
CLUTCH SIZE 3–5

DISTRIBUTION Summer visitor to Greece, Turkey, and countries northeast of the Black Sea. Spends winter in Africa.

LEVANT SPARROWHAWKS feed mainly on insects as well as small lizards. The cock can be easily distinguished from the Eurasian Sparrowhawk by its grey rather than rufous cheek coloration, while hens have reddish-brown, rather than greyish, barring on their underparts. The habits of these two species are also different, because Levant Sparrowhawks migrate in sometimes large flocks of hundreds of individuals, although at other times, they will be seen individually or in pairs.

TREE NEST Levant Sparrowhawks breed off the ground in a tree, constructing a small nest of twigs and vegetation.

Northern Goshawk

FAMILY Accipitridae
SPECIES *Accipter gentilis*
LENGTH 56 cm (22 in)/ wingspan 150 cm (59 in)
HABITAT Forest
CLUTCH SIZE 3–4

DISTRIBUTION Resident in most of Europe; absent from or has a restricted range in central Scandinavia, Ireland, Britain, Italy, and Turkey.

THESE POWERFUL PREDATORS hunt both mammals and birds. Owls can fall victim to these goshawks, as may other diurnal birds of prey, such as the Honey Buzzard (*see* p 109). Among mammals, squirrels and rabbits are popular targets.

Female Northern Goshawks are predominantly brown in colour, whereas the cock birds are mainly grey.

BULKY NEST Northern Goshawks breed in a forest setting, building a bulky structure as their nest.

Eurasian Sparrowhawk

FAMILY Accipitridae

SPECIES *Accipter nisus*

LENGTH 34 cm (13½ in)/ wingspan 62 cm (24½ in)

HABITAT Woodland/parks

CLUTCH SIZE 4–6

DISTRIBUTION Widely found in Europe, except northern Scotland and northern Scandinavia, though a summer visitor here and into Russia.

THESE RELATIVELY small birds of prey are quite commonly seen in city parks, where they hunt small birds such as sparrows and starlings. In the countryside, they can prey on species as big as the Common Pheasant (*see* p 127). They are very agile, able to twist their bodies in flight to grab prey, as well as being capable of pursuing an individual trying to escape at high speed. Their nest is made of twigs, and built in a tree. The incubation period lasts about five weeks, with the young fledging a month later.

YOUNGSTER Dark brown upperparts characterize a juvenile Eurasian Sparrowhawk. Adults have slate-grey upperparts, with a rufous tinge on the underparts in the case of the cock.

Common Buzzard

FAMILY Accipitridae

SPECIES *Buteo buteo*

LENGTH 58 cm (23 in)/ wingspan 120 cm (47¼ in)

HABITAT Wooded areas

CLUTCH SIZE 2–4

DISTRIBUTION Resident in western Europe to the Caspian Sea. Widespread in summer from Sweden to west Russia. Overwinters in the south.

THESE ARE CONSPICUOUS and common birds of prey throughout most of their range. Common Buzzards hunt a wide variety of small mammals, birds, reptiles, and amphibians, and this adaptability helps to explain why the species is so widespread. They will even catch earthworms and other invertebrates, especially when food is scarce. When breeding, the pair will build a large nest of sticks and other vegetation, constructed up to about 25 m (80 ft) high in a tree. It will take around five weeks for the eggs to hatch; the young buzzards leave the nest about two months later.

VIEWPOINT Common Buzzards will perch on fence posts, as shown here, looking for small mammals such as voles in their vicinity.

Rough-legged Buzzard

FAMILY Accipitridae

SPECIES *Buteo lagopus*

LENGTH 59 cm (23¼ in)/ wingspan 135 cm (53 in)

HABITAT Upland areas

CLUTCH SIZE 3–4

DISTRIBUTION Summer visitor to the far north of Europe, from Norway to European Russia. Winter range from northern Italy up and around the Black Sea.

THE BREEDING RANGE of these buzzards over the summer months extends right up to the tundra, forcing them to nest on the ground as there are no trees growing here because of the extreme cold. Lemmings form a significant part of their diet in this environment, as does carrion. Over the winter, Rough-legged Buzzards prey to a greater extent on rabbits and birds.

HIGH PERCH A large pile of sticks serves as the basis for the Rough-legged Buzzard's nest. It may be built on a cliff face, as here.

Long-legged Buzzard

FAMILY Accipitridae

SPECIES *Buteo rufinus*

LENGTH 61 cm (24 in)/
wingspan 135 cm (53 in)

HABITAT Arid areas

CLUTCH SIZE 3–4

DISTRIBUTION Summer visitor to Greece, and to northeast of the Black Sea, into European Russia. Winters in Turkey, east to the Caspian Sea and into Asia.

IT IS NOT UNKNOWN for these buzzards to turn up in Spain, but such birds are likely to be members of the slightly smaller North African race (*Buteo rufinus cirtensis*). There is also a dark-coloured morph, which is seen most often in birds from eastern areas. Pairs create a large nest that is usually built in a relatively inaccessible area, often on a cliff face, although occasionally they may take over an abandoned nest.

VARIED DIET Long-legged Buzzards feed mainly on rodents in some areas, whereas in largely arid country, lizards and snakes will feature more prominently in their diet.

Honey Buzzard

FAMILY Accipitridae

SPECIES *Pernis apivorus*

LENGTH 59 cm (23¼ in)/
wingspan 142 cm (56 in)

HABITAT Wooded areas

CLUTCH SIZE 2

DISTRIBUTION Summer range from southeast England and the Iberian Peninsula to south Scandinavia and European Russia. Overwinters in Africa.

AS ITS NAME IMPLIES, the Honey Buzzard will seek out the nests of bees and wasps, breaking into them to feed on the combs and grubs, as well as the adults. These birds seem largely immune to the stings of the insects buzzing around them as they plunder the nest. When food of this type is in short supply, Honey Buzzards will feed on other invertebrates and small creatures such as amphibians, resorting to hunting other birds on occasions too.

SCARCE The species is rare in parts of its range – for example only about 15 pairs breed in Britain – but common elsewhere.

Lanner Falcon

FAMILY Falconidae

SPECIES *Falco biarmicus*

LENGTH 51 cm (20 in)/
wingspan 100 cm (39½ in)

HABITAT Arid country

CLUTCH SIZE 3–4

DISTRIBUTION Resident in parts of southern Europe, mainly the eastern Mediterranean, including Greece and Crete. Also present in North Africa.

LIVING IN OPEN arid country, these falcons tend to hunt small birds, using their aerial agility and speed to catch their quarry in midair. It is not uncommon for both members of a pair to hunt collaboratively. Lanner Falcons are scarce in Europe, with their population thought to be a maximum of 360 pairs. They usually breed on cliff faces, laying their eggs in a bare scrape on the ground.

BIRD HUNTER Small gamebirds, such as quails, are a favoured target of these falcons, but they will also hunt birds of prey, with Lesser Kestrels (*see* p 112) regularly caught by them in Sicily.

Saker Falcon

FAMILY Falconidae

SPECIES *Falco cherrug*

LENGTH 55 cm (21¾ in)/
wingspan 114 cm (45 in)

HABITAT Wooded steppes

CLUTCH SIZE 3–5

DISTRIBUTION Summer visitor from north of the Black Sea to Russia, and resident in areas to the west. Overwinters on Sardinia, Sicily, and eastwards.

AS A HUNTER, the Saker Falcon generally targets small mammals, although birds may also form a significant part of its diet. The species is not especially widespread in Europe, however, where its total population is estimated to be comprised of a maximum of 700 pairs; it is far more common in Asia. When breeding, a pair may colonize an existing nest built in a tree by a heron or stork, for example. The incubation period lasts a month, with the young leaving the nest by seven weeks old.

ADAPTABLE Sakers feed on whatever prey is available and nest on electricity pylons where trees are uncommon.

Merlin

FAMILY Falconidae

SPECIES *Falco columbarius*

LENGTH 33 cm (13 in)/ wingspan 56 cm (22 in)

HABITAT Open country

CLUTCH SIZE 3–6

DISTRIBUTION Summer visitor to Scandinavia, the Baltic States, and Russia. Resident over the United Kingdom. Overwinters here and in southern Europe.

THESE BIRDS OF PREY of the far north are recognizable partly by their size, as they are the smallest of all falcons. They prey on small birds, which they pursue and catch in flight, as well as flying insects such as butterflies and dragonflies. Before they have mastered the aerial agility that is necessary to seize prey in flight, young Merlins more often feed on rodents caught on the ground. Merlins may hunt together in pairs or groups.

CHOICE OF HABITAT Merlins are to be found in a wide range of different habitats, with much depending on the time of year.

Eleonora's Falcon

FAMILY Falconidae

SPECIES *Falco eleonorae*

LENGTH 42 cm (16½ in)/ wingspan 120 cm (47¼ in)

HABITAT Coastal cliffs

CLUTCH SIZE 2–3

DISTRIBUTION Summer visitor through the Mediterranean, from the Balearics eastwards. Particularly common in the Aegean. Overwinters in Africa.

UNLIKE MOST BIRDS of prey, Eleonora's Falcons are gregarious in their habits. There are about a hundred colonies scattered across Europe, each comprised of up to 20 pairs, although larger groups numbering about 300 pairs have been recorded. They often nest on the ground, typically on cliff ledges near the sea. Hatching coincides with the period in the year, usually August, when songbirds are starting to migrate back from Europe to Africa, as food will be more abundant then.

EARLY LEARNING Young Eleonora's Falcons often have to migrate within two weeks of fledging.

Lesser Kestrel

FAMILY Falconidae

SPECIES *Falco naumanni*

LENGTH 37 cm (14½ in)/
wingspan 65 cm (25½ in)

HABITAT Open country

CLUTCH SIZE 3–5

DISTRIBUTION Summer visitor
across southern Europe and
into Russia, with a small
resident population in southern
Spain. Overwinters in Africa.

LESSER KESTRELS often lives in colonies.
These are typically comprised of up to 30
pairs, although as many as 250 have been
recorded at a single locality. The birds
will often select tall buildings for their
colonies, typically nesting high up on a
cathedral or church roof, for example.
Other popular nesting areas are
abandoned quarries and similar
workings. However, they may even make
use of nestboxes put out for them. The
young hatch after about 28 days, fledging
in a further five to six weeks.

AT RISK The Lesser Kestrel's numbers have fallen
dramatically across Europe over the past 50 years or
so. It feeds largely on invertebrates.

Peregrine Falcon

FAMILY Falconidae

SPECIES *Falco peregrinus*

LENGTH 45 cm (17¾ in)/ wingspan 105 cm (41½ in)

HABITAT Open country

CLUTCH SIZE 3–4

DISTRIBUTION Resident in the Iberian Peninsula, parts of the United Kingdom, and southern Europe. Summer visitor to Scandinavia and Russia.

A HUNTING PEREGRINE will dive from the sky onto a bird flying beneath it, closing on its target at speeds that may approach 400 kph (250 mph). Peregrines frequently target pigeons, which has made them unpopular with those who race these birds, but these falcons may also hunt starlings and other birds of similar size, as well as rodents and even insects. They are naturally found in craggy areas, often breeding on cliff ledges, and this has helped them to adapt to living in cities. Here they hunt from tall buildings, swooping down to catch pigeons.

LARGE HEN The female Peregrine Falcon is significantly larger and heavier than her mate.

Gyrfalcon

FAMILY Falconidae

SPECIES *Falco rusticolus*

LENGTH 63 cm (25 in)/ wingspan 145 cm (57 in)

HABITAT Wooded areas

CLUTCH SIZE 3–4

DISTRIBUTION Resident from northern Norway into European Russia. Overwinters also over a wider area to the south.

GYRFALCONS RANK as the largest of the falcons, with the whitish plumage seen in some individuals helping to provide camouflage in the snowy landscape where they occur. They have the ability to fly quickly, thanks to their powerful wings, but also with relatively little effort. Gyrfalcons hunt birds such as Ptarmigans (*see* p 117), knocking them out of the sky, and also rodents, particularly lemmings. When nesting, a pair may utilize a ledge on a cliff face. Incubation period lasts about a month and it is a further seven weeks before the young falcons fly for the first time.

SHADES OF GREY This is a grey morph of the Gyrfalcon. There is a dark morph with blackish-brown upperparts, and a striking all-white form.

Eurasian Hobby

FAMILY Falconidae

SPECIES *Falco subbuteo*

LENGTH 35 cm (13¾ in)/ wingspan 88 cm (34¾ in)

HABITAT Open woodland

CLUTCH SIZE 3

DISTRIBUTION Summer visitor across the Iberian Peninsula, but rarer in France; occurs in southern England, north to southern Scandinavia and east.

ALSO KNOWN AS the Northern Hobby, this species flies long distances annually, to and from its winter range in southern Africa. In Europe, it is essentially a solitary species, although sometimes seen in pairs or family groups after the breeding season; within its African range, however, these hobbies often roost communally. Invertebrates form the mainstay of their diet, although they are more inclined to hunt small birds during the breeding period. They are sufficiently agile to prey on swifts and swallows. Pairs nest on the fringes of woodland, usually taking over

the nests of crows, but this can prove to be their undoing. It is thought that up to half of the nests of Eurasian Hobbies may be plundered by crows, and squirrels too will steal their eggs. The weather can have a marked influence on the level of breeding success. In wet summers, pairs struggle to obtain sufficient food to raise their young.

RED MARKS Young hobbies lack the red markings, described as 'trousers', on the legs of adult birds.

Common Kestrel

FAMILY Falconidae

SPECIES *Falco tinnunculus*

LENGTH 37 cm (14½ in)/
wingspan 76 cm (30 in)

HABITAT Open country

CLUTCH SIZE 3–6

DISTRIBUTION Widely
resident throughout southern
Europe. Summer visitor north
of the Caspian Sea, apart from
parts of Scandinavia.

THESE KESTRELS LIVE IN both rural and city environments. The Common Kestrel's keen eyesight enables it to spot potential prey on the ground as it hovers overhead. Sometimes, it may be seen resting on a telephone wire, from where it will also dive down if a hunting opportunity presents itself. Rodents and invertebrates are the main items in their diet, although they are opportunistic, preying on small birds and other creatures.

HEN BIRD Cock birds can be distinguished from hens by having a greyish head and no barring on the upper side of the tail.

Red-footed Falcon

FAMILY Falconidae

SPECIES *Falco vespertinus*

LENGTH 34 cm (13½ in)/
wingspan 72 cm (28½ in)

HABITAT Open country

CLUTCH SIZE 3–4

DISTRIBUTION Summer visitor
to eastern Europe, west of the
Caspian Sea, north to the Baltic
states, and southern Finland.

THE WEATHER can play a significant role in the summer distribution of the Red-footed Falcon, with anticyclones causing these birds to be seen well outside their normal range. They may then be sighted in Sweden and westwards to the United Kingdom. Red-footed Falcons migrate some 11,000 km (6,875 miles) to Africa usually in September, returning to their breeding grounds from April onwards, where they may nest communally.

FEET AND LEGS One of the most evident features of these falcons is their red feet; the colour extends up their legs, too.

GALLIFORMES

Pheasants, partridges, and grouse

These birds are generally ground-dwellers, well adapted to move on foot, although they can fly if danger threatens. Their flight tends to be quite clumsy, however, and they will glide down to another suitable area of cover relatively nearby. Cock birds are generally more brightly coloured. In some species, polygamy occurs, with a male being surrounded by a group of hens, while in other cases, communal displays serve to permit the hens to choose their own mates. Young birds are able to follow their parents directly after hatching, although they cannot fly at this stage.

Willow Grouse

FAMILY Tetraonidae
SPECIES *Lagopus lagopus*
LENGTH 38 cm (15 in)
HABITAT Tundra/shrub
CLUTCH SIZE 7–12

DISTRIBUTION Occurs in parts of Ireland and Scotland, with the main area of distribution extending from Scandinavia eastwards through Russia and south to the Baltic States.

WILLOW GROUSE typically occur in areas of moorland, right up into the far north where it is too cold for trees to grow. Here they may feed to a large extent on willow, eating the catkins in the spring, and pecking off buds and even twigs to sustain them over the bleak winter. The appearance of the Willow Grouse alters to match the seasons, helping to prevent them being exposed to predators in the open landscape where they occur. During the winter, their plumage becomes snow-white, reflecting the frozen landscape, and they are more likely to be seen in small flocks. In summer, their brownish plumage enables them to merge very effectively with the earth. Those occurring in Ireland and on the Scottish moorlands are often called Red Grouse, having very prominent red combs, with this population not acquiring white winter plumage.

FIDELITY Pairs of these grouse will stay together throughout the nesting period, watching over the chicks.

Rock Ptarmigan

FAMILY Tetraonidae
SPECIES *Lagopus mutus*
LENGTH 36 cm (14 in)
HABITAT Tundra/rocky country
CLUTCH SIZE 6–9

DISTRIBUTION Occurs in the Pyrenees, between France and Spain, in the Alps, and in northern Scotland, Iceland, and northern Scandinavia, extending north along the coast of European Russia.

THESE PTARMIGANS occur at relatively high altitudes within the Arctic region, in rocky areas of countryside. They undergo a seasonal change in appearance at the start of winter, becoming white at this stage, apart from their black tails and a characteristic black stripe above each eye.

INSULATION Feathering extends right down the legs and on to the toes in the case of the Rock Ptarmigan.

Black Grouse

FAMILY Tetraonidae
SPECIES *Lyrurus tetrix*
LENGTH 58 cm (23 in)
HABITAT Moorland/forest
CLUTCH SIZE 6–11

DISTRIBUTION Resident in Scotland and northern England, the Alpine region of mainland Europe, and in northeastern parts of the continent, extending to Norway and Russia.

OUTSIDE THE nesting period, these grouse generally live in flocks, which usually consist of either cocks or hens. They are often forced to forage for food in the branches of birch trees in winter, pecking at buds when the ground below is covered in snow. Each spring, male Black Grouse congregate on traditional open display grounds, known as leks, where they compete against each other in the search for a mate.

DISTINCTIVE PLUMAGE The female Black Grouse is tawny-brown, with heavily barred plumage. A narrow white wing bar is apparent in flight.

BLACK GROUSE DISPLAY These male Black Grouse are displaying to each other on a lek. Their strongly curved, lyre-shaped tail feathers are very apparent at this stage, when the tail is raised and fanned open.

Caucasian Snowcock

FAMILY Phasianidae

SPECIES *Tetraogallus caucasicus*

LENGTH 60 cm (23¾ in)

HABITAT Montane areas

CLUTCH SIZE 5–8

DISTRIBUTION The Caucasus Mountains between Black Sea and Caspian Sea. Reports of sightings in northeastern Turkey are not universally accepted.

CAUCASIAN SNOWCOCKS have a very distinctive coloration. There is a pale area on the crown, with alternating rusty-red stripes running down the sides of the head. Cock birds are more brightly coloured. They roam up to heights of 4,000 m (13,123 ft), coming down to lower altitudes in the winter when snow carpets the ground. Occupying rocky areas, they hide among the boulders, and may nest in these surroundings. Pairs breed on their own, but are likely to be seen in small groups at other times of the year.

VEGETARIAN DIET These snowcocks feed on vegetation throughout the year, ranging from bulbs to leaves and also grass seeds. Unusually, not even their chicks eat insects.

Capercaillie

FAMILY Tetraonidae

SPECIES *Tetrao urogallus*

LENGTH 90 cm (35½ in)

HABITAT Coniferous forest

CLUTCH SIZE 7–11

DISTRIBUTION Resident in northern Europe, from Scandinavia through to Russia. Scattered distribution in north Spain, the Alps, and the Balkan region, and present in Scotland.

THESE MASSIVE GROUSE are hard to spot, as they are shy by nature. Only in late spring, when cock birds are displaying on their leks, will they be more conspicuous, particularly as both sexes become more vocal at this stage as well. Capercailles normally spend most of their time on the ground, eating plant matter and berries. During the winter, they will then feed up in trees, eating pine needles here, when the ground is likely to be covered by snow.

ON DISPLAY This male Capercaillie is displaying. They fan their tail feathers out at the same time as calling, in a similar way to a turkey.

PROTECTION This Hen Capercaillie shows the plumage extending over the legs and toes. This gives additional protection against the cold, especially over the winter period in the northern areas where these birds occur.

Hazel Grouse

FAMILY Tetraonidae
SPECIES *Bonasa bonasia*
LENGTH 39 cm (15½ in)
HABITAT Mixed coniferous forest
CLUTCH SIZE 7–11

DISTRIBUTION Resident from northeastern France and Germany down to west of the Caspian Sea. Also southern parts of Scandinavia, to north Russia.

THE WIDE RANGE of these grouse, extending right across Asia to Japan, has led to the recognition of a dozen distinctive subspecies across their range. As a general guide, there is a white streak extending from the sides of the bill down to each side of the chest. This borders the characteristic black throat patch of the cock bird. Hazel Grouse are essentially forest dwellers, preferring areas where there is dense undergrowth. Their mottled plumage means they are hard to observe in the dappled woodland light, although unlike some gamebirds, they will fly if disturbed, rather than hiding in vegetation. These birds will sometimes venture up into the trees, wandering along the branches, and will usually roost off the ground. Hazel buds provide one of their main sources of food. If the winter weather is

very severe, they may actually construct what are effectively mini-igloos in the snow to keep warm. They may also roost inside trees at this stage, to stay warm. Pairing occurs in the autumn, with male Hazel Grouse establishing territories at this stage. The breeding period extends from the end of March through until June, depending on the latitude, being later in the far north. The hen builds a nest, which is a simple scrape in the ground, with leaves and grass providing a lining.

TERRITORIAL The cock Hazel Grouse will whistle from tree stumps and rocks, laying claim to his territory.

Black Francolin

FAMILY Phasianidae

SPECIES *Francolinus francolinus*

LENGTH 36 cm (14 in)

HABITAT Open country

CLUTCH SIZE 6–9

DISTRIBUTION Resident in Turkey, Iran, Iraq, Afghanistan, with its range continuing further eastwards into Asia. Also occurs into various parts of the Middle East.

ONE OF THE MOST obvious features of the Black Francolin is its upright posture. The cock bird is easily distinguished by his black-coloured head, with a prominent white cheek patch. A chestnut-red area encircles the lower neck. Much of the chest and also the underparts are black, broken with white markings. Hens, in contrast, have a less distinctive neck band, and a yellowish edge to their cheeks, with a stripe extending down the neck from the eyes. They are shy birds by nature. Various reintroduction schemes are now taking place in Europe, where the species formerly occurred right across to the Iberian Peninsula.

EVASIVE ACTION If flushed from cover, these francolins will glide down into nearby undergrowth again, in a manner reminiscent of pheasants. They tend to occur in pairs.

Common Quail

FAMILY Phasianidae

SPECIES *Coturnix coturnix*

LENGTH 18 cm (7 in)

HABITAT Open farmland

CLUTCH SIZE 7–18

DISTRIBUTION Summer visitor across mainland Europe, apart from the far north. Occurs in the United Kingdom and Ireland. Resident in areas along the southern Mediterranean coast.

WHEN SEEN IN FLIGHT, these birds have particularly long wings. They fly fast, dropping back into cover rapidly. Their small size and narrow body shape means they can move largely unseen through the grassland areas where they occur, while their mottled plumage helps them to blend in against this background. Common Quail have a distinctive three-syllable call, and this is often a better guide to their presence in an area than sightings. They are rarely evident unless dust-bathing along a track adjacent to a field.

PLUMAGE DISTINCTIONS This is a hen Common Quail. The cock bird can be identified by the presence of black plumage in the throat area.

Chukar Partridge

FAMILY Phasianidae
SPECIES *Alectoris chukar*
LENGTH 36 cm (14 in)
HABITAT Arid country
CLUTCH SIZE 10–15

DISTRIBUTION Resident from northern Italy eastwards and south through the former Yugoslavia to Greece and Bulgaria. Also present in parts of central Italy and on Sicily.

THE CHUKAR PARTRIDGE, or simply Chukar, is similar to the Rock Partridge, but has a cream rather than white area around the throat down onto the chest. This species is named after the sounds of its calls. These partridges spend most of their time on the ground, running at the hint of danger. Occurring in arid areas,

they do not stray far from water. Hens lay in a secluded spot on the ground, often under a rock or bush. They generally incubate on their own, with incubation lasting for just over three weeks. The young partridges are able to walk as soon as they hatch, and they are shepherded together by the adult hen. Once they are about two weeks old, the chicks from several nearby nests join up together into larger groups. Young Chukar Partridges then remain in coveys right up until the flocks split up to breed in due course.

SEASONAL JOURNEY Chukar Partridges move down to lower altitudes during the winter, when the weather is at its harshest.

Rock Partridge

FAMILY Phasianidae
SPECIES *Alectornis graeca*
LENGTH 36 cm (14 in)
HABITAT Rocky alpine country
CLUTCH SIZE 8–14

DISTRIBUTION Eastern Mediterranean region, extending northwards to the southern part of the Caspian sea and from the eastern shore. Present also on Crete and Cyprus.

GROUPS OF Rock Partridges split up early in the year into individual pairs. The hen lays in a shallow scrape on the ground, and the chicks are then watched over and guarded by both adult birds. Although they tend to be found in upland areas, Rock Partridges occur down to sea level in some parts of their range, as in Sicily.

DIET Rock Partridges feed mainly on seeds and vegetation, although invertebrates feature prominently in the diet of young birds over the summer period.

Red-legged Partridge

FAMILY Phasianidae
SPECIES *Alectoris rufa*
LENGTH 35 cm (13¾ in)
HABITAT Open country
CLUTCH SIZE 11–14

DISTRIBUTION Across most of the Iberian Peninsula into France and along the Mediterranean to northern Italy. Also widespread over southern England.

THE RED-LEGGED Partridge is generally a lowland species that has been introduced successfully in various localities, notably in parts of the United Kingdom. Black speckling extending from the throat on to the upper breast helps to identify the species, which has a typically corpulent body shape. The sexes are identical in terms of their plumage, but cock birds can be distinguished by the spur present on each of the hind legs, which is not present in hens, and they also tend to be larger in size. Female Red-legged Partridges usually only produce one clutch of eggs annually, but occasionally a hen may lay two clutches in rapid succession. The cock bird will then assume the incubation duties for the second batch of eggs. The group will then stay together right round until the following spring. Young Red-legged Partridges will be fully grown by the time they are about two months of age. They eat vegetation of various types, foraging for beechmast in woodland areas from the autumn onwards and sometimes digging for roots over the winter. These partridges often rest during the day, sometimes concealing themselves by crouching down in plough furrows in fields at this stage, where available cover is limited. If disturbed, they will fly off, and then run when they return to the ground.

PAIR OF RED-LEGGED PARTRIDGES The cock bird (*behind*) adopts an upright posture when calling.

Grey Partridge

FAMILY Phasianidae

SPECIES *Perdix perdix*

LENGTH 32 cm (12½ in)

HABITAT Grassland

CLUTCH SIZE 12–16

DISTRIBUTION Northern Spain, southern France, and across much of Europe north to southern Scandinavia. Resident across much of the United Kingdom; absent from southern parts of Ireland.

THESE GAMEBIRDS have a very wide range across much of Europe, with seven different races being identified through this vast area, differing in slight respects from each other. Although naturally occurring in grassland, Grey Partridges are now often to be seen in areas of farmland. They spend most of their time on the ground, usually near the edges of fields where there is more likely to be cover available. If disturbed, a Grey Partridge will only fly a relatively short distance, soon dropping down into cover again. Outside the breeding period, they associate in small flocks, called coveys, numbering up to 25 individuals, feeding primarily early in the day, and then at dusk. They eat seeds and invertebrates. A cock bird usually pairs with a single hen at the start of the breeding period, and she will then nest in a well-hidden locality.

GENDER DIFFERENCES In this pair of Grey Partridges, the cock, with brighter facial feathering, is on the left.

Common Pheasant

FAMILY Phasianidae

SPECIES *Phasinus colchicus*

LENGTH 60–84 cm (23¾–33 in)

HABITAT Lightly wooded country

CLUTCH SIZE 7–14

DISTRIBUTION Occurs across most of western Europe up into southern Scandinavia, down to southern Italy and north of the Black Sea. Populations topped up by released birds.

THIS SPECIES IS NATIVE to Asia, and was introduced into Europe about a millennium ago, being brought to the United Kingdom as a gamebird. These pheasants have since become established across much of the country and indeed, the continent. Cock birds are significantly larger than hens, showing extensive red areas of skin on the face, with a white ring of plumage often evident around the back of the neck. Hens are duller, being buff in colour, with barring on their plumage. There are still some local variations in the appearance of cocks, however, reflecting the fact that several races were originally brought over, and introduced into different areas. Some populations may for example be darker in colour, or lack the white neck collar.

TYPICAL GROUP A cock pheasant is usually seen with several hens, foraging in the open. Although Common Pheasants breed on the ground, they will roost on branches.

Golden Pheasant

FAMILY Phasianidae

SPECIES *Chrysolophus pictus*

LENGTH 80–105 cm (32–41½ in)

HABITAT Forest

CLUTCH SIZE 5–12

DISTRIBUTION Originates from central China. Introduced to the United Kingdom, notably parts of southern and eastern England, southwestern Scotland, and the Isle of Anglesey.

THE RICH GOLDEN head coloration of the cock Golden Pheasant helps to identify this species, although in reality, there is no other bird with which it could be confused. Hens, however, are far less colourful, and have strongly barred underparts, compared with the Common Pheasant, whose underparts are spotted. Golden Pheasants were first released in the United Kingdom soon after they were brought here in the 1800s as an ornamental species. They have not spread far beyond their original haunts here in the wild, favouring pine and larch forests.

SPECTACULAR PLUMAGE The stunning beauty of a mature cock Golden Pheasant is portrayed in this photograph. This species is also polygamous, with a cock bird living in the company of several hens.

GRUIFORMES

Cranes, coots, and rails

There is a wide variation in size between members of this Order, from the large cranes down to the small rails, but all are usually linked in some way to an aquatic environment. Their habitat can vary from saltwater through to freshwater, with some species being adaptable to either. Members can be migratory too, as in the case of cranes. Many of these species are shy birds by nature, and not easy to observe; the relatively upright and slender body shape of rails in particular enables them to slip through reedbeds essentially unnoticed. Their fairly plain coloration also helps to conceal their presence.

Little Button Quail

FAMILY Gruidae
SPECIES *Turnix sylvaticus*
LENGTH 17 cm (6¾ in)
HABITAT Heathland
CLUTCH SIZE 3–4

DISTRIBUTION Restricted to southern areas of the Iberian Peninsula in Europe; also occurs on the Mediterranean coast of North Africa.

IN SPITE OF their common name, Little Button Quails are unrelated to true quails, although they look rather like them and share a similar lifestyle. Their alternative name is the Andalusian Hemipode. This species operates something of a role reversal during breeding since it is the cock bird that incubates the eggs.

BRIGHT HEN The hen is more brightly coloured than the cock bird, with orange-brown feathering over the breast. Little Button Quails also have very short tails.

Common Crane

FAMILY Gruidae
SPECIES *Grus grus*
LENGTH 180–220 cm (71–86¾ in)/wingspan 175 cm (69 in)
HABITAT Wetland areas
CLUTCH SIZE 1–2

DISTRIBUTION In summer, breeds through northeastern Europe and Scandinavia. Resident south of the Black Sea.

THESE CRANES fly long distances to and from their northern breeding grounds. Once there, it is not just their display but also their loud duetting calls echoing across boggy ground that command attention. They build a bulky nest on the ground. When feeding, cranes walk slowly and deliberately, looking for prey such as amphibians.

YOUNG AND OLD An adult stands with a less brightly coloured juvenile. Males are larger than females. The short tail plumes are covered by bushy tertial feathers.

Demoiselle Crane

FAMILY Gruidae

SPECIES *Anthropoides virgo*

LENGTH 85–100 cm (33½–39½ in)/wingspan 232 cm (91¼ in)

HABITAT Steppes/waterways

CLUTCH SIZE 1

DISTRIBUTION Summer range from northern–central parts of the Black Sea northeastwards, occurring in southern Russia. Overwinters in Asia. Seen on Cyprus when migrating.

THE DEMOISELLE is smaller in size than the Common Crane, and has elongated black breast feathering, and lacks the bushy plumage in the vicinity of the tail. There are also distinctive long, white 'ear tufts' of plumage extending back down the neck from behind the eyes, which are a striking shade of red. Pairs nest communally in dry steppe areas, but are more likely to be sighted in wetlands over the winter period, sometimes in the company of other cranes. In flight, cranes generally can be easily distinguished from storks, because they fly with their necks extended, usually adopting a V-shaped formation in a group, although sometimes flying in a straight line. When migrating, flocks fly at high altitude, taking advantage of thermal air currents to assist their flight.

FAMILY GROUP In this group of Demoiselle Cranes, the slightly larger cock bird is on the right. The hen is in the centre; the juvenile on the left is distinguishable by a lack of long ear tufts and breast plumes.

CRANES DISPLAYING The dance of breeding cranes is one of the most famous rituals in the natural world. At intervals, the birds leap into the air, throwing up twigs and other items as part of their display.

Water Rail

FAMILY Rallidae

SPECIES *Rallus aquaticus*

LENGTH 23–26 cm (9–10¼ in)

HABITAT Shallow lakes/ marshland

CLUTCH SIZE 6–11

DISTRIBUTION Resident in western Europe and along the Mediterranean. Summer visitor to eastern Europe, north up to southern Scandinavia.

THIS IS AN ADAPTABLE species that is found in both freshwater and brackish areas. The Water Rail is hard to spot, however, hiding away in reedbeds and similar vegetation at any hint of danger. The sexes can be distinguished by the hen's smaller size, as well as her narrow bill. They catch small vertebrates such as fish and amphibians, and will also feed on a variety of plant matter.

FORAGING FOR FOOD Water Rails generally look for food in shallow water, but they can swim and may occasionally even dive.

Corncrake

FAMILY Rallidae

SPECIES *Crex crex*

LENGTH 25 cm (10 in)

HABITAT Damp meadows

CLUTCH SIZE 8–12

DISTRIBUTION Summer visitor mainly from France westwards across Europe, north to areas of Scotland and southern Scandinavia. Overwinters largely in eastern Africa.

CORNCRAKES ARE found in drier areas than other members of their family, but their numbers have declined significantly in some areas. This has been linked to changes in agricultural practices: it is thought that fewer chicks are reared in the fields where pairs traditionally breed because nests are destroyed by earlier harvesting. The species still remains common where agriculture is less intensive.

PRESERVATION Populations have been helped by changes in farming practices, such as mowing fields from the centre out, and reserves.

Little Crake

FAMILY Rallidae
SPECIES *Porzana parva*
LENGTH 19 cm (7½ in)
HABITAT Reedbeds
CLUTCH SIZE 7–9

DISTRIBUTION Breeds in scattered areas in western Europe; more common in eastern parts, to the north of the Black Sea. Overwinters in north and eastern Africa.

PAIRS OF LITTLE CRAKES establish individual territories, building a cup-shaped nest usually in a site that can only be reached over water. The incubation period lasts for about three weeks. Chicks are covered in a glossy black down, and can move around immediately after hatching. They will be fully weaned before they can fly at the age of seven weeks old, with the adult pair then laying again.

COLOURED BILL The Little Crake's bill is short yet pointed, being red at its base and yellowish-green along its length.

Spotted Crake

FAMILY Rallidae
SPECIES *Porzana porzana*
LENGTH 22 cm (8¾ in)
HABITAT Sedge bogs
CLUTCH SIZE 8–12

DISTRIBUTION In summer, occurs in parts of the United Kingdom and western Europe, to south Scandinavia; more widespread in eastern parts. Overwinters mainly in Africa.

FINE WHITE SPOTTING is apparent on the chest, neck, and underparts of these crakes, but these markings tend to become more elongated and barred along the flanks. Spotted Crakes have a very distinctive call, resembling a wolf whistle, but are rather shy by nature. They do not occur in reedbeds, but favour more open countryside, sometimes venturing out into wet meadowland.

DISTINCTIVE The colour of the bill of these crakes is reddish-orange at the base, paler with dark markings towards the tip.

Baillon's Crake

FAMILY Rallidae
SPECIES *Porzana pusilla*
LENGTH 18 cm (7 in)
HABITAT Sedge bogs
CLUTCH SIZE 4–11

DISTRIBUTION Scattered in southerly areas of western Europe; more widespread north and east of the Black Sea. Recorded in 14 countries. Overwinters in Africa.

IT IS NOT EASY to distinguish the sexes in this species, but hens may have paler throats; adults have bluish-grey colouring whereas juveniles have black-and-white barring. After hatching the young start to be able to feed themselves within a few days, but it will take at least ten days before their plumage starts to emerge through their down.

WATERY HOME Baillon's Crakes nest on platforms in shallow water. The platform allows young birds to rest.

Common Moorhen

FAMILY Rallidae
SPECIES *Gallinula chloropus*
LENGTH 36 cm (14 in)
HABITAT Freshwater areas
CLUTCH SIZE 8–12

DISTRIBUTION Resident in most of western Europe and Turkey; absent from the far north of the United Kingdom. Summer visitor throughout the east, to southern Scandinavia.

THESE MOORHENS are mainly dark, with a characteristic red shield on the forehead, merging into the bill, which is yellow at its tip. Common Moorhens can be encountered in a wide range of habitats, from ponds and marshes to rivers. They are quite shy by nature, and may be seen skulking along the edge of a pond, disappearing into reeds at any hint of a threat.

PROTECTIVE A Common Moorhen watches over its young chick. These birds can swim well.

Purple Swamp-hen

FAMILY Rallidae
SPECIES *Porphyrio porphyrio*
LENGTH 50 cm (19¾ in)
HABITAT Marshland/lakes
CLUTCH SIZE 3–5

DISTRIBUTION Mainly from southern Spain east to Sardinia in Europe, having contracted over recent years. Also from the Caspian Sea ranging to Australia, and in Africa.

THIS IS A PARTICULARLY striking and colourful member of the family, thanks to its predominantly purplish-blue body, offset by white plumage under the tail. The bill is large and red, with a large frontal plate that extends back above the red eyes. Its long legs and equally lengthy agile toes are reddish. The toes allow the Purple Swamp-hen to walk effectively over aquatic vegetation, helping to disperse its body weight so it does not sink down into the water. These birds are mainly vegetarian in their feeding habits, but will catch aquatic invertebrates, plus small vertebrates such as fish. The hen lays her eggs in a nest of grass and reeds, anchored to aquatic plants. The chicks are covered in blackish down when they hatch, and will start following their mother soon after emerging from the eggs. By three months of age, they resemble adults, but are paler overall in colour, being more of a greyish-blue shade.

WALK THE WALK These birds prefer to walk, although they can swim if necessary, too, as well as fly. They have a loud and varied range of calls.

Eurasian Coot

FAMILY Rallidae

SPECIES *Fulica atra*

LENGTH 42 cm (16½ in)

HABITAT Slow-flowing waters/parks

CLUTCH SIZE 6–10

DISTRIBUTION Resident in western Europe through Italy, into Denmark, and south of the Black Sea. Summer visitor in southern Scandinavia and east.

ATHOUGH IT IS greyish-black overall, the Eurasian Coot does have white edging at the tips of its secondary flight feathers. This is apparent when the wings are open. There is a conspicuous white frontal plate on the forehead, merging into the bill beneath, which has a slight pinkish hue. The toes of these coots are not webbed, but expanded with flaps of skin, called lobes, aiding their swimming ability. When breeding, pairs are highly territorial, but in the winter, they may form relatively large flocks on larger stretches of water such as reservoirs, and are seen in coastal areas.

VEGETARIAN Coots feed mainly on vegetation, both on land and in the water. They may even dive for food.

Red-knobbed Coot

FAMILY Rallidae

SPECIES *Fulica cristata*

LENGTH 44 cm (17½ in)

HABITAT Slow-flowing waterways/swamps

CLUTCH SIZE 5–7

DISTRIBUTION European range is restricted to southern Spain; occurs on the opposite side of the Straits of Gibraltar in Morocco and North Africa.

THE NUMBERS of the Red-knobbed Coot have fallen in Europe, to the point that it is now on the verge of extinction, although it remains numerous further south. In some areas, it can be seen alongside the Eurasian Coot, being distinguishable by the red nodules on the forehead, which are apparent during the breeding season. A lasting point of distinction, however, is that the bill has a bluish-grey hue. Their calls are very different, too.

WATER FEEDERS Red-knobbed Coots prefer to feed on aquatic vegetation, but may graze on grass near the water's edge.

Little Bustard

FAMILY Otididae
SPECIES *Tetrax tetrax*
LENGTH 45 cm (17¾ in)
HABITAT Open country
CLUTCH SIZE 2–4

DISTRIBUTION Resident in much of the Iberian Peninsula, and various localities along the Mediterranean. Present in more northern areas, including France, during the summer.

AS ITS NAME SUGGESTS, the Little Bustard can be distinguished partly on the basis of its size. While the hen is speckled overall, cock birds are recognizable by the prominent area of black plumage on the neck. This part of the body can appear swollen, as the male bustard inflates his throat and raises the feathers as part of his courtship display. During courtship the head is thrown back repeatedly in rapid succession, emphasizing the white areas too, and every so often, the bird leaps up into the air. Little Bustards are often seen in small flocks, pairing off for the nesting season. They feed on a variety of plant matter and invertebrates.

LOOK OUT This is a male Little Bustard. Living in open country and being ground-dwellers, these birds are very watchful by nature.

Great Bustard

FAMILY Otididae
SPECIES *Otis tarda*
LENGTH 85–105 cm (33½– 41½ in)
HABITAT Open country
CLUTCH SIZE 2–4

DISTRIBUTION Resident in parts of the Iberian Peninsula and other suitable down areas around the Black Sea. Summer visitor in parts of eastern Europe.

THE COCK Great Bustard is the largest bird found in Europe, being significantly larger and heavier than the hen, weighing up to 2.3 kg (5 lb). They have particularly heavy chests, with this musculature being essential to get them airborne. The neck of the male has blue-grey plumage, which is less extensive in the hen. The cock's display is called a foam bath, because of the way in which he inflates his throat, lifting and shaking the wings, with white plumage being predominant and essentially hiding the head.

BARKING Cock birds are usually quiet, but they may utter a sound rather like a barking dog during the breeding season.

GROUP OF BUSTARDS The numbers of Great Bustards are
declining in many areas. They became extinct in the
United Kingdom in 1832, but a recent reintroduction
scheme offers hope that flocks may be re-established.

CHARADRIIFORMES

Waders, gulls, terns, and auks

Members of this Order are a diverse group of birds, divided into 19 families, whose representatives are often seen either in coastal areas or in grasslands. They include typical shorebirds, observed wandering along the coastline, following tidal movements and congregating on mudflats. They may then move inland to grassland areas during the breeding season. Some of the other families that are also included under this heading, such as the gulls and terns, can be encountered some distance out at sea, and also inland, while others, like auks and razorbills, spend most of their lives on the world's oceans.

Eurasian Oystercatcher

FAMILY Haematopodidae
SPECIES *Haematopus ostralegus*
LENGTH 44 cm (17½ in)
HABITAT Coasts/tidal flats
CLUTCH SIZE 2–4

DISTRIBUTION Summertime visitor north to the Scandinavian coast, also inland areas northeast of the Black Sea and elsewhere.

OYSTERCATCHERS often move inland in summer, sometimes being sighted away from water in fields, feeding on invertebrates. They congregate along the coasts of western Europe in winter, with the sharp, chisel-like tip to the bill then allowing them to open up mussels and cockles, which form their main food source at this stage.

SEASONAL CHANGE This adult is in summer plumage. During the winter, a white band runs across the throat. Juveniles have greyer legs and a dark tip to the bill.

Avocet

FAMILY Recurvirostridae
SPECIES *Recurvirostra avosetta*
LENGTH 46 cm (18 in)
HABITAT Lagoons/mudflats
CLUTCH SIZE 4

DISTRIBUTION Summer visitor to south Scandinavia, various parts of United Kingdom, around Mediterranean and Black Sea.

THE AVOCET looks unmistakeable, thanks to its slender, upcurved black bill. It feeds by sweeping this from side to side through an area, detecting food such as shrimps by touch. It may sometimes peck for food on mudflats. If necessary, Avocets can swim well, although they are usually seen wading in the shallows.

GENDER DIFFERENCES Male Avocets have longer, less sharply curved bills than hens. Their black areas of plumage are well defined and do not have a brownish tinge.

Ruff

FAMILY Scolopacidae
SPECIES *Philomachus pugnax*
LENGTH 22–32 cm (8½–12½ in)
HABITAT Marshland/meadows
CLUTCH SIZE 4

DISTRIBUTION Summer visitor to northeastern Europe in Scandinavia and Russia. Also in the United Kingdom. Overwinters here, and south of the Black Sea, and in Africa.

THIS SPECIES is so called because of the spectacular ruff of longer feathers around the neck of the cock bird. During the breeding season, the males display on leks, which are communal display grounds, fluffing up their plumage for this purpose. There may be as many as 20 males on some sites of this type. The coloration of their ruff is highly variable, as is that of the body itself, ranging from white through buff to chestnut and even black. During the winter period, when cock birds lose this distinctive characteristic and resemble hens in appearance, it will still be possible to distinguish them by their larger size.

SPECTACULAR PLUMAGE This cock bird has a ruff with white-and-dark brown barring. The facial coloration in all cases is yellowish.

Black-winged Stilt

FAMILY Recurvirostridae

SPECIES *Himatopus himatopus*

LENGTH 36 cm (14 in)

HABITAT Wetland

CLUTCH SIZE 4

DISTRIBUTION Summer visitor through scattered localities mainly across southern Europe, extending north to the French Channel coast, and northeast of the Black Sea. Overwinters in Africa.

THE APPEARANCE of these slender stilts is quite distinctive. Black plumage extends back down over the back and wings, which often have a slightly browner hue, notably in the case of the hen. The crown and neck can vary from white through to greyish-black, underparts being white, with cock birds generally tending to have darker heads. Young birds of both sexes resemble hens, although there is a light edging apparent over their wings. The long, straight bill is black, while the long legs are red. Its height enables the Black-winged Stilt to feed in relatively deep waters. The species occurs in a variety of habitats, ranging from freshwater lagoons through to estuaries. These stilts breed close to water, laying on the ground, with pairs nesting in colonies. The buff coloration of the eggs helps to disguise them, as they are generally laid simply in a scrape in the ground.

QUIET NATURED Only during the breeding period do Black-winged Stilts tend to become very vocal.

Stone-curlew

FAMILY Burhinidae
SPECIES *Burhinus oedicnemus*
LENGTH 45 cm (17¾ in)
HABITAT Open country
CLUTCH SIZE 2

DISTRIBUTION Resident through much of the Iberian Peninsula; summertime visitor to France and southern England, also through much of the Mediterranean and sporadically further north.

THE STONE-CURLEW'S plumage enables these birds to merge very effectively into the arid landscape where they occur, particularly when they are nesting and in direct contact with the ground. As a further protection against potential predators in this exposed environment, these birds are primarily nocturnal in their habits. Stone-curlews are able to run quickly on their long legs in pursuit of prey such as invertebrates or lizards. The sexes are identical in appearance, with the eggs being laid in a simple scrape. These too are well camouflaged. Young Stone-curlews can be distinguished by their less distinctive wing bars.

DISTINCTIVE FEATURES The large yellow eyes are characteristic of the Stone-curlew, along with the yellow area at the base of the bill. They are instinctively shy and nervous birds.

Black-winged Pratincole

FAMILY Glareolidae
SPECIES *Glareola nordmanni*
LENGTH 28 cm (11 in)
HABITAT Damp areas
CLUTCH SIZE 2–3

DISTRIBUTION Restricted to the northern and eastern areas of the Black Sea during the summer months, generally overwintering in southern Africa, migrating over the Middle East.

IT IS STRAIGHTFORWARD to identify the Black-winged Pratincole in flight, since it lacks white edging to the rear of the wings. On the ground, a more evident point of distinction from the similarly coloured Common Pratincole (*see* p 144) is the length of the tail feathers, which are shorter than the wing tips in this case. Their range does overlap in eastern areas, although the Black-winged tends to occur in less arid surroundings. Nevertheless, there are occasional records of these particular pratincoles being seen in western Europe as vagrants.

BEHAVIOUR These birds nest in colonies in open countryside, and hunt invertebrates. They overwinter in southern parts of Africa.

Common Pratincole

FAMILY Glareolidae
SPECIES *Glareola pratincola*
LENGTH 28 cm (11 in)
HABITAT Arid country
CLUTCH SIZE 2–3

DISTRIBUTION From the Iberian Peninsula along the Mediterranean to various localities around the Black Sea in the summer, overwintering in Africa south of the Sahara.

ALTHOUGH ALSO DESCRIBED as the Collared Pratincole, this species displays the same black marking running around the throat from eye to eye as its Black-winged cousin (*see* p 143). In some areas where their range overlaps, they are even reported to have hybridized. The Common Pratincole has longer tail feathers, however, and may be a slightly lighter shade of brown on the upperparts. The bill too is more colourful, with red coloration here being more prominent. The sexes can be distinguished because the lores of hens tend to be of a browner shade than those of cock birds. Pratincoles are agile birds in flight, able to catch insects on the wing, although they will also pursue them on the ground. Their tail feathers often form a V-shaped pattern when flying.
They nest colonially on the ground.

COMMUNAL LIVING Common Pratincoles occur in large flocks, and will hunt invertebrates in flight, particularly after dawn and towards dusk.

Cream-coloured Courser

FAMILY Glareolidae
SPECIES *Cursorius cursor*
LENGTH 27 cm (10¾ in)
HABITAT Arid country
CLUTCH SIZE 2–3

DISTRIBUTION Recorded as a vagrant widely across Europe, but otherwise restricted to an area east of the Mediterranean during the summer. Overwinters in Africa.

AS ITS NAME SUGGESTS, the coloration of this species is mainly a sandy-buff colour overall, but adults have a bluish-grey area of plumage on the crown with prominent white-and-black stripes extending back from the eyes. Young birds have pale spots over their wings. Black areas in the wings are prominent in flight. Cream-coloured Coursers often run in the sandy areas where they are found, however, rather than taking to the wing. They have a very distinctive upright gait, keeping their heads raised.

SPECIALIZATION The bill of the Cream-coloured Courser is curved at its tip, helping these birds to catch invertebrates on the ground.

Ruddy Turnstone

FAMILY Scolopacidae
SPECIES *Arenaria interpres*
LENGTH 24 cm (9½ in)
HABITAT Rocky coasts/
beaches
CLUTCH SIZE 4

DISTRIBUTION Summer visitor right around the Scandinavian coast, overwintering around the shores of the United Kingdom and Ireland, as well as the coast of western Europe.

THE DESCRIPTION of 'turnstone' for these waders comes from the way in which they feed, turning over pebbles and pushing aside seaweed searching for invertebrates. The Ruddy Turnstone's summer coloration is very distinctive, with adults developing orange-red plumage on the back, and contrasting black feathering on the head and chest, complete with bright orange legs. Hens are duller in color than cocks. In the winter, their upperparts become dark brown with black streaking, while the underparts are white. Young birds have scaled rather than streaked patterning on their backs.

COASTAL DWELLERS Ruddy Turnstones rarely stray far from the shore, even breeding in areas close to the sea.

Eurasian Curlew

FAMILY Scolopacidae
SPECIES *Numenius arquata*
LENGTH 58 cm (23 in)
HABITAT Wetland/grassland
CLUTCH SIZE 3–4

DISTRIBUTION Summer visitor through northeastern Europe, and in central parts. Winters on the coast from southwestern Denmark to the Mediterranean.

THE CURLEW IS the largest of the waders occurring in Europe. It has a very long, down-curving bill, which tends to be bigger in hens, measuring up to 15 cm (6 in) overall. These birds have dark brown markings on their plumage, with their mottling helping to disguise their presence on the ground. Their back and rump are white, and this is especially evident in flight, with barring here being restricted to the tip of the tail. Pairs breed inland in grassland areas, occupying what can be quite large individual territories. These areas can range across boggy areas of ground in the far north through to moorland and meadows, depending on their locality. During the winter, Curlews tend to form flocks, occurring in large numbers in estuaries, where they will probe in the mud for worms and similar edible items. They may also pick up potential prey at the surface such as crabs and molluscs. Strangely, in contrast to most migrants that head south as winter approaches, some Curlews will fly north to Iceland, spending this period here. The migratory behaviour of these birds is quite variable: some fly long distances down into Africa, while others tend not to move far from their breeding grounds. Young birds, which do not breed in their first year, will remain resident on their wintering grounds through their first summer.

WARY AND CAUTIOUS The Curlew is quite a shy bird by nature, especially over the breeding period.

Whimbrel

FAMILY Scolopacidae
SPECIES *Numenius phaeopus*
LENGTH 37 cm (14½ in)
HABITAT Open country/coasts
CLUTCH SIZE 4

DISTRIBUTION Occurs in the summer in the far north from Scotland to Iceland, and from northern Scandinavia eastwards into northern Russia. Overwinters on the coast of Africa.

THE SHORTER, STOCKIER BILL of the Whimbrel gives some insight into how its behaviour differs in comparison to that of related species. During the winter period, when they are found largely in coastal areas, these birds prefer to feed not by probing deeply but rather by searching for edible items lying on top of the mud. They are relatively territorial, as far as feeding areas are concerned, with individuals often patrolling a stretch of beach on their own. When migrating, they may be observed in areas of farmland.

GENDER DIFFERENCES
These particular curlews cannot be sexed visually, but on their breeding grounds, the male's display flight enables members of a pair to be distinguished.

Slender-billed Curlew

FAMILY Scolopacidae
SPECIES *Numenius tenuirostris*
LENGTH 41 cm (16¼ in)
HABITAT Wet meadows
CLUTCH SIZE 4

DISTRIBUTION Breeds in summer in Siberia; overwinters around the Mediterranean, including Italy and North Africa. Also a vagrant seen in Poland, the Netherlands, and Germany.

THIS PARTICULAR SPECIES now ranks as one of the rarest birds in Europe, being regarded as critically endangered. The largest number of Slender-billed Curlews recorded during recent years was a flock of some 20 birds, seen in southeastern Italy. The white background colour of the plumage on the head, throat, and breast helps to distinguish this species, and the bill is fine, as its name suggests, and also relatively short. This serves to distinguish the occasional vagrant that may join up with flocks of other curlews.

UNDER THREAT Appearances of Slender-billed Curlews in Europe have become increasing scarce over recent years. The reasons for their decline are unclear.

Kentish Plover

FAMILY Charadriidae

SPECIES *Charadrius alexandrinus*

LENGTH 17 cm (6¾ in)

HABITAT Open country/mudflats

CLUTCH SIZE 4

DISTRIBUTION Summer visitor to western Europe, the Black Sea, and the Mediterranean. Winters around the Mediterranean.

THESE PARTICULAR PLOVERS tend to breed near the coast but, especially in eastern Europe, they may nest in open country, laying directly on the ground. Sexing is quite possible when the birds are in breeding plumage, with the cock bird having a black streak extending around the sides of the neck with a reddish-brown crown. Hens have a much broader, brown area on the neck, with brown extending over the head. Pairs tend to nest near beaches on the coast. Both members of the pair share the task of incubation, but then the hen is likely to abandon her offspring, which can move soon after hatching, leaving them under the care of the cock bird. She will then often lay again, and so produces two broods of chicks over the summer. Outside the breeding season, the sexes are similar in appearance, resembling hens.

BREEDING A pair of Kentish Plovers on their nest site, with the cock bird on the left.

Little Ringed Plover

FAMILY Charadriidae

SPECIES *Charadrius dubius*

LENGTH 18 cm (7 in)

HABITAT Sandy areas/
            estuaries

CLUTCH SIZE 4

DISTRIBUTION Occurs
through the summer across
most of Europe from southern
Scandinavia to the
Mediterranean. Restricted to
eastern parts of the United
Kingdom. Overwinters in Africa.

AREAS OF FRESHWATER are the favoured breeding haunts of the Little Ringed Plover. They are rarely seen along the coast itself, although they may frequent estuaries. These plovers are particularly adaptable in their habits, often colonizing reclaimed areas such as gravel pits. Pairs will nest on the adjacent land, usually preferring sandy areas as a breeding site. Their nest consists of a scrape on the ground. The sexes can be distinguished during the breeding season, with cock birds having a prominent black band encircling the area below the throat, and distinctive black markings on the head too, whereas these areas are browner in hens.

APPEARANCE A male Little Ringed Plover in breeding plumage. Note the relatively dark bill and the colour of the legs, which help to distinguish these birds.

Ringed Plover

FAMILY Charadriidae

SPECIES *Charadrius hiaticula*

LENGTH 19 cm (7½ in)

HABITAT Open country/
            coasts

CLUTCH SIZE 4

DISTRIBUTION Occurs in
Iceland, northern Scandinavia,
and adjacent parts of Russia in
summer. Resident along coasts
of western Europe.

RINGED PLOVERS ARE likely to be seen in larger groups than the Little Ringed Plover, and are generally more common overall. They also tend to occupy a slightly different habitat, being more commonly observed in coastal areas. Flocks of several hundred birds may be observed at high tide. Pairs may sometimes nest inland though, in the far north on the tundra as an example, and can be sighted around estuaries. Although their markings are quite similar to those of their relative, the bill is orange in colour with a black tip, and the legs are a bright shade of yellowish-orange.

SEASONAL MOVEMENTS The majority of Ringed Plovers leave Europe in the autumn to overwinter further south, along the coast of the Iberian Peninsula into Africa, but there are also resident populations in western parts of the continent.

Eurasian Dotterel

FAMILY Charadriidae

SPECIES *Charadrius morinellus*

LENGTH 24 cm (9½ in)

HABITAT Upland areas/open country

CLUTCH SIZE 3–4

DISTRIBUTION Summer resident in northern Scotland, central Scandinavia, and various localities in southern parts of Europe. Overwinters in northern Spain and Africa.

THIS SPECIES FAVOURS mountainous areas in Europe for nesting purposes, and also breeds in the far north on the open tundra. Eurasian Dotterel spend a relatively short period here, usually extending from the middle of June through to mid-August. Having laid, the hen is likely to leave much of the task of incubation to her partner, and she is unlikely to care for the young. Instead, she may mate again with another partner during this period. This allows more chicks to be reared in a relatively short time. The hen has a consistent shade of grey across

UNUSUAL The Eurasian Dotterel is the only plover where the hen is more brightly coloured than her mate.

the throat, while the underparts are rufous in color. Cocks have a similar colour scheme, but are paler overall. Outside the breeding period, the sexes are indistinguishable, and they have predominantly white underparts, with no rufous markings. When migrating, they are not encountered in large groups, although occasional sightings of small numbers may be made, typically in fairly open countryside, such as in areas of grassland.

European Golden Plover

FAMILY Charadriidae
SPECIES *Pluvialis apricaria*
LENGTH 28 cm (11 in)
HABITAT Moorland/pasture
CLUTCH SIZE 4

DISTRIBUTION Summer visitor to Iceland, Scotland, and northern Scandinavia east into Russia. Overwinters in Denmark and sporadically in parts of Spain, Portugal, and the Mediterranean.

ONCE AGAIN, the sexes in this case can only be distinguished during the summer breeding period. At this stage, the cock bird has a very distinctive black area encircling the eyes and extending down over the chest and broadening out over the underparts. Hens in comparison are much paler, notably on the sides of the face, with white plumage intruding into the black of their underparts, although there are individual variations in this respect. Pairs nest in open country, sometimes on mountainsides above the treeline. They simply lay in a scrape on the ground, often in among vegetation. During the winter, these Golden Plovers will form large flocks at lower altitude, quite often being seen in the company of lapwings at this stage. They generally do not occur in wetland areas.

FORAGING Berries as well as a variety of invertebrates and seeds feature in the diet of these birds.

Grey Plover

FAMILY Charadriidae
SPECIES *Pluvialis squatarola*
LENGTH 29 cm (11½ in)
HABITAT Tundra/tidal flats
CLUTCH SIZE 4

DISTRIBUTION Breeds on the tundra of northern Russia. Overwinters along the Channel coast of mainland Europe to Spain, and also through the Mediterranean and in Africa.

THIS IS A SPECIES that is most likely to be seen in Europe outside the summer months. Many of these birds will be passage migrants, heading to and from their breeding grounds in the high Arctic, overwintering in Africa, although some will remain on the continent at this stage. They are most likely to be observed on mudflats over the winter.

COLOUR CHANGE A Grey Plover in winter plumage. During the summer, they are predominately black-and-white in colour, with hens having flecked black underparts.

Sociable Lapwing

FAMILY Charadriidae
SPECIES *Vanellus gregarius*
LENGTH 30 cm (12 in)
HABITAT Steppes/sandy areas
CLUTCH SIZE 4

DISTRIBUTION Breeds in central parts of Asia and southwestern Siberia, being seen as a passage migrant in southeastern Europe, heading to northeastern Africa.

THE BLACK STRIPE running through the eye of this species is far more prominent when these birds are in summer plumage, with the lower cheek area being yellowish. The underparts are grey at this stage, becoming black below, with the sexes being indistinguishable. In winter plumage, the breast is brownish-grey, with the remainder of the underparts being white. The population of the Sociable Lapwing has declined significantly over recent years, possibly because of changes in grazing patterns by farmstock affecting its breeding habitat, and increased predation of nests by Rooks (*see* p 333). In Europe, these birds may associate with flocks of Lapwings.

HABITS Sociable Lapwings feed on the ground, seeking invertebrates of various types, including beetles and grasshoppers. As their name suggests, they are social birds by nature.

Red-wattled Lapwing

FAMILY Charadriidae
SPECIES *Vanellus indicus*
LENGTH 35 cm (13¾ in)
HABITAT Grassland
CLUTCH SIZE 4

DISTRIBUTION Breeding grounds are centred in southern Asia, eastwards to Malaysia, but not uncommon in southeastern Turkey, around Cizre on the River Tigris.

THE BARE RED AREAS of skin running from the bill back to the eyes serve to identify this species, with the bill too being red along most of its length. When seen in flight, they have a prominent black band with a white area below, across the tail feathers. Their light brown upperparts serve to conceal the presence of these birds when they are nesting on the ground. Red-wattled Lapwings are surprisingly noisy by nature, not infrequently calling at night. They often feed under cover of darkness, too.

LONG LEGS These lapwings are relatively tall. They are often seen on cultivated land, looking for invertebrates, especially near water.

Spur-winged Lapwing

FAMILY Charadriidae
SPECIES *Vanellus spinosus*
LENGTH 28 cm (11 in)
HABITAT Open country
CLUTCH SIZE 4

DISTRIBUTION Occasionally breeds in southeastern parts of Europe, extending to the Middle East. May also be sighted as a vagrant in western Europe.

AS ITS NAME SUGGESTS, there is actually a small, spur-like projection along the front edge of each wing of this species, which will be apparent in flight. The black plumage extending down the chest in a line and broadening out over the underparts also helps to distinguish these lapwings from similar species.

NOT UNIQUE In spite of its name, the Spur-winged is not the only lapwing with a spur on its carpal joint.

Northern Lapwing

FAMILY Charadriidae
SPECIES *Vanellus vanellus*
LENGTH 31 cm (12¼ in)
HABITAT Open country/ farmland
CLUTCH SIZE 4

DISTRIBUTION Summer visitor across much of eastern Europe up into Scandinavia, resident in northwestern Europe, being seen more commonly in southern Europe in the winter.

THE DISTINCTIVE CREST of the Northern Lapwing is hidden in flight, lying flat over the back of the head. It is short and relatively indistinct in the case of young birds. These lapwings are often to be seen in fields in large flocks during the winter, typically close to areas of water, hunting for invertebrates. They are also known as Peewits, because of the sound of their calls. Their short-legged stance also helps to distinguish them from other lapwings.

FAMILY GROUP A male Lapwing with a young chick. The black area on the chest is broken by white plumage in the case of hens.

Bar-tailed Godwit

FAMILY Scolopacidae
SPECIES *Limosa lapponica*
LENGTH 41 cm (16 in)
HABITAT Tundra/mudflats
CLUTCH SIZE 4

DISTRIBUTION Northern Scandinavia and tundra of northern Russia in summer. Overwinters around coastal areas of the British Isles, western Europe through the Mediterranean, and in Africa.

THE BARRING ACROSS the upper surface of the tail feathers helps to identify Bar-tailed Godwits throughout the year. In breeding plumage, the back of the cock bird is a mottled shade of brown, with the the head, neck, and underparts being chestnut and free from any markings. Their appearance is then transformed at the end of the breeding season, when brownish-grey streaking becomes evident over the back, while whitish plumage is apparent below. Hens can be identified by their paler coloration, and a slightly longer bill. This is upturned towards the tip, allowing the godwit to probe for food such as worms under water. The difference in bill length between the sexes allows the hens to feed in somewhat deep water and so lessens the competition for food.

JOINT RESPONSIBILITIES A male Bar-tailed Godwit in breeding plumage. Both parents share the task of incubation.

Black-tailed Godwit

FAMILY Scolopacidae
SPECIES *Limosa limosa*
LENGTH 42 cm (16½ in)
HABITAT Marshland/estuaries
CLUTCH SIZE 4

DISTRIBUTION Summer breeding range in Iceland and northern Europe, especially Germany and Denmark eastwards. Overwinters in coastal areas and through the Mediterranean, into Africa.

FEEDING GROUNDS Farmland and estuaries are habitats favoured by these godwits outside the breeding period. They use their long bill to probe into the mud for edible items.

THIS IS THE TALLEST of the godwits, with a comparatively slim profile. The bill is relatively straight, yellowish-orange along much of its length and blackish at the tip. The tail feathers are short and predominantly black, with a narrow white band across the tip. Males in the summer have a more rufous shade to the plumage on their upperparts with barring extending from here down onto the white feathering of the abdomen. Pairs nest on the ground in wetland areas, inland from the coast, and often form loose colonies. If threatened by a would-be predator, the birds in the colony then mob the intruder. On their wintering grounds, there may be thousands of individuals in some areas. The population of the Black-tailed Godwit has increased significantly in parts of western Europe over recent years.

Sanderling

FAMILY Scolopacidae
SPECIES *Calidris alba*
LENGTH 20 cm (8 in)
HABITAT Sandy beaches
CLUTCH SIZE 4

DISTRIBUTION Breeds in the high Arctic. Overwinters around the British Isles, and Denmark southwards to Spain, in coastal areas. Also occurs through the Mediterranean and in Africa.

IN BREEDING PLUMAGE, this member of the sandpiper clan has blackish, rust, and white mottling on its chest and upperparts, with more evident streaking on the head, while the underparts are white. During the winter, however, its appearance is transformed with the mottling being replaced by grey plumage above, occasionally with a blackish area at the shoulders. Young birds resemble adults in winter plumage, but they are a darker shade of grey, often with white scaling evident on the back as well. The sexes are similar in appearance.

DIET Sanderlings are opportunistic feeders, running along the shore and using their short bill to grab invertebrates exposed in the surf.

BLACK-TAILED GODWIT The long legs of this species extend out beyond the end of the tail when the bird is in flight. Like many waders, these particular godwits fly long distances every year, to and from their breeding grounds

Dunlin

FAMILY Scolopacidae
SPECIES *Calidris alpina*
LENGTH 22 cm (8½ in)
HABITAT Tundra/mudflats
CLUTCH SIZE 4

DISTRIBUTION Breeds in Iceland, northern Scandinavia, Scotland, and other areas of northern Europe. Overwinters in coastal areas of southern England, western Europe, and the Mediterranean.

IN THE WINTER MONTHS, Dunlin are brownish-grey above, with white underparts. During the summer, they display rufous feathering over the back, and a prominent black patch on the belly. Dunlin move slowly through the shallows when feeding, probing for small crustaceans and similar invertebrates.

BILL SHAPE The Dunlin's black bill is much thicker at its base compared with its tip. It is also slightly down-curved towards the tip.

Red Knot

FAMILY Scolopacidae
SPECIES *Calidris canutus*
LENGTH 27 cm (10½ in)
HABITAT Sandy beaches/ mudflats
CLUTCH SIZE 4

DISTRIBUTION Breeds in the high Arctic. Winters around the coasts of the British Isles and western Europe to the Mediterranean and north Africa.

THE REDDISH UNDERPARTS of this species are only evident during the summer breeding period, offset against greyish-brown, black, and chestnut mottling on the upperparts. In the winter, Red Knots are transformed to a pale grey colour on the back and wings, with their underparts being white. At this time of year, they often join up to create large flocks.

COLOUR AND PATTERN An adult Red Knot in summer plumage. The sexes cannot be distinguished by any variance in their appearance. Young birds are grey.

Curlew Sandpiper

FAMILY Scolopacidae

SPECIES *Calidris ferruginea*

LENGTH 20 cm (8 in)

HABITAT Open country/ marshland

CLUTCH SIZE 4

DISTRIBUTION Breeding grounds in the Arctic region of Siberia, and seen as a passage migrant heading to Africa. Sometimes overwinters in the Mediterranean, uncommonly in western Europe.

THESE SANDPIPERS ARE most likely to be seen as transitory visitors to Europe during the autumn, as they are heading back to their wintering grounds in Africa, rather than in the spring. There are a few records of Curlew Sandpipers occasionally overwintering in Europe too. Males, which have a reddish head and underparts in breeding plumage, moult first. They will then start to leave their breeding grounds as early as June, flying southwest across Europe in the direction of Africa. Hens tend to depart later, along with their young, which migrate south in August or September. They are most likely to be seen in areas where there are mudflats, either inland or along the coast. Curlew Sandpipers may be encountered in mixed flocks with other waders, although when feeding, they often wade out into deeper water too. They can pick up edible items directly or probe down into the mud, with their down-curved black bill extracting worms and other invertebrates.

LONG LIMBED Curlew Sandpipers have long legs, so that they can wade into deep water. In flight, their toes extend out beyond their tail feathers.

Purple Sandpiper

FAMILY Scolopacidae
SPECIES *Calidris maritima*
LENGTH 22 cm (8¾ in)
HABITAT Marshland/coasts
CLUTCH SIZE 4

DISTRIBUTION Summer visitor inland to northern Scandinavia and Iceland; resident in coastal areas. Winters on western coasts down to northern Spain.

THESE SANDPIPERS WILL often nest inland, well away from the coast, usually frequenting boggy ground, with the hen laying in a simple depression on the ground. After nesting, they moult before moving on to their permanent wintering grounds. During winter, Purple Sandpipers occur in coastal areas, forming mixed flocks, often with Ruddy Turnstones (*see* p 145). They are quite bold, and frequently forage over seaweed-covered rocks rather than sandy areas, and can swim if necessary. Their diet is mainly small molluscs.

LEG COLOUR The legs of the Purple Sandpiper are a yellowish-orange shade in winter, being more brightly coloured than in the summer, when they are greyer.

Pectoral Sandpiper

FAMILY Scolopacidae
SPECIES *Calidris melanotos*
LENGTH 22 cm (8¾ in)
HABITAT Marshland/mudflats
CLUTCH SIZE 4

DISTRIBUTION This North American native is probably the commonest vagrant in Europe, certainly in the United Kingdom and the Irish Republic.

PECTORAL SANDPIPERS spend more time inland than many related species, even being observed in flooded fields. They are often seen in mainland Europe during the early summer, but are more commonly sighted as autumn visitors in the United Kingdom and Irish Republic. They are rarely seen in this area in winter. Their basic coloration is similar to that of related species, but there is a very noticeable dividing line between the grey-brown mottling extending down over the breast, and the white feathering on the underparts.

RANGE Pectoral Sandpipers breed in areas from North America to northeastern Siberia, and overwinter in the southern hemisphere.

Little Stint

FAMILY Scolopacidae
SPECIES *Calidris minuta*
LENGTH 15 cm (6 in)
HABITAT Tundra/coasts
CLUTCH SIZE 4

DISTRIBUTION Breeds in the tundra and the extreme north of Scandinavia, overwintering south in the Mediterranean and into northern parts of Africa.

THIS SPECIES is most likely to be seen during the spring and especially the early autumn in Europe, flying south to its wintering grounds. At these times of year, Little Stints frequently congregate on inland waters rather than at the coast, often with Dunlin (*see* p 158).

BROWN BACK The brown plumage evident on the back is replaced by silvery-grey feathering over winter.

Temminck's Sandpiper

FAMILY Scolopacidae
SPECIES *Calidris temminckii*
LENGTH 15 cm (6 in)
HABITAT Marshland/coasts
CLUTCH SIZE 4

DISTRIBUTION Breeds in northern Scotland and Scandinavia up into the tundra. Overwinters in a few areas of southern Europe, from northern Italy eastwards, and in Africa.

ALSO SOMETIMES called Temminck's Stint, this species tends not to fly as far east when migrating, so it is not as commonly seen as the Little Stint in the more westerly parts of Europe, including Ireland. Its plumage is duller, noticeably over the wings, but the most evident point of distinction between these two species is the yellow rather than blackish legs of Temminck's Sandpiper. This species is also more vocal, uttering its trilling call repeatedly in flight.

CREEPING These sandpipers flex their legs noticeably when searching for food, making them appear as if they are creeping along.

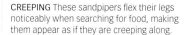

Spotted Redshank

FAMILY Scolopacidae
SPECIES *Tringa erythropus*
LENGTH 33 cm (13 in)
HABITAT Tundra/marshland
CLUTCH SIZE 4

DISTRIBUTION Breeds in the far north of Scandinavia into the Arctic. Overwinters on the coasts of western Europe, the Mediterranean, and into Africa.

THIS SPECIES UNDERGOES a very dramatic transformation in appearance at the start of the breeding period, changing from greyish plumage with white underparts to being predominately black. Even the legs darken in colour during this period. Barring remains evident along the flanks, with spotted patterning clearly evident on the wings. Pairs nest on the ground. When migrating, they may be seen in small groups, with hens tending to leave the breeding grounds first, followed by their partners, and finally the offspring. Young birds that are not breeding may stay in their wintering grounds the following summer, but often fly some distance back north, to parts of northern Europe.

WHISTLER A Spotted Redshank calling from a tree. These birds utter a series of whistling notes.

Wood Sandpiper

FAMILY Scolopacidae
SPECIES *Tringa glareola*
LENGTH 21 cm (8¼ in)
HABITAT Woodland/lakes
CLUTCH SIZE 4

DISTRIBUTION Breeds in Scotland, Scandinavia, and northern Europe. Overwinters in sub-Saharan Africa, but may seen on Mediterranean coasts.

NESTING SEASON A Wood Sandpiper on its breeding grounds. Their nesting season extends from May to July. Young birds have prominent brown markings on their wings.

CONSPICUOUS MOTTLING over the wings, with white blotches as well, helps to identify this sandpiper. There is a pale stripe running above the eyes, and dark streaking extending down the neck. The relatively long legs are yellowish, and extend back beyond the short tail feathers when the bird is flying. The bill is dark. There is not a great difference between winter and summer plumage in this species, although the barring on the flanks is not evident outside the nesting period, and the upperparts are less heavily streaked. Their name reflects their breeding behaviour, with pairs nesting in close proximity to wooded areas, usually on the ground, but sometimes up in a tree, using the abandoned nest of another bird. They spend the winter mainly in freshwater habitats, flying long distances southwards.

Greenshank

FAMILY Scolopacidae
SPECIES *Tringa nebularia*
LENGTH 34 cm (13½ in)
HABITAT Pine forest/coasts
CLUTCH SIZE 4

DISTRIBUTION Breeding range extends from central Scotland and Scandinavia east. Winters in southern Ireland and England, Spain, and into Africa.

THE GREY-GREEN coloration of the Greenshank's legs is only apparent during the winter; the legs are yellowish in summer. The dark markings on the upper breast, extending down onto the underparts, and black areas on the wings are more pronounced in summer too. Greenshanks are very nimble, catching not just aquatic invertebrates but also fish fry in the shallows, especially over the winter period. Pairs nest in forested areas, usually close to water.

FEEDING Greenshanks may pursue aquatic prey by running through the water, although usually they feed at a more sedentary pace.

Green Sandpiper

FAMILY Scolopacidae
SPECIES *Tringa ochropus*
LENGTH 24 cm (9½ in)
HABITAT Wet woodland/ponds
CLUTCH SIZE 4

DISTRIBUTION Breeds in Scandinavia and northern Europe. Overwinters in southern England southwards to northern Africa.

CLEAR WHITE UNDERPARTS with no markings on the flanks help to identify the Green Sandpiper. The wings are dark brown with fine spotting, and the legs are greyish-green. When these sandpipers are observed in flight, their feet extend back roughly to the end of the tail feathers, rather than beyond them. The tail feathers have broad black bars running across their tips. During the winter, the plumage of the upperparts and breast is much darker than in the breeding season. Unlike many related species, these sandpipers breed off the ground in trees, adopting the nests of other birds, such as thrushes and pigeons, for this purpose. They are most likely to be seen in boggy areas, which provide them with feeding opportunities. They frequent small stretches of open water at other times of the year, often occurring inland rather than in coastal areas.

TIMID Green Sandpipers are rather nervous birds by nature and are not encountered in large flocks.

Marsh Sandpiper

FAMILY Scolopacidae
SPECIES *Tringa stagnatilis*
LENGTH 25 cm (10 in)
HABITAT Wet grassland/ponds
CLUTCH SIZE 4

DISTRIBUTION Summer visitor to eastern Europe, north of the Caspian Sea, and scattered elsewhere. Overwinters in the Mediterranean and Africa.

THE SLENDER, STRAIGHT BILL of the Marsh Sandpiper, and its long legs, helps to set it apart from other related species. The feet are clearly visible in flight, extending well beyond the tail feathers, which have narrow barring at the tip. In summer plumage, there are black spots evident over the wings, and streaking extending down the neck onto the chest, and down onto the flanks. During winter, the Marsh Sandpiper has a plainer appearance: the underparts from the throat are almost completely white, and the wings are a uniform shade of brown. Pairs nest in open country, either individually or sometimes in small groups. Both members of the pair share the task of incubating the eggs and then caring for the chicks.

WINTER COLOURS A Marsh Sandpiper in winter plumage. These birds may occur in larger numbers, often feeding in groups, grabbing aquatic invertebrates in the water during winter.

Redshank

FAMILY Scolopacidae
SPECIES *Tringa totanus*
LENGTH 33 cm (13 in)
HABITAT Damp areas/coasts
CLUTCH SIZE 4

DISTRIBUTION Summer visitor from Iceland to Scandinavia and eastern Europe. Resident in parts of the United Kingdom, Denmark, and further south.

THE BRIGHT RED 'SHANKS', or legs, enable this species to be distinguished easily throughout the year. It is widespread across Europe, being resident in various localities, and overwinters in southern Europe. The bill too is red, particularly at the base, with darker markings towards the tip. Dark streaking is very evident on the underparts during the summer, with dark markings on the wings too. The tail feathers are heavily barred. Redshanks are vociferous birds, calling loudly at any hint of danger, alerting other waders nearby, so that it is difficult to approach them closely. They are often to be seen feeding in large flocks.

WINTER COLOURS Dull brown colouring predominates in Redshanks over the winter. These waders can prove quite territorial in some localities.

Lesser Yellowlegs

FAMILY Scolopacidae
SPECIES *Tringa flavipes*
LENGTH 26 cm (10¼ in)
HABITAT Tundra/coasts
CLUTCH SIZE 4

DISTRIBUTION A North American species sighted each year in Europe as a vagrant, including in the United Kingdom.

SPECKLED DARK PLUMAGE over the back and wings, paler underparts, and yellow legs help to identify this wader. Lesser Yellowlegs are typically observed in late summer through to autumn in Europe, mainly in summer plumage: at this stage, their flanks are entirely white or just display slight barring, in comparison with the Greater Yellowlegs, which is heavily marked. In winter plumage, the only means of distinguishing between these two species is by size. Lesser Yellowlegs catch small invertebrates by wading through shallow water, and may join up with other waders. They are most likely to be seen in marshland areas.

TRAVELLER Even in their North American homeland, Lesser Yellowlegs undertake long flights to and from their breeding grounds, which are in northern latitudes.

Greater Yellowlegs

FAMILY Scolopacidae
SPECIES *Tringa melanoleuca*
LENGTH 36 cm (14 in)
HABITAT Shallow wetland
CLUTCH SIZE 3–4

DISTRIBUTION A primarily North American species, usually sighted each year in Europe, particularly in parts of the United Kingdom and Ireland.

APART FROM SIZE, the Greater Yellowlegs is basically identical in appearance to its smaller relative. It breeds over a wide area in Canada, with odd individuals crossing the Atlantic and being sighted later in the year in European localities. It is most likely to be confused with the Greenshank (*see* p 163) in terms of its overall appearance, although the bright yellow colour of its legs is an easy distinction. Just as in its homeland, Greater Yellowlegs will form mixed flocks with other waders, hunting for invertebrates and small fish.

CHARACTERISTIC A slightly upturned bill, a long neck, a heavily mottled back, and yellow legs are all features of this species.

PERCH Common Sandpipers may be seen perching in trees as well as on the ground near water.

Common Sandpiper

FAMILY Scolopacidae
SPECIES *Actitis hypoleucos*
LENGTH 20 cm (8 in)
HABITAT Forest/coasts
CLUTCH SIZE 3–4

DISTRIBUTION Occurs across much of Europe in the summer, but more patchily distributed in the west, being absent from southern parts of both England and Ireland.

THIS SPECIES has a somewhat short-legged appearance, with pure white underparts, and dark streaking across the breast. The wings and tail are brown with black markings; the tail is relatively long. Common Sandpipers have a very distinctive style of walking, with a pronounced bobbing action not seen in related species. When breeding, pairs seek out forested areas that are close to water; the nest itself is well hidden on the ground. However, they may also choose areas near the coast, being seen in Europe typically from April to August, after which they fly to Africa where they overwinter. Very few Common Sandpipers remain in southern Europe during the winter. They fly under cover of darkness sometimes individually or in small groups but are rarely seen in large flocks. Unlike many waders, Common Sandpipers may sometimes be seen feeding alongside roads away from water.

Spotted Sandpiper

FAMILY Scolopacidae
SPECIES *Actitis macularia*
LENGTH 19 cm (7½ in)
HABITAT Streams/marshland
CLUTCH SIZE 3–4

DISTRIBUTION A visitor from North America, recorded in small numbers annually, most commonly in the United Kingdom and Ireland.

THE SPOTTED SANDPIPER has an extensive breeding area in North America, being seen in a variety of habitats close to water, in coastal areas as well as inland. It moves with a very distinctive bobbing gait, and flies in quite a stiff way, revealing the white area on each wing. Its back is brown, as is the breast in winter plumage; the underparts are white during winter. The spotted patterning is a feature seen in the summer, extending down onto the abdomen, with the underlying coloration remaining white. Although the majority of European sightings are made during late summer and early autumn, the Spotted Sandpiper has been known to overwinter in Europe, and can be seen occasionally in the spring. Unlike most vagrants, this species has even attempted to breed in Europe – recorded in Scotland. The eggs are laid in a scrape near water, and often the cock bird incubates for much of the time on his own, with the hen leaving and laying again with another partner.

LONG TOES The long toes of this and other waders are often not especially obvious except on dry land.

Terek Sandpiper

FAMILY Scolopacidae
SPECIES *Xenus cinereus*
LENGTH 25 cm (10 cm)
HABITAT Rivers/lakes
CLUTCH SIZE 3–4

DISTRIBUTION A summer visitor mainly to northeastern Europe and eastwards into Asia. European birds fly around the eastern Mediterranean to their African wintering grounds.

A COMBINATION OF short legs and upturned bill helps to identify this sandpiper quite easily. The legs are orange-yellow, and there is a dark stripe running down the back from the vicinity of the shoulder. Pairs breed alongside larger stretches of water, arriving on their breeding grounds in May and staying relatively briefly, heading south again in July. The nest itself is a scrape on the ground, concealed in among grasses. There is some indication, based on sightings, that these sandpipers may be extending their range further westwards. Certainly, there are larger numbers now breeding in Finland. Its feeding pattern helps to identify it among other waders, as it is very quick and changes direction rapidly too.

BILL SHAPE Even from the front, the upturned shape of the bill of the Terek Sandpiper is clearly evident.

Broad-billed Sandpiper

FAMILY Scolopacidae
SPECIES *Limicola falcinellus*
LENGTH 18 cm (7¼ in)
HABITAT Bogs/coasts
CLUTCH SIZE 3–4

DISTRIBUTION Most likely to be seen in Scandinavia during the summer months, and glimpsed further south when migrating from and to Africa.

THE RELATIVELY BROAD BILL of these sandpipers is not entirely straight. Instead, it curves down slightly at its tip. In winter plumage, the wings are mainly grey, with dark streaks down the centre of the individual feathers. Black coloration predominates over the breeding period, however, with the feathers here having white-and-brown edging. The dark markings on the underparts are also more pronounced. The eggs are laid in a nest on the ground, often concealed in a tussock of grass and lined with some vegetation.

LONG JOURNEY Adults start to migrate south in late July, with youngsters following in August. They may not reach their winter quarters until October.

Grey Phalarope

FAMILY Scolopacidae

SPECIES *Phalaropus fulicarius*

LENGTH 22 cm (8½ in)

HABITAT Tundra/sea

CLUTCH SIZE 2–4

DISTRIBUTION Breeds in the Arctic and on Iceland; migrates south, sometimes passing the British Isles, overwintering in the Atlantic off western Africa.

THE APPEARANCE OF these birds changes dramatically according to the season. The sexes are clearly discernible over the summer, with males having white streaking breaking up the red coloration of their breast and underparts. (This explains why this species is also, rather confusingly, described as the Red Phalarope.) During the winter, however, both cocks and hens become predominantly grey. Grey Phalaropes are most likely to be seen in the autumn, when stormy seas may force them to move closer to the shore. Hens compete for mates at the start of the breeding season rather than vice-versa, associating in groups at this stage, with the cocks then assuming the parental duties.

SUMMER COLOURS A hen Grey Phalarope in summer plumage. Migration unusually occurs over the sea.

Red-necked Phalarope

FAMILY Scolopacidae
SPECIES *Phalaropus lobatus*
LENGTH 19 cm (7½ in)
HABITAT Tundra/coasts
CLUTCH SIZE 2–4

DISTRIBUTION Iceland, Scandinavia, and the far north in the summer, also northern Scotland and Ireland. Migrates southeastwards across Europe to overwinter on the Arabian Sea.

THE PLUMAGE OF this phalarope alters significantly during the year. During the winter, it is difficult to see why it is called a Red-necked Phalarope as its coloration is relatively subdued: grey upperparts with white below. The back is streaked with lighter markings, and there is black feathering behind the eyes and on the crown. Just prior to the breeding season, the birds moult and, unusually among birds, the hen's breeding plumage is more colorful than that of her partner. She can be recognized by the two yellow bars present on each wing. The neck and upper chest are rusty-red, with the throat area being white. After laying, the hen will guard the nest site from interlopers, leaving it to the cock bird to incubate the eggs. The chicks should hatch three weeks later.

WINTER COLOURS An adult Red-necked Phalarope in winter plumage. The sexes cannot be distinguished visually at this stage. They will spend most of this period at sea.

Buff-breasted Sandpiper

FAMILY Scolopacidae
SPECIES *Tryngites subruficollis*
LENGTH 20 cm (8 in)
HABITAT Coasts/grassland
CLUTCH SIZE 3–4

DISTRIBUTION A native of North America, but seen each year in Europe, particularly in the United Kingdom and Ireland.

THESE SANDPIPERS ARE seen not just as odd vagrants, but unusually, they are often to be witnessed in Europe in small flocks. Their plumage does not vary through the year; the underparts are buff on the breast with black spotting on the sides of the chest, and there is white plumage lower down on the abdomen. The legs and feet are yellowish. When they are seen from below in flight, there are dark grey, crescent-shaped markings towards the wing tips, with the underside of the wing otherwise being white.

VISITOR Buff-breasted Sandpipers are sometimes seen on open land such as golf courses. They breed in the Arctic tundra.

Eurasian Woodcock

FAMILY Scolopacidae

SPECIES *Scolopax rusticola*

LENGTH 30 cm (12 in)

HABITAT Damp woodland/
fields

CLUTCH SIZE 4

DISTRIBUTION A summer visitor over much of eastern and northern Europe. Winters in the Mediterranean. Resident in west to northern Spain.

THE RELATIVELY LARGE EYES of the Eurasian Woodcock are an indicator of its nocturnal lifestyle. Males even undertake their elaborate courtship dance at night. Hiding in woodland areas during the day, these birds emerge into nearby fields under cover of darkness to hunt for worms, which they can grab with their long bill. Their mottled plumage conceals their presence, and their short legs allow them to drop to the ground to escape detection. They prefer to hide rather than fly from danger.

WELL HIDDEN This shy, cryptic species is very hard to spot, with its plumage providing excellent camouflage, even at close quarters. It tends to be solitary by nature.

Common Snipe

FAMILY Scolopacidae

SPECIES *Gallinago gallinago*

LENGTH 28 cm (11 in)

HABITAT Wetland/pasture

CLUTCH SIZE 4

DISTRIBUTION Summer visitor to Iceland and northern Europe, tending to be resident further west. Overwinters in Iberia and the southeastern Mediterranean.

WHITE UNDERPARTS and a pale stripe running down the centre of the crown help to identify this species, which also has a long, straight bill. The sexes are identical in appearance, although hens on average have slightly longer bills. Common Snipes are shy birds, and their nest is carefully hidden, usually among tussocks of grass. Outside the breeding season, which typically extends between April and August, large flocks of Common Snipe may gather, comprised of hundreds of individuals. Flocks in flight are traditionally called 'wisps'.

FENCE POST PERCH It is not uncommon for Common Snipes to perch on fence posts, especially during the breeding season.

Great Snipe

FAMILY Scolopacidae
SPECIES *Gallinago media*
LENGTH 30 cm (12 in)
HABITAT Wet meadows/
mountains
CLUTCH SIZE 4

DISTRIBUTION A summer visitor to eastern Europe, also occurs in parts of northern Scandinavia and the former USSR. Overwinters in Africa.

GREAT SNIPE MALES perform their courtship displays at communal grounds, or leks, where they call to their would-be mates, which assemble here at dusk.

Females nest on their own. Great Snipes may be seen further west in Europe, occasionally being sighted in the British Isles, typically in autumn.

AT RISK The populations of Great Snipe have declined significantly over recent years.

Jack Snipe

FAMILY Scolopacidae
SPECIES *Lymnocryptes
minimus*
LENGTH 20 cm (8 in)
HABITAT Bogs/muddy pools
CLUTCH SIZE 4

DISTRIBUTION Breeds in east Scandinavia into the former USSR. Overwinters in the British Isles, from Denmark to Portugal, and parts of the Mediterranean.

THE BILL OF THE Jack Snipe is relatively short, and it is also the smallest member of this group of birds, in terms of its overall size. It has two very distinctive yellowish-orange stripes running down along the length of each wing. These streaks are particularly important for camouflage, with the birds using them to align their bodies with twigs, helping them to blend into the background if danger threatens. They are exceedingly reluctant to fly off.

LATE TO LEAVE Pairs remain on their breeding grounds until their autumn moult is complete in September, and may return by the following April.

Great Skua

FAMILY Stercorariidae

SPECIES *Stercorarius skua*

LENGTH 58 cm (23 in)/
wingspan 140 cm (55 in)

HABITAT Open sea/coasts

CLUTCH SIZE 1–2

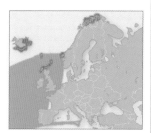

DISTRIBUTION Breeds in northern parts of Scandinavia, and from Iceland to Scotland. Ranges across the Atlantic, and to the Mediterranean in winter.

THESE SKUAS ARE STOCKY BIRDS, with streaky brown plumage and a short tail. They nest on the ground, often near other seabirds, where they will try to steal eggs or even young chicks. They will also harry other birds such as Puffins (*see* p 194) that might be carrying fish back to their offspring, stealing their catches. After the breeding season, they leave land and wander across the Atlantic Ocean. Great Skuas feed on fish and other marine life during this time, although they will also scavenge on carrion such as dead seals, or edible items thrown overboard from boats. By March, they will be returning once more to their breeding grounds.

WELL TRAVELLED Great Skuas that nest in Europe are not uncommonly seen off the Americas, and may travel as far southwards as the coast of Brazil.

Long-tailed Skua

FAMILY Stercorariidae

SPECIES *Stercorarius longicuadus*

LENGTH 40 cm (15¾ in)/
wingspan 115 cm (45¼ in)

HABITAT Sea/coasts

CLUTCH SIZE 1–2

DISTRIBUTION Breeds in Scandinavia and the former USSR. Winters in southern seas, as far as the Antarctic waters.

IN SPITE OF THE tremendous distances which it travels, the Long-tailed Skua is the smallest member of its group. Its long tail plumes account for nearly a quarter of its overall body length. Its wings are long and pointed. Perhaps due to its size, the Long-tailed Skua is particularly agile in flight, and uses this ability to harry other more cumbersome seabirds into dropping their catches, which it can then retrieve from the surface of the sea, assisted by its sharp bill.

VOYAGER Few birds travel as far over the course of a year than the Long-tailed Skua. They briefly spend time on land when nesting.

Arctic Skua

FAMILY Stercorariidae

SPECIES *Stercorarius parasiticus*

LENGTH 44 cm (17½ in)/ wingspan 115 cm (45¼ in)

HABITAT Sea/coasts

CLUTCH SIZE 1–2

DISTRIBUTION Breeds along northern coasts of Europe, from Scandinavia eastwards to the former USSR, and Iceland south to Scotland, wandering widely over the rest of the year.

ARCTIC SKUAS ARE also known as Parasitic Jaegers, because of the way in which they will try to steal the catches of other seabirds rather than catching their own prey. They do not wander widely over the oceans, essentially being more of a coastal species.

WEBBED FEET Like other skuas, the Arctic Skua has webbed feet. Both sexes are similar in appearance.

Pomarine Skua

FAMILY Stercorariidae

SPECIES *Stercorarius pomarinus*

LENGTH 50 cm (20 in)/ wingspan 125 cm (49¼ in)

HABITAT Sea/coasts

CLUTCH SIZE 1–2

DISTRIBUTION Summer visitor to the far north of Europe to breed on the Arctic tundra. Seen during spring or autumn migration.

NESTING IN THE FAR NORTH where food is scarce has resulted in these seabirds adapting to hunting lemmings. The numbers of these small rodents fluctuate on a cyclical basis, however, and this affects the breeding success of the skuas, with more chicks being reared when food is plentiful. At other times, they may resort to hunting other birds and scavenging generally. After leaving their breeding grounds, they spend their time at sea, feeding largely on fish.

NO NEST Pomarine Skuas lay their eggs on the ground, not attempting to build a nest. Some individuals are much blacker in colour than others.

Ivory Gull

FAMILY Laridae

SPECIES *Pagophila eburnea*

LENGTH 47 cm (18½ in)/ wingspan 112 cm (44 cm)

HABITAT Coasts/sea

CLUTCH SIZE 2–3

DISTRIBUTION Occurs in the high Arctic region, as far south as northern Iceland; often seen as a vagrant in the British Isles.

THE PURE, SNOW-WHITE appearance of the Ivory Gull helps to distinguish it from other species, with the bill being bluish at the base and yellow at its tip. The legs and feet are black. These latter characteristics serve to distinguish it from albino gulls of other species, which are occasionally reported. Young birds, however, display a variable pattern of dark spots over the wings and also on the tips of the flight feathers through their first winter, until they moult into adult plumage during the following spring. The area between the eyes and around the base of the bill is also dark in colour up until this stage.

OPPORTUNISTIC FEEDER The Ivory Gull is a scavenger, seeking out corpses of seals, although it will also follow fishing boats.

Herring Gull

FAMILY Laridae

SPECIES *Larus argentatus*

LENGTH 63 cm (25 in)/ wingspan 146 cm (57½ in)

HABITAT Coasts/lakes

CLUTCH SIZE 2–3

DISTRIBUTION Resident from Iceland south around the British Isles and the French coast up to Scandinavia. Also occurs in summer in southern Scandinavia and the adjacent area.

ADULTS OF THIS SPECIES can be identified by their yellowish bill colour with a prominent red spot on the lower mandible, near its tip. In winter plumage, the neck is streaked with brown, and the red spot becomes less distinctive. Herring

Gulls naturally feed on fish, but are also scavengers, eating anything edible. This has seen them move further inland, away from the coast, often into cities where they may nest on the roofs of buildings. Pairs have very protective parental instincts, dive-bombing people who venture too close to the nest or chicks here.

PARENTAL DUTIES An adult Herring Gull at its rooftop nest about to feed its two young chicks, discernible by their mottled brown plumage and dark bills.

Audouin's Gull

FAMILY Laridae

SPECIES *Larus audouinii*

LENGTH 52 cm (20½ in)/ wingspan 125 cm (49¼ in)

HABITAT Coasts/sea

CLUTCH SIZE 2–3

DISTRIBUTION Resident mainly on islands through the Mediterranean region, having become more numerous in western parts over recent years.

THIS PARTICULAR SPECIES ranks as one of the rarest gulls in the world. When adult, these birds can be recognized by their red bill with a darker subterminal band and a yellow tip. The legs are greyish in colour. Immatures are brown in colour, gaining grey feathering over the course of their first winter. Audouin's Gull feeds largely on fish, sometimes diving to catch its food.

APPEARANCE Audouin's Gull has long wings extending back beyond the tail. A young bird can be seen in the background here.

Yellow-legged Gull

FAMILY Laridae

SPECIES *Larus cachinnans*

LENGTH 58 cm (23 in)/
wingspan 140 cm (55¼ in)

HABITAT Coasts/lakes

CLUTCH SIZE 2–3

DISTRIBUTION Resident from northern France throughout much of the Mediterranean region, with a summer breeding population in eastern Europe in particular being located far from the sea.

A PROMINENT RED DOT on the base of the yellow lower bill, grey wings, and a white body help to distinguish this species. It resembles the Herring Gull (*see* p 177) overall, but can be easily distinguished by its legs, which are yellow rather than pink. Young Yellow-legged Gulls are usually lighter in colour than immatures of that species, with whiter heads and dark markings on the underparts, although individuals do display some variations. The signs are that this adaptable gull is now becoming more widespread and starting to expand its range further afield, particularly heading further north along the coast of the English Channel.

ADAPTABLE These gulls will seek food out over the sea, or forage on land, sometimes congregating at rubbish dumps for edible waste.

Common Gull

FAMILY Laridae

SPECIES *Larus canus*

LENGTH 41 cm (16 in)/
wingspan 108 cm (43½ in)

HABITAT Coasts/lakes

CLUTCH SIZE 2–3

DISTRIBUTION Resident in northwestern parts of Europe, from Scotland to southern Scandinavia, and a summer visitor in northern areas.

A NARROW YELLOW BILL and yellow legs help to distinguish the Common Gull. The plumage over the back and wings is greyish, with the underparts being white. Over the winter period, the white area on the head and neck has a brownish suffusion. Common Gulls nest in colonies and overwinter along the coast. This species feeds on invertebrates such as worms and molluscs, rather than scavenging. Young birds can be recognized by their brown, mottled appearance, and it takes three years for them to acquire full adult plumage.

CALL The call of the Common Gull is like that of a miaowing cat, accounting for its alternative name of Mew Gull.

Lesser Black-backed Gull

FAMILY Laridae

SPECIES *Larus fuscus*

LENGTH 56 cm (22 in)/ wingspan 130 cm (51¼ in)

HABITAT Coasts/sea

CLUTCH SIZE 2–3

DISTRIBUTION Summer visitor to the far north of Europe. Resident in areas of western Europe; overwinters on the Black and Caspian Seas and around the Mediterranean.

IN SPITE OF ITS NAME, the dark plumage over the back and wings of the Lesser Black-backed Gull can vary from black through to grey, depending on the area where the birds originate, with those from western Europe being paler than those occurring to the north. They have yellow legs, which, combined with their smaller size, help to separate them from the Greater Black-backed Gull (*see* page 182). Young birds both have brown mottled plumage, but in the case of the Lesser Black-backed, the dark brown flight feathers have only a very narrow band of white at their tips.

STRONG FLYERS These gulls can migrate long distances, with those occurring in the far northeastern parts of Europe flying not just to the Mediterranean, but sometimes further down into Africa.

Slender-billed Gull

FAMILY Laridae

SPECIES *Larus genei*

LENGTH 40 cm (15¾ in)/
wingspan 100 cm (39½ in)

HABITAT Coasts/lakes

CLUTCH SIZE 2–3

DISTRIBUTION Summer visitor right across southern Europe, often seen on the coast, but also inland. Overwinters in areas throughout the Mediterranean, extending to Africa.

THE SLENDER-BILLED GULL is not especially common, although occasionally it does crop up well outside its normal range, having been observed, for example, in southern England. The relatively long bill of these birds changes in colour through the year, being dark in the summer and then lightening to yellow in the winter, with only the tip remaining dark at this stage. When feeding, another distinguishing characteristic of the Slender-billed Gull will be apparent: its long neck.

Pairs nest in colonies on the ground; after the breeding period, some birds may fly as far south as the Horn of Africa, where they spend the winter.

JUVENILE This bird is in its second year, as reflected by the remaining traces of brown plumage.

Iceland Gull

FAMILY Laridae
SPECIES *Larus glaucoides*
LENGTH 64 cm (25¼ in)/
wingspan 135 cm (53¼ in)
HABITAT Coasts/sea
CLUTCH SIZE 2–3

DISTRIBUTION Its breeding grounds lie across the Atlantic in northern Canada and Greenland. Wintertime visitor only to Iceland and parts of the British Isles.

IDENTIFICATION Aside from catching fish on occasion themselves, these gulls will scavenge for food. This is a young bird, as shown by its bill colour.

ADULT ICELAND GULLS are white in colour, with pale grey plumage over the back and wings, and streaking on the sides of the head and neck. Young birds start off pale brown with white markings on the wings, and undergo a series of moults with their plumage becoming whiter overall. The bill coloration undergoes a progressive transformation too, from being pinkish with a black tip to more of a bluish shade before finally becoming yellowish, with a red spot near the tip of the lower bill in the case of adults. The sexes are identical in appearance. The birds that are seen in Iceland tend to be those that nest on the northeastern side of Greenland, with the more southerly population there being resident throughout the year.

Glaucous Gull

FAMILY Laridae
SPECIES *Larus hyperboreus*
LENGTH 69 cm (27 in)/
wingspan 156 cm (61½ cm)
HABITAT Coasts/sea
CLUTCH SIZE 2–3

DISTRIBUTION Wintertime visitor to Europe, breeding in North America. Seen mainly around the coasts of Iceland, Scandinavia, and the British Isles.

THESE GULLS ARE UNUSUAL in breeding entirely in the far north, on the Arctic tundra and along the North American coast. Their large size and very pale coloration help to distinguish them from other species. They have glaucous-grey plumage over the back and wings, and the rest of the body is white. Pale brown streaking on the head is apparent in the winter, with the sexes being identical in appearance. It takes four years for young birds to gain their adult plumage. Glaucous Gulls may associate with flocks of other large gulls, and usually remain close to the shore.

FEEDING The Glaucous Gull is a predatory species, which will seize eggs and nestlings of other birds, and harries sea ducks to drop fish, although these birds may also scavenge.

Greater Black-backed Gull

FAMILY Laridae

SPECIES *Larus marinus*

LENGTH 76 cm (30 in)/
wingpan 165 cm (65 in)

HABITAT Coasts/lakes

CLUTCH SIZE 2–3

DISTRIBUTION Summer visitor
to Iceland and Scandinavia; also
resident here, in the British Isles,
and the coast of western Europe.

THESE LARGE AND AGGRESSIVE gulls
have expanded their range from the coast,
moving inland in some areas, where they
will visit rubbish dumps for the remains of
anything edible. They may also be seen
occasionally around lakes. Around the
coast, Greater Black-backed Gulls nest in
association with other seabirds, and are
well recognized as nest-raiders in these
surroundings. They will also rob seabirds
of their catches as they fly back to land,
and can even catch and kill smaller birds
such as Puffins (*see* p 194). Pairs may
breed either on their own, or sometimes
in small colonies. Their speckled eggs are
laid in a nest of detritus and vegetation on
the ground. The extensive black plumage
over their back and wings, combined with
their large size, helps to identify Great

Black-backed Gulls. The bill is yellow, with
a prominent red spot near the end of the
lower bill. Young birds are again white,
heavily marked with brown streaks and
spots; the tips of the flight feathers are,
however, predominantly white. It will take
four years for these birds to acquire full
adult plumage. Like most gulls, they are
potentially long-lived, with a life
expectancy of possibly 20 years or more.
They face few predators, although they
are vulnerable to pollution such as oil
spillages in coastal areas.

AQUATIC These gulls can swim well, often spending
time out at sea, particularly over the winter period.

Mediterranean Gull

FAMILY Laridae

SPECIES *Larus melanocephalus*

LENGTH 40 cm (15¾ in)/
wingspan 100 cm (39½ in)

HABITAT Rivers/coasts

CLUTCH SIZE 2–4

DISTRIBUTION Breeds in various localities from Denmark west to England and France, and through the Mediterranean, as well as some areas inland, overwintering in coastal areas.

THERE IS A MARKED variance between summer and winter plumage for these birds, with the head coloration of adult Mediterranean Gulls tending to be dusky during the winter, and then becoming jet black in the summer, contrasting with the blood-red coloration of the bill and legs. The area around the eyes is white, with the chest and underparts also being white. The back and wings are pale grey. Young birds have paler edging to the brownish plumage over the back, with the bill and legs being dark in colour. It takes approximately three years for these gulls to acquire their adult coloration.

NESTING A pair of adult Mediterranean Gulls on their breeding grounds. Pairs nest in close proximity to each other. The sexes are identical in coloration.

Little Gull

FAMILY Laridae

SPECIES *Larus minutus*

LENGTH 27 cm (10¾ in)/
wingspan 67 cm (26½ in)

HABITAT Marshland/coasts

CLUTCH SIZE 2–4

AS ITS NAME SUGGESTS, this is the smallest of the gulls. They are agile on the wing, feeding both at the water's surface, and also by catching flying insects. Breeding occurs on freshwater marshes, with pairs nesting communally. Young birds are an unmistakeable combination of black and white when they fledge, with prominent pale edging to the black feathers on the wings. These black areas reduce over successive moults, being replaced by grey plumage.

DISTRIBUTION Breeds in parts of southern Scandinavia and through eastern Europe into Asia. Overwinters along the coast of western and southern Europe.

COLORATION This is a Little Gull in summer plumage, with black plumage evident on the head. This becomes mainly white over the winter.

STORMY WEATHER A flock of gulls flying over a stormy sea. They will dart down to scavenge on edible items thrown up by the churning of the waves, almost hovering in flight, before diving down to the surface of the water.

Black-headed Gull

FAMILY Laridae

SPECIES *Larus ribidundus*

LENGTH 38 cm (15 in)/
wingspan 96 cm (37¾ in)

HABITAT Marshland/inland/
coasts

CLUTCH SIZE 2–4

DISTRIBUTION Breeds in the
summer over most of eastern
Europe and Iceland. Resident in
western Europe, overwinters
on the coast from southern
Scandinavia down to the
Mediterranean.

ONE OF THE MOST commonly seen
species of gull in Europe, the Black-
headed can actually be distinguished
by the dark chocolate-brown colour
of its plumage on this part of its
body over the summer months. It
is not jet black, as in some other
species. In the winter, there is just
a black area behind the eye and a
dark streak running up above here.
The bill, too, is lighter at this stage,
being red with a dark tip. Black-
headed Gulls are highly social by
nature, and can be seen in flocks
even inland, often being attracted
to agricultural areas.

ADAPTABLE Black-headed Gulls are versatile
when feeding. They will follow a ploughing
tractor, seeking invertebrates in the soil, or
congregate in city parks, taking handouts.

Sabine's Gull

FAMILY Laridae

SPECIES *Larus sabini*

LENGTH 35 cm (13¾ in)/
wingspan 85 cm (33½ in)

HABITAT Tundra/sea

CLUTCH SIZE 3

DISTRIBUTION Breeds in the
Arctic Circle, and birds of North
American origins are often seen
on the west coast of Europe,
especially in the British Isles.

ALTHOUGH ONLY seen as a
vagrant in the region, Sabine's
Gull is often encountered
during the period from August
to October when birds are
crossing the Atlantic to their
wintering grounds off the
southwestern coast of Africa.
They are sometimes forced
further northwards during
this period, depending on the
wind patterns, and may be
sighted off Europe. In winter
plumage, there is a prominent
black area on the open wings,
and a broad black collar.

BILL COLOUR Another distinguishing
feature of Sabine's Gull is its dark bill,
which ends in a yellow tip.

Black-legged Kittiwake

FAMILY Laridae

SPECIES *Rissa tridactyla*

LENGTH 43 cm (17 in)/ wingspan 105 cm (41 in)

HABITAT Coasts/sea

CLUTCH SIZE 2

DISTRIBUTION Breeds on coast from Iceland and northern Scandinavia to the Iberian Peninsula. Overwinters at sea.

THESE OCEAN-DWELLING GULLS live on the coast, and are unlikely to be seen inland. Agile in flight, Black-legged Kittiwakes can swim well, aided by their webbed feet. They do not feed exclusively at the surface, however, but can dive effectively as well, pursuing fish underwater. They sometimes follow fishing boats too, feeding on the waste thrown overboard. The bill is yellow, and the legs and feet are black, which aids their identification. This species is described as the Black-legged Kittiwake for this reason, with the name of Kittwake originating from the sound of their rather shrill calls. When breeding, pairs nest in large colonies often numbering thousands of individuals on very narrow and often quite exposed cliff faces, constructing a

nest of seaweed for their eggs. It is thought that choosing a very narrow shelf helps to protect them against potential predators, including other, larger members of the gull family such as the Greater Black-backed Gull (*see* p 182). Young Kittiwakes have a black collar around the back of the neck, with a black area behind each eye, with the bill too being black. It takes three years for them to acquire full adult plumage. In winter plumage, adult Kittiwakes have a relatively narrow dark streak across the neck, whereas in summer, their heads are completely white.

TYPICAL PLUMAGE Like many gulls, these kittiwakes have a white head and body, offset against grey wings.

Whiskered Tern

FAMILY Laridae

SPECIES *Chlidonias hybridus*

LENGTH 28 cm (11 in)/ wingspan 62 cm (24½ in)

HABITAT Lakes/rivers

CLUTCH SIZE 2–3

DISTRIBUTION Breeds widely in various localities across southern Europe; overwinters in some areas of the Mediterranean but the majority of birds head further south into Africa.

IN SUMMER, these terns have a black area on the top of the head, encompassing the eyes, with a white area below. The back and underparts are otherwise grey, apart from a white area around the vent. The wings are long, as in other terns, extending to the tip of the tail. During the winter, however, their appearance is transformed: the black cap is reduced to streaking on the back of the head, and the chest and underparts become completely white. The relatively powerful bill is dull blackish-red throughout the year, and the sexes are identical in appearance. Young birds have brown-and-black markings evident over the back.

NESTING A Whiskered Tern returns to its nest on the ground, where its speckled egg is just visible.

White-winged Black Tern

FAMILY Laridae

SPECIES *Chlidonias leucopterus*

LENGTH 24 cm (9½ in)/ wingspan 55 cm (21¾ in)

HABITAT Marshland

CLUTCH SIZE 2–3

DISTRIBUTION Its breeding grounds lie essentially in eastern parts of Europe, mainly to the north of the Black and Caspian Seas. These terns overwinter in Africa.

TERNS IN GENERAL are long-distance travellers, as reflected by their wing shape, and it is actually not uncommon for sightings of this species to be made on a regular basis in parts of Europe outside their normal area of distribution, even as far west as in parts of the British Isles where the closely related Black Tern is more likely to be seen. These two species can be told apart very easily in summer plumage, however, because as its name suggests, the White-winged Black Tern has prominent white wing coverts. Even during the winter, whereas the Black Tern has a consistent black cap, the head markings of its white-winged relative are reduced to pale black streaks extending back from behind the eye, with an isolated black spot on each side of the head behind the eye.

DIET AND BEHAVIOUR These terns feed mainly on invertebrates which they catch either in flight or at the water's surface, rather than diving for fish. They nest in colonies.

Black Tern

FAMILY Laridae

SPECIES *Chlidonias niger*

LENGTH 24 cm (9¾ in)/ wingspan 62 cm (24½ in)

HABITAT Lakes/marshland

CLUTCH SIZE 2–3

DISTRIBUTION Summer visitor throughout much of central and eastern Europe, nesting more sporadically in western parts. Overwinters in Africa.

THESE TERNS ARE mainly black in colour, with grey wings and a relatively short, forked tail. They also have white undertail coverts. During the winter, their appearance is transformed: they are mainly white, with an area of black plumage on the head and at the shoulders. Black Terns breed inland, in small colonies using mats of floating vegetation to support their eggs. They often nest in the company of Black-headed Gulls.

FEEDING A Black Tern resting. These birds will also catch insects in flight, hawking them in a similar way to swallows.

Little Tern

FAMILY Laridae

SPECIES *Sterna albifrons*

LENGTH 22 cm (8¾ in)/
wingspan 46 cm (18 in)

HABITAT Beaches/lakes

CLUTCH SIZE 2–3

DISTRIBUTION Main breeding area is in eastern Europe, but nests quite widely in other parts, too, although not common in the north. Overwinters in Africa.

THE SMALL SIZE OF THESE TERNS helps to set them apart. In summer plumage, they have a white forehead, with black markings extending through the eyes and down the neck. The bill is bright yellow, becoming black in the autumn. The area of white plumage on the head extends further back in winter. Little Terns feed on small fish, hovering and watching intently, and then diving into the water.

COURTSHIP A male Little Tern courts a female with the offer of a fish. Pairs nest on the ground on sand bars and beaches, in colonies.

Roseate Tern

FAMILY Laridae

SPECIES *Sterna dougallii*

LENGTH 35 cm (13¾ in)/
wingspan 75 cm (29½ in)

HABITAT Beaches

CLUTCH SIZE 2–3

DISTRIBUTION Breeds at various points around the coast of the British Isles and along the northern coast of France. Overwinters in West Africa.

A RARE SPECIES that has suffered from hunting pressure in its winter range, the Roseate Tern is so called because of the rosy suffusion evident on the plumage of the breast area. These terns nest in colonies on beaches, with the incubation period typically lasting for about 24 days, all the young fledging approximately four weeks later. They will not breed for the first time until they are at least three years old, but typically only one in five chicks will survive through to this stage.

COLOUR CHANGE At the start of the breeding season, the base of the Roseate Tern's bill turns red, rather than being entirely black.

Common Tern

FAMILY Laridae

SPECIES *Sterna hirundo*

LENGTH 37 cm (14½ in)/ wingspan 80 cm (31½ in)

HABITAT Beaches/inland waters

CLUTCH SIZE 2–3

DISTRIBUTION Breeds throughout much of Europe, although far less common in southwestern parts. Occurs around the Scandinavian coast. Overwinters in western and southern Africa.

PAIRS WILL NEST on the ground, seeking out sandy areas close to water for this purpose, including islands. In the breeding season, Common Terns have brownish rather than grey markings on the back. They will dive into the water to obtain their food, eating mainly small fish.

PLUMAGE In the summer, these terns have tail streamers, which are roughly the same length as the folded wings, visible on the right here.

Arctic Tern

FAMILY Laridae

SPECIES *Sterna paradisaea*

LENGTH 39 cm (15½ in)/ wingspan 75 cm (29½ in)

HABITAT Tundra/beaches

CLUTCH SIZE 2–4

DISTRIBUTION Summer visitor to northern parts, up into the Arctic Circle. Found south around parts of the British Isles and south of Denmark along the coast.

THESE TERNS FLY almost from one end of the earth to the other, being summer visitors to the far north. They are the ultimate long-distance migrants, although having flown south to the Antarctic, young Arctic Terns may not immediately undertake the return journey north during the following spring, remaining here instead until the following year. These terns are very defensive of their nest sites, not hesitating to mob any would-be intruders with the aim of driving them away.

IDENTIFICATION They have a black cap in breeding plumage, with pale grey coloration on the body and a whitish area around the cheeks.

Gull-billed Tern

FAMILY Laridae
SPECIES *Sterna nilotica*
LENGTH 36 cm (14 in)/
wingspan 42 cm (16½ in)
HABITAT Marshland/beaches
CLUTCH SIZE 3–5

DISTRIBUTION Tends to occur mainly in southern parts of Europe, but range in the summer extends up to Denmark. Overwinters south in Africa.

THIS SPECIES HAS A DISTINCTIVE black beak, which is relatively short and stout in appearance, being more similar to that of a gull than a typical tern. In breeding plumage, there is an extensive black area present on the crown of the head that extends back down the neck. Gull-billed Terns catch flying insects on the wing, and also fish and amphibians, but they do not dive into the water to catch their prey on the coast. They have a remarkably varied diet, also being recorded as catching voles and lizards, seizing them by swooping low over the ground.

SHELTERING These Gull-billed Terns are facing away from the direction of the prevailing wind, sheltering on the sand as far as possible. They also nest in colonies.

Caspian Tern

FAMILY Laridae
SPECIES *Sterna caspia*
LENGTH 53 cm (21 in)/
wingspan 110 cm (43½ in)
HABITAT Coasts/inland waters
CLUTCH SIZE 2–4

DISTRIBUTION Breeds in Europe around the coast of southern Scandinavia, and the Caspian and Black Seas; migrates to west Africa for the winter.

THIS SPECIES IS the largest European tern, and is easily recognizable in breeding condition by its black cap and pale grey body coloration, which is darker over the wings. In winter plumage, these terns have white streaking on the head. They have a distinctive pattern of feeding, diving in search of fish from high above the surface, and may feed over 60 km (37 miles) from their breeding grounds.

SHORES The migratory passage of the Caspian Terns follows the routes of the major European rivers, giving them feeding opportunities.

Sandwich Tern

FAMILY Laridae

SPECIES *Sterna sandvicensis*

LENGTH 38 cm (15 in)/
wingspan 95 cm (37½ in)

HABITAT Beaches/islands

CLUTCH SIZE 1–2

DISTRIBUTION Breeds at various localities around the British Isles and northwestern Europe. Also occurs in the Mediterranean, Caspian, and Black Seas, overwintering here and in Africa.

A BLACK CAP with a ragged crest at the back of the head and black legs help to identify this species. Its bill is black, with a yellow tip. These terns then start to moult quite early, with the black cap being replaced by a white forehead, which may show some darker speckling, while the rear of the head, including the crest, remains black. The Sandwich Tern is a plunge diver, as far as obtaining food is concerned, feeding in among shoals of fish, especially sand eels and squid. Birds may dive down from heights of over 10 m (33 ft) into the sea for this purpose. In suitable areas, a number of birds may congregate together to feed. Breeding occurs in large colonies, with hens laying their eggs directly on the ground. Sandwich Terns are usually only likely to be seen in coastal areas, tending not to venture inland. They are noisy birds by nature, with their calls having been likened to the grinding sound of a loose cartwheel. These terns used to be heavily hunted in the 1800s for their crest feathers, which were used to decorate hats, but their populations have now recovered.

COURTSHIP BEHAVIOUR A pair of Sandwich Terns courting on their breeding grounds. The sexes are identical in appearance, but can be distinguished by their behaviour.

Little Auk

FAMILY Alcidae

SPECIES *Alle alle*

LENGTH 21 cm (8¼ in)

HABITAT Rocky coasts/shore

CLUTCH SIZE 1

DISTRIBUTION Up through the North Sea from southern England, to the waters around Iceland and eastwards to northern Scandinavia over the winter. Breeds in the Arctic.

THIS SPECIES, which is also sometimes known as the Dovekie, has a distinctive small, stubby bill. Its head and breast, as well as the back and wings, are black in colour, and the underparts are white. In winter plumage, the breast is white, with white extending up behind the eyes. The sexes are identical in appearance. When swimming, their compact body shape is very apparent, and they will dive regularly. They can also fly well, with a series of fast wingbeats propelling them just above the waves. Occasionally, groups or 'wrecks' may be driven ashore by gales.

DIET Little Auks eat small shrimps and other planktonic creatures, which they catch at sea.

Puffin

FAMILY Alcidae

SPECIES *Fratercula arctica*

LENGTH 32 cm (12½ in)

HABITAT Open sea/islands

CLUTCH SIZE 1

DISTRIBUTION Breeds around the coasts of northern Europe, including Iceland, Scandinavia the British Isles, and France, but may wander to the Mediterranean and further south.

THE PUFFIN'S LARGE and brightly coloured bill is only evident in the breeding season. Pairs nest in colonies in underground burrows, although they may occasionally nest under rocks. The hen incubates alone, with the male bringing her food. The incubation period lasts for about 30 days, with the chick fledging after about seven weeks. Its bill is greyish at this stage, and the distinctive coloration only develops slowly, over the course of about five years.

NESTING Puffins live mainly at sea, only coming ashore for breeding purposes each spring, and they prefer to nest on islands where there will be less disturbance.

Razorbill

FAMILY Alcidae
SPECIES *Alca torda*
LENGTH 43 cm (17 in)
HABITAT Cliffs/sea
CLUTCH SIZE 1

DISTRIBUTION Breeds widely through northern coastal areas of Europe, from Iceland down to northern France and also in Scandinavia. Range may extend to the Mediterranean in winter.

THE FLATTENED, BROAD razor-like shape of the bill helps to identify this species. It is also short and encircled by a white band. The head, back, wings, and throat are black, apart from white edging across the rear of the wings, with the sexes being identical. The underparts are white, too, with white feathering extending over the throat when Razorbills are in winter plumage. They are able to walk effectively on land, waddling in a rather similar way to a penguin. Furthermore, Razorbills are able to fly well, often skimming close to the waves, and they will dive, too, down to depths of 18 m (60 ft), in search of squid, fish, and crustaceans.

HEAD MARKINGS
A white stripe connects the eyes with the bill when Razorbills are in breeding condition.

Common Guillemot

FAMILY Alcidae
SPECIES *Uria aalge*
LENGTH 44 cm (17½ in)
HABITAT Open sea
CLUTCH SIZE 1

DISTRIBUTION Breeds from Iceland and Scandinavia down to France and the Iberian Peninsula. Its winter range does not extend as far south as the Mediterranean.

THIS SPECIES, also called the Common Murre, is the largest living alcid. Its appearance resembles that of most seabirds, being predominantly black-and-white in colour. In the summer, pairs nest in colonies on narrow cliff ledges. The egg of the Common Guillemot is pear-shaped to prevent it rolling off the edge here.

COLOUR CHANGE When in breeding plumage, the Common Guillemot has a white stripe running from each side of the bill across the cheeks to the eyes.

Brünnich's Guillemot

FAMILY Alcidae
SPECIES *Uria lomvia*
LENGTH 40 cm (15¾ in)
HABITAT Rocky shores/sea
CLUTCH SIZE 1

DISTRIBUTION Found only in the far north, breeding on the coasts of Iceland and northern Scandinavia. Overwinters further to the south, reaching the tip of Scandinavia.

THE PRESENCE OF a white stripe running along the bill helps to distinguish Brünnich's Guillemot. The flanks are pure white, too, not being streaked, and the bill is shorter and stockier than that of the Common Guillemot. In flight, a further area of distinction emerges, with a white area underneath each wing.

BREEDING GROUNDS Brünnich's Guillemots nesting on cliff ledges, with a speckled egg visible in the foreground. These birds, like other guillemots, have a relatively upright stance.

Black Guillemot

FAMILY Alcidae
SPECIES *Cepphus grylle*
LENGTH 33 cm (13 in)
HABITAT Rocky shores/sea
CLUTCH SIZE 1–2

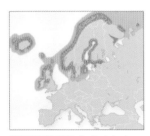

DISTRIBUTION An isolated population breeds around the Icelandic coast, and also from Ireland via Scotland to Scandinavia. Even in winter, does not range further south.

THESE GUILLEMOTS undergo a marked change in appearance from their winter to summer plumage. The underparts and wing coverts are white, with their wings otherwise being black. There is also black-and-white speckling over the back. At the onset of the breeding season, however, they appear totally black, aside from their white wing patches. Although the bill is black, the inside of the mouth and their legs and feet are bright red. The wings are quite broad and rounded in shape, not only enabling Black Guillemots to fly effectively, but also to swim well underwater, with their webbed feet acting as flippers. Pairs breed on rocky coasts, sometimes nesting on their own rather than in the company of others of their own kind.

VOCAL Black Guillemots often rest on rocks, calling loudly. They utter whistles and high-pitched sounds resembling screams.

GUILLEMOTS ON CLIFF A rocky stack is home to a large number of Common Guillemots (*see* p 196). The social instincts of these birds is such that serious squabbling is unlikely to take place, in spite of the crowded conditions.

COLUMBIFORMES

Sandgrouse, doves, and pigeons

Sandgrouse are compact, sturdy, ground-feeding birds, closely related to pigeons, with small heads and short necks, giving them the look of small gamebirds. They are powerful flyers often seen in flocks visiting drinking pools at dawn and dusk. They are all ground-nesting birds. Pigeons and doves are less terrestrial in habit, usually nesting in trees. They tend to have plump bodies and small heads, and their flight is rapid and powerful. Doves are smaller than pigeons but there is no real difference between them. Both can drink by sucking up water, unlike other birds.

Pin-tailed Sandgrouse

FAMILY Pteroclididae
SPECIES *Pterocles alchata*
LENGTH 28–37 cm (11–14½ in)
HABITAT Arid lowland plains
CLUTCH SIZE 2–3

DISTRIBUTION Resident in dry lowland areas of Iberian Peninsula and southern France, favouring uncultivated sandy areas and dried out riverbeds.

FLOCKS OF thousands of Pin-tailed Sandgrouse visit water holes in the morning then disperse to feed in open dry countryside. In flight, the underside and underwings are pure white, and the overall build is slimmer than the similar Black-bellied Sandgrouse. This species' harsh grating flight call recalls that of the Mediterranean Gull (*see* p 183).

PLUMAGE The black-framed breast patch and long narrow central tail feathers are seen in both sexes, but the male has a longer tail and bolder coloration.

Black-bellied Sandgrouse

FAMILY Pteroclididae
SPECIES *Pterocles orientalis*
LENGTH 30–35 cm (12–13½ in)
HABITAT Arid plains
CLUTCH SIZE 2–3

DISTRIBUTION Resident in arid, sparsely vegetated plains, avoiding open deserts, in Iberian Peninsula and North Africa, but also moves to upland areas.

THIS SPECIES IS best identified by its short tail, large black belly patch in both sexes, and bulkier size than the Pin-tailed Sandgrouse. The wings show a distinctive black trailing edge in flight. The female has more mottled plumage than the male and has a pale patch between the black belly and spotted breast. Both sexes show black throat patches.

WARY VISITORS Black-bellied Sandgrouse are shy, nervous birds, especially at waterholes, which they may have flown many miles to reach every morning.

Rock Dove

FAMILY Columbidae
SPECIES *Columba livia*
LENGTH 31–34 cm (12–13½ in)
HABITAT Sea cliffs/mountains
CLUTCH SIZE 2

DISTRIBUTION Resident in rocky habitats over most of Europe, North Africa, and Scandinavia, but absent from the far north. Very similar Feral Pigeon is resident in towns and cities.

A SLIM, streamlined dove with overall grey coloration, showing two black wing bars in flight and a pale rump. The red eye has a yellow ring around it. It has a similar 'coo-coo-coo' call to the domestic pigeon. The Feral Pigeon is very similar in appearance, but has more variable plumage.

HABITAT At home on sea cliffs, the Rock Dove seeks shaded ledges and rock crevices. High-rise buildings provide a similar habitat for the urban Feral Pigeon.

Stock Dove

FAMILY Columbidae
SPECIES *Columba oenas*
LENGTH 32–34 cm (12½–13½ in)
HABITAT Open woodland/ parkland/farmland
CLUTCH SIZE 2

DISTRIBUTION Resident over a large area of western Europe, but summer visitor to eastern Europe, favouring a range of habitats.

SIMILAR IN BUILD to the Rock Dove and Feral Pigeon, the Stock Dove lacks their black wing bars and pale rump. Rather shy, it is often located by its 'ooh-look' call, usually given from tree cover near to nesting holes. It has a slimmer build than the Wood Pigeon, from which it stands out in mixed flocks. It gives a circular display flight, gliding on raised wings, but otherwise remains in woodland cover.

COLORATION When alighting near a nesting hole, the raised wings reveal the characteristic uniform grey underside and plain appearance of the stock dove. Juveniles lack the green sheen.

Wood Pigeon

FAMILY Columbidae

SPECIES *Columba palumbus*

LENGTH 40–42 cm (15¾–16½ in)

HABITAT Woodland/parkland/ gardens/urban areas

CLUTCH SIZE 2

DISTRIBUTION Resident in western Europe and widespread in summer across all of region. Large flocks move west in winter.

THIS IS THE LARGEST PIGEON with a much plumper appearance than other species, although its head appears smaller and tail longer in flight. It is best recognized by the white patch on the neck and broad white bands on the wings. The sexes are alike, but juveniles lack the white neck patch and are much duller than the adults. A wing-clapping circular display flight is often seen near breeding sites, but otherwise Wood Pigeons may live in large flocks, feeding together on fields of crops, especially in winter. A five-note monotone call is heard from perched birds; the stress is on the second note. There is also a gruff disyllabic call heard mainly in the breeding season. Once a very shy bird, Wood Pigeons are increasingly seen in urban areas and parks, and in winter, huge flocks, often numbering many thousands, move west to Britain and Ireland, making it the commonest bird in many areas. The spread of crops like oil-seed rape has helped the Wood Pigeon to increase its range and its population. It nests in trees and shrubs, almost through the year in milder areas, and like other pigeons is able to feed young, called squabs, on 'pigeon milk' from the crop.

MOTHER AND CHICKS The Wood Pigeon's nest is a simple platform of woven twigs with no soft lining.

Collared Dove

FAMILY Columbidae

SPECIES *Streptopelia decaocto*

LENGTH 31–34 cm (12–13½ in)

HABITAT Urban areas/farmland/parkland

CLUTCH SIZE 2

DISTRIBUTION Resident across most of Europe, in urban and farming areas in the west, and drier open habitats in the east.

A MUCH PALER and slimmer dove than other species with generally sandy-brown colouring, a black half-collar, and black wing tips and outer tail feathers, most easily seen in flight. The repetitive, three-note call, emphasizing the second note, is a familiar, and to some, irritating call of wooded urban areas. A choked squawk is also heard from birds taking off or landing. The Collared Dove has greatly increased its range by colonizing western Europe in the second part of the 20th century. Since first arriving in Britain in the 1950s, it has spread to become a common inhabitant of towns and gardens, although it is not common in the open countryside.

FORAGING Collared Doves feed on the ground, often seeking out farmland grain spills or bird feeders provided in town gardens.

Oriental Turtle Dove

FAMILY Columbidae

SPECIES *Streptopelia orientalis*

LENGTH 30–35 cm (12–13½ in)

HABITAT Taiga/forest-steppe

CLUTCH SIZE 2

DISTRIBUTION A rare visitor to north and west Europe from its breeding grounds in Siberian taiga and forests of Central Asia.

THE ORIENTAL TURTLE DOVE is similar to the Turtle Dove (*see* p 204), but is a bulkier bird with more prominent neck markings and darker coloration on the underside; its richer coloration overall gives it the alternative name of Rufous Turtle Dove. The wings are boldly spotted and show one or two pale wing bars. In flight it has a more pigeon-like appearance than the slimmer Turtle Dove. The hoarse call is a repetitive series of four notes.

IDENTIFICATION The pale tips on the flight feathers distinguish this species from the more common Turtle Dove.

Laughing Dove

FAMILY Columbidae

SPECIES *Streptopelia senegalensis*

LENGTH 23–26 cm (9–10¼ in)

HABITAT Oases/palm groves/ wooded urban areas

CLUTCH SIZE 2

DISTRIBUTION Resident in lowland areas of north Africa, eastern Mediterranean (Israel, Turkey), and Middle East.

A SMALL, slim dove, that in flight shows a relatively long tail and short wings. The overall reddish-brown colours with a blue-grey panel on the wings are more obvious at close range. The distinctive black-mottled patch on the crop area is unique to this species. Its alternative name of Palm Dove indicates its preferred habitat, but it is also known, in India, as the Little Brown Dove due to its small size. The Laughing Dove's typical five-note dove call sounds like 'oh-cook-cook-oo-oo'.

WATER LOVERS Small flocks of Laughing Doves regularly visit desert oases to drink and bathe.

Turtle Dove

FAMILY Columbidae

SPECIES *Streptopelia turtur*

LENGTH 26–28 cm (10¼–11 in)

HABITAT Open woodland/parks/ farmland/scrubland/

CLUTCH SIZE 2

DISTRIBUTION A summer visitor to most of Europe apart from far north and Scandinavia, favouring lowland arable areas and open country.

A SMALL, slim dove with chestnut-and-black upperparts and prominent black-and-white neck patches. The distinctive fanned black-and-white tail aids identification in flight. Juveniles lack the neck patches and have more dull brown coloration. This dove gives a continuous 'turrrr turrrr' call from high perches. It feeds on open ground, but is shy and difficult to approach. It is hunted on migration through the Mediterranean region.

ELUSIVE Turtle Doves like to perch in concealed places high in tree canopies, but they can be traced by their calls.

PSITTACIFORMES

Parrots

The parrots are a family of brightly coloured tropical birds, none of them native to Europe, but introduced, either accidentally through escapes, or deliberately, into a range of habitats. The characteristic stout hooked bill is designed to cope with tough fruits and seeds; the larger upper mandible fits over the lower and there is often a colourful cere surrounding the bill.

The short wings and long tail are suited to flight in woodland habitats where they seek out large holes in trees for nest sites. Parrots are usually noisy and conspicuous in flight, sometimes gathering in pre-roost flocks at dusk.

Indian Ring-necked Parakeet

FAMILY Psittacidae

SPECIES *Psittacula krameri*

LENGTH 38–42 cm (15–16½ in)

HABITAT Well-wooded urban areas

CLUTCH SIZE 3–4

DISTRIBUTION Introduced into Europe from parts of Asia and now found in scattered urban areas in Britain, France, and Germany, where populations are increasing.

IDEAL SETTING Ring-necked Parakeets favour large mature trees where they can find suitable hollows for nesting and fruits, seeds, and buds to feed on.

A VERY LONG-TAILED, small parrot with overall green plumage, slightly yellow under the tail, and a striking bright red bill; males have a thin rosy partial collar on the nape merging with a black chin and lower mandible. The female is similar but lacks any neck markings. Juveniles are like females but paler with shorter tails. This species is very conspicuous in flight with characteristic rapid clipped wing-beats and a loud screeching call. In some suburban areas large numbers converge on trees and rooftops before going into communal roosting areas. In winter, they feed on buds of trees making them unpopular with gardeners, but elsewhere they are encouraged by the provision of food in gardens.

CUCULIFORMES

Cuckoos

The cuckoos are medium-sized, streamlined birds with long tails, raptor-like in appearance when in direct flight. When perched they are seen to have very short legs. They are usually solitary in habit, but loud calls signal their presence. Their most notable characteristic is nest parasitism in which they lay their eggs in the nests of a range of other bird species, relying on foster parents to raise their young in which they take no interest. Slender down-curved bills are specialized for feeding on insects such as large caterpillars. All are summer visitors, returning south as soon as the breeding season is over.

European Cuckoo

FAMILY Cuculidae
SPECIES *Cuculus canorus*
LENGTH 33 cm (13 in)
HABITAT Open woodland/ tundra/marshland
CLUTCH SIZE 1–25

DISTRIBUTION Widespread in summer in wide range of suitable habitats where prey species live across Europe and Scandinavia, returning to Africa in winter.

THE MALE Cuckoo's arrival in spring is heralded by its unmistakable onomatopoeic call; the female has a frantic bubbling call. Females seek out the nests of prey species such as Meadow Pipits or Reed Warblers and lay a single matching egg in each nest. The Cuckoo hatchlings then evict the remaining eggs or chicks. This species is aso known as the Common Cuckoo.

PLUMAGE The adult bird is mostly grey with a barred breast and graduated lightly spotted tail. Juveniles can be grey or brown with more barring on the breast.

Great Spotted Cuckoo

FAMILY Cuculidae
SPECIES *Clamator glandarius*
LENGTH 39 cm (15½ in)
HABITAT Open dry areas
CLUTCH SIZE 5 (in single nest)

DISTRIBUTION Summer visitor to southwest Europe and eastern Mediterranean region, rare vagrant elsewhere, overwintering mainly in Africa. Commonest in areas where there are many Magpies.

A LARGE STRIKING bird with spotted plumage, a conspicuous crest, and long white-bordered tail. It is often noticed when pursued by chattering Magpies, its usual host species. It makes a variety of harsh calls, often given in flight. It seeks out nests of Magpies and crows in olive groves and open woodlands, and feeds on caterpillars, beetles, and small lizards.

ALERT Great Spotted Cuckoos often perch out in the open, keeping a watch for their host species as they head for their nests or looking out for food.

Oriental Cuckoo

FAMILY Cuculidae

SPECIES *Cuculus saturatus*

LENGTH 31 cm (12 in)

HABITAT Spruce and pine forests

CLUTCH SIZE 1–25

DISTRIBUTION Forests and taiga in Russia and Siberia, very rare vagrant outside this region. Overwinters in southeast Asia.

VERY SIMILAR TO the European Cuckoo, but much more secretive and with a quiet 'du-du, du-du' call, rather like a muted hoopoe; this is the most reliable way to separate the two species. It is slightly smaller than the European Cuckoo but with a heavier bill and darker colours. There is a brown phase, during which the bird has much bolder markings than the similar brown phase European Cuckoo. The undertail area may be yellow-buff, but this is not a good distinction from the European Cuckoo. It is a nest parasite of Leaf Warblers, whose alarm calls may give away its presence.

IDENTIFICATION The Oriental Cuckoo is almost indistinguishable from the European Cuckoo unless it calls. It normally remains hidden high in the canopy of pine or spruce forests.

STRIGIFORMES

Owls

The owls are largely nocturnal birds of prey, with compact bodies, long rounded wings, short tails, and usually feathered legs and feet. Their large heads have large forward-looking eyes surrounded by a flattened facial disc; the short hooked bill is usually hidden by the feathers. The sexes are alike in most species, although females may be larger. Some owls have ear tufts, which are simply feathering, but all have good hearing. Larger species have a slow, buoyant flapping flight; smaller species are usually faster. All have an upright posture when perched. Nest sites may be holes, old bird nests, or hollows on the ground.

Barn Owl

FAMILY Tytonidae

SPECIES *Tyto alba*

LENGTH 34 cm (13½ in)/ wingspan 85–93 cm (33–36 in)

HABITAT Farmland/open country

CLUTCH SIZE 4–6

DISTRIBUTION Widespread resident across much of Europe and North Africa, but not common in most areas. Mainly in open lowland areas with scattered trees.

APPEARING VERY white when caught in lights at night, the Barn Owl has pure white underparts and golden-buff colourings above. Males are usually paler than females. Its calls are ghostly screeches and hisses uttered in flight and from nest sites in barns, churches, or holes in trees or rocks. It preys on small mammals, frogs, and insects.

SILENT HUNTER The heart-shaped face frames the dark eyes of the Barn Owl; at night, its acute eyesight and hearing help it locate prey in complete darkness and its soft plumage makes its flight silent.

Pale Scops Owl

FAMILY Strigidae

SPECIES *Otus brucei*

LENGTH 21 cm (8¼ in)/
wingspan 55–64 cm (21¾–25 in)

HABITAT Cultivated land/
desert

CLUTCH SIZE 4–6

DISTRIBUTION The exact range of this owl is still uncertain, but it occurs to the northeast of the Mediterranean during the summer, overwintering in southern Israel.

A PALER, MORE STRIATED version of the Scops Owl, with two distinct colour phases. Individuals may be yellowish or grey-brown, but both lack white spots on head. It is best separated from the Scops Owl by its much quieter call, which is a series of low, slowly repeated cooing sounds.

BLENDING IN The Pale Scops Owl shows excellent camouflage when perched quietly during the day in dense tree cover.

Scops Owl

FAMILY Stigidae

SPECIES *Otus scops*

LENGTH 19cm (8¼ in)/
wingspan 47–54 cm (18–21 in)

HABITAT Woodland/orchards/
farmland/palm groves

CLUTCH SIZE 4–6

DISTRIBUTION Summer visitor to southern Europe and Middle East, wintering in Africa; year-round resident in Mediterranean.

THIS HARD-TO-SEE OWL is most easily detected by the far-carrying monotone call, an endless repetition of 'piu piu piu'. Females sometimes perform duets with males. If it is located in a roost site, the Scops Owl will sit up straight with eyes closed and ear tufts raised. It nests in holes in walls or trees, or uses old corvid nests, feeding young on large insects.

HIDDEN The Scops Owl relies on its camouflage to remain concealed during the day and sits motionless for hours on end, often returning to the same perch every day.

BARN OWL (*see* p 208) The Barn Owl's buoyant, silent flight enables it to approach its prey without being heard and then locate the prey by the sound it makes; its forward-pointing eyes make it easy to pinpoint its target.

Eagle Owl

FAMILY Strigidae

SPECIES *Bubo bubo*

LENGTH 66–71 cm (26–28 in)/ wingspan 175 cm (69 in)

HABITAT Dense forest/rocky gorges/desert

CLUTCH SIZE 2–3

DISTRIBUTION Mountainous and forested parts of Scandinavia, Europe, Russia, and North Africa.

THE LARGEST OWL in the region has the proportions of an eagle, and its dense plumage, large staring orange eyes, and long ear tufts give it an intimidating appearance. When alarmed it can stretch itself upwards to appear even larger and more threatening. From its roosting place on rocky crags or large conifers it can launch attacks on a range of large mammals and birds, being able to cope with prey like hares, hedgehogs, gulls, crows, small deer, and even other birds of prey. Eagle Owls need a large territory to provide sufficient food and so are very thinly spread over suitable habitats, and very difficult to observe being almost entirely nocturnal in habit. Its harsh 'kveck kveck' alarm calls may be heard at dusk and in darkness its deep 'oo hu' or 'boo hoo' calls are far-carrying. In flight the sheer size of the bird makes recognition easy, but note that the ear tufts are flattened and the feathered legs and feet look disproportionately large. It glides rather like a buzzard, but the flight is lower over the ground on powerful wingbeats. If discovered by other birds, especially crows, they will mob it furiously, drawing attention to its presence. Across the region there is some variation in colouring, with paler birds being found in Siberia. Slightly smaller birds occur in southwest Europe. The Eagle Owl has been introduced into the United Kingdom, but it is not widespread in any part of its range.

POWER STRIKE The impressive wingspan and powerful talons of the Eagle Owl enable it to tackle prey as large as small deer.

Little Owl

FAMILY Strigidae

SPECIES *Athene noctua*

LENGTH 22 cm (8½ in)/ wingspan 50–56 cm (20–22 in)

HABITAT Farmland/open country/desert/islands

CLUTCH SIZE 3–4

DISTRIBUTION Widespread across most of Europe and North Africa, but not Ireland, Scandinavia, and far northern tundra and steppe areas.

HAVING LARGELY diurnal habits, the diminutive Little Owl is one of the most familiar owls of open countryside, often being spotted perched on a fence post or tree stump. When alarmed, it will bob and flatten itself, and also turn its head through 180°. Its cat-like 'goo-eek' calls are heard at dusk, and young in the nest make a persistent hissing sound when begging for food. Prey consists of large insects and small birds, reptiles, and rodents. It can hover over grassland in order to hunt large beetles, whose wing cases are found in its pellets.

CLUES A Little Owl will often choose a small tree hollow as a safe nesting site, and littered around it will be the pellets containing remains of their meals.

Tengmalm's Owl

FAMILY Strigidae

SPECIES *Aegolius funereus*

LENGTH 25 cm (10 in)/
wingspan 50–62 cm (20–24½ in)

HABITAT Dense northern and
upland forest

CLUTCH SIZE 3–6

DISTRIBUTION Widespread
across coniferous forests in
upland regions of Europe,
especially where there are
boggy glades. May migrate
south in winter to escape
harsh conditions.

THIS STRICTLY NOCTURNAL small
owl is very difficult to see unless
discovered near a nest site, which
is usually in an abandoned Black
Woodpecker nest hole or a nest
box. Facial markings give it the
appearance of having raised
eyebrows or looking permanently
startled, and it adopts a very upright
posture, unlike the similar Little Owl
(*see* p 213). Adults are brownish and
spotted with a black-rimmed pale
facial disc, but the young are a
more uniform dark brown. The call
resembles a rising succession of
hoopoe-like notes given from dense
cover and there is also a shrill 'chiak'
alarm note. Their main prey is voles
caught at night on the forest floor.

WELL CAMOUFLAGED Sitting upright on its
high perch, the Tengmalm's Owl is a very
difficult bird to locate in dense conifer forests,
especially as it is rarely active during the day.

Tawny Owl

FAMILY Strigidae

SPECIES *Strix aluco*

LENGTH 38 cm (15 in)/
wingspan 94–104 cm (37–41 in)

HABITAT Broad-leafed forest/
parkland/urban areas

CLUTCH SIZE 2–3

DISTRIBUTION Widespread
across most of Europe but
absent from Ireland, northern
Scandinavia, Russia, and Siberia.

THIS IS THE COMMONEST medium-
sized brown owl to occur in most of
Europe and is often seen in daytime
perched in a tree being harassed by
a flock of small birds. Its overall
mottled brown plumage separates it
from the Barn Owl (*see* p 208) and
the black eyes and lack of ear tufts
separate it from Long-eared and
Short-eared Owls (*see* pp 216–17).
In flight, it appears compact and
short-winged and is completely
silent as it hunts. The sharp 'ke-wick'
call is heard in autumn, and the
quavering 'hoooo-ooooo' calls are
heard during courtship.

BEHAVIOUR Although nocturnal in habit the
Tawny Owl can often be spotted during daylight
roosting on a high branch in a broad-leafed tree.

KEEN EARS The Great Grey Owl can locate voles and lemmings beneath the snow by detecting the sounds they make as they run through burrows.

Great Grey Owl

FAMILY Strigidae

SPECIES *Strix nebulosa*

LENGTH 69 cm (27 in)/ wingspan 130–150 cm (52–60 in)

HABITAT Northern coniferous forest

CLUTCH SIZE 3–5

A VERY LARGE mostly grey owl with a thick neck and proportionately large head, likened to a tree stump in profile when the bird is observed perched in the open. The yellow eyes look small in comparison to the large facial disc, which has concentric dark rings and a sooty black chin. The Great Grey Owl is similar in stature to the Eagle Owl but without the ear tufts and much greyer in appearance. In flight, the

DISTRIBUTION Resident for most of year in boreal forests of Scandinavia and Russia, often near boggy areas, but may migrate south or west to avoid harsh weather and follow prey.

long tail shows a dark terminal band. The voice recalls the Tawny Owl but is much deeper in tone. It is likely to be seen hunting during the day when it seeks small mammals, including squirrels, on the woodland floor. Breeding success depends on the abundance of prey species so in some years Great Grey Owls wander in search of food. Eggs are laid in abandoned nests of other large birds like crows or ravens. Young birds just out of the nest resemble their parents but have darker faces; females are larger than males.

Ural Owl

FAMILY Strigidae

SPECIES *Strix uralensis*

LENGTH 61 cm (24 in)/
wingspan 115–125 cm (45–49 in)

HABITAT Forest/wooded
urban areas

CLUTCH SIZE 3–4

DISTRIBUTION Widespread in
boreal forests across northern
Europe and in upland forests in
parts of southern Europe.
Often found in areas of
clearings, near lakes and
habitation.

SIMILAR TO THE rather larger Great Grey Owl (*see* p 215), the Ural Owl differs in having dark eyes, a pale, unlined facial disc and no black mark on the chin. It can be separated from the much smaller Tawny Owl (*see* p 214) by its longer tail, which droops in flight, and smaller eyes. It is an aggressive bird near the nest, which may be in a tree hollow, an old crow's nest or even on the ground, and likely to repel any intruders. It sits on a perch to watch for variety of prey species ranging from frogs and small mammals to large birds and even other owls. The call of the male is a deep rhythmic hooting, and there are also harsh alarm calls.

IDENTIFICATION The large Ural Owl's
streaked grey plumage and the long tail
are very distinctive features of this aggressive
bird, which should not be approached
when nesting.

Short-Eared Owl

FAMILY Strigidae

SPECIES *Asio flammeus*

LENGTH 38 cm (15 in)/
wingspan 90–105 cm (35–41 in)

HABITAT Plains/moorland/
downland/marshland

CLUTCH SIZE 4–8

DISTRIBUTION Widespread
across most of Europe,
spreading north in summer to
breed; moving south for winter.

THIS IS THE OWL most likely to be seen during the day, soaring and gliding on strikingly long wings, or perched in the open watching for prey, with a rather frowning expression and yellow eyes. Black 'elbow patches' show on the wings when in flight. The short ear tufts are usually not visible. During the wing-clapping high display flight, a short triple hoot call may be heard and there is also a harsh barking flight call. Its prey consists of small birds and rodents, and in winter, birds may congregate in good feeding areas.

CONSPICUOUS Short-eared Owls are regularly
seen perched in a prominent open position in
the daytime and will also roost on the ground.

Long-Eared Owl

FAMILY Strigidae

SPECIES *Asio otus*

LENGTH 36 cm (14 in)/
wingspan 84–95 cm (33–37 in)

HABITAT Wooded areas/open
country with copses

CLUTCH SIZE 4–5

DISTRIBUTION Widespread
resident across most of Europe
apart from the far north. Some
move north during breeding
season and others migrate
short distances south to avoid
harsh winter conditions.

A SMALLER, slimmer owl than the
Tawny Owl (*see* p 214) and best
distinguished by the bright orange eyes
and prominent long ear tufts, which are
raised when the bird is alarmed, or
during courtship; in flight they do not
show at all. This is a very secretive owl
in its habits and is a nocturnal hunter of
small mammals; during the day they
roost in trees and even if discovered sit
motionless showing remarkable
camouflage. In winter, several birds may
roost in close proximity. Old crows' nests
are taken over for nesting, preferably
located in conifers, but the owls will
hunt over open country, sometimes
being spotted in car headlights at night.
Calls are not often heard, but are a
series of deep single hoots.

DEFENSIVE The staring orange eyes and long
ear tufts of the Long-eared Owl present an
intimidating appearance, making the bird
appear larger than it really is.

Pygmy Owl

FAMILY Strigidae

SPECIES *Glaucidium passerinum*

LENGTH 17 cm (6½ in)/ wingspan 37–41 cm (14½–16 in)

HABITAT Coniferous forest/ mountain slopes

CLUTCH SIZE 4–6

DISTRIBUTION Found throughout the year in coniferous or mixed woodlands across northern Europe and Scandinavia, preferring upland areas in southern parts of its range.

THE SMALLEST OWL of the area, comparable in size to a starling, the Pygmy Owl is most likely to be seen at dusk on a high treetop where its diminutive size, relatively small head, and habit of flicking its tail help identification. It has a rather severe expression with white eyebrows over the yellow eyes and no visible ear tufts. Various piping and squeaking calls are uttered and males will respond rapidly to an imitation of their call. For its size, this is an aggressive bird, tackling prey species such as thrushes that may be larger than it is, although voles are the most common prey. Old woodpecker holes are usually chosen as nest sites.

CREPUSCULAR HABITS The Pygmy Owl usually hunts at dusk, having rather poor night vision, so is often seen perched prominently as the light fades, looking for prey.

Hawk Owl

FAMILY Strigidae

SPECIES *Surnia ulula*

LENGTH 36–40 cm (14–16 in)/ wingspan 78 cm (30¾ in)

HABITAT Boreal forest/boggy areas/mountains

CLUTCH SIZE 3–10

DISTRIBUTION Mainly resident in forests of north Scandinavia, Russia, and Siberia, but will sometimes migrate south.

THE HAWK OWL has a very distinctive appearance while perched and in flight. No other owl has such a long tail, and in flight this gives it the appearance of a small hawk, although the large head and scowling face with its bright yellow eyes and black-edged white facial disc is a more owl-like feature. Perched birds often choose a high tree stump as a look out. Merlin-like chattering calls are uttered by alarmed birds and the display call is a more liquid trill. The favourite prey is voles, spotted from the high vantage point, but this fearless owl will also take birds as large as Hazel Grouse (*see* p 122).

RECOGNITION The Hawk Owl is frequently seen during the day on a conspicuous open perch and from a distance presents a hawk-like appearance.

Snowy Owl

FAMILY Strigidae

SPECIES *Nyctea scandiaca*

LENGTH 53–66 cm (21–26 in)/ wingspan 154 cm (60½ in)

HABITAT Arctic tundra/high open areas

CLUTCH SIZE 4–10

DISTRIBUTION Thinly spread over tundra regions in far north of Scandinavia, Russia, and Siberia, often in areas beyond the Arctic Circle. Moves south slightly in winter to find prey.

THIS ENORMOUS, strikingly white owl with large yellow eyes cannot be mistaken for any other species of owl. Unusually, the sexes differ in appearance with mature males having almost pure white plumage, while the much larger females are white with dark spots on the head and wings and narrow bars on the underside. In flight, the Snowy Qwl looks relatively short-winged as it flies on slow powerful wingbeats. In the breeding season, adults may be seen sitting on a rock showing up from a great distance in contrast to vegetation and rocks around them. Usually silent, they sometimes utter a harsh barking call or a very deep hoot. The main prey is lemmings and in good years where food is plentiful they raise large clutches. They will also feed on birds and larger mammals. Good lemming years are often followed by irruptions of Snowy Owls to new areas.

GENDER DIFFERENCES The female Snowy Owl is much larger than the male, and has strongly barred plumage.

CAPRIMULGIFORMES   Nightjars

Nightjars are secretive, nocturnal birds, only likely to be seen during the day if flushed from the ground or when perched along a branch. Nightjars rely on perfectly camouflaged brown, mottled plumage to remain undetected and they will sit still even if approached very closely. Long wings and tail make them very agile in flight, able to catch night-flying large insects such as moths and beetles. They also perform nocturnal display flights. All species in this Order have a very distinctive far-carrying call uttered at night on breeding grounds.

Egyptian Nightjar

FAMILY Caprimulgidae
SPECIES *Caprimulgus aegypticus*
LENGTH 25 cm (10 in)
HABITAT Desert/arid country
CLUTCH SIZE 2

DISTRIBUTION North Africa and deserts of Middle East, overwintering further south in similar arid areas, but often near settlements.

THE PALEST OF THE NIGHTJARS, the Egyptian Nightjar still has remarkably cryptic coloration to give it camouflage in the desert environment. There is a pale throat patch, but the wing and tail markings are rather less distinct than in the other species. At night, the song is a persistent 'kre-kre-kre' or series of 'toc-toc' notes, which seem to come from several different places as the bird turns its head. Nomadic desert encampments are an attraction as their livestock encourage flies, so these nightjars hunt near them, flying on slower wingbeats than other nightjars. The eggs are laid in a small scrape on the ground, usually in a shaded area, and often near a spring or streambed. Sometimes during the day in the open desert, resting birds are forced to move as the ground warms up.

BEHAVIOUR Nightjars rest directly on the ground or branches as their swift-like legs are too short to support them on other perches.

European Nightjar

FAMILY Caprimulgidae

SPECIES *Caprimulgus europaeus*

LENGTH 27 cm (10½ in)

HABITAT Open woodland/ heathland/semi-desert

CLUTCH SIZE 2

DISTRIBUTION The most widespread nightjar occurring in suitable habitats across almost the whole of Europe, apart from the far north, but overwintering in Africa.

THE EUROPEAN NIGHTJAR is most often detected by its persistent churring call which starts about one hour after sunset. It also utters a quiet 'cu-ic' call and makes a wing-clapping display flight. It looks like a small bird of prey in flight but has a very small straight bill and shows white patches on the wings.

HARD TO SEE The nightjar's perfect camouflage and ability to keep perfectly still protect it while nesting on the ground.

Red-necked Nightjar

FAMILY Caprimulgidae

SPECIES *Caprimulgus ruficollis*

LENGTH 31 cm (12 in)

HABITAT Dry open country/ semi-desert

CLUTCH SIZE 2

DISTRIBUTION Summer visitor to localized arid regions of far southwest Europe and north Africa, returning to deserts of Africa in winter.

THE LARGEST NIGHTJAR of the region, this species has a conspicuous rufous collar and a prominent white throat patch. In flight, the wings and tail also show more prominent white patches than the European Nightjar. Its distinctive call is a staccato, repetitive 'kutuk', which has a resonant, echoing quality. Excellent camouflage makes it very difficult to see unless it is accidentally flushed or observed in flight at night.

PERFECT CAMOUFLAGE On its nest site under trees, it is often only the large gleaming eyes of a nocturnal bird that give it away.

APODIFORMES

Swifts

The swifts are fast-flying, streamlined birds superbly adapted to life in the open sky. Their legs and feet are very small and are needed only for clinging onto walls before entering nest sites. Almost every aspect of their lives is conducted in the air, including feeding, mating, and even sleeping. They are capable of flying up to 1 km (0.6 miles) above the ground and feed on insects caught on the wing. They need to settle to nest and choose high buildings, cliff ledges, and, rarely, large tree holes. Nesting material is collected on the wing and consists of feathers, animal hair, and wisps of plant material all bound together with saliva.

Little Swift

FAMILY Apodidae
SPECIES *Apus affinis*
LENGTH 12 cm (4¾ in)
HABITAT Arid country with scattered settlements
CLUTCH SIZE 2–3

DISTRIBUTION Resident in arid areas of north Africa and Middle East, and summer visitor to eastern Mediterranean region; seen on migration elsewhere.

THE SMALLEST swift is best distinguished by its conspicuous white rump, extending on to the flanks, and the squared-off tail, similar in appearance to the slightly larger, forked-tailed House Martin (*see* p 248). The flight is rather fluttering compared with larger swifts and the quiet twittering call is also diagnostic. It is often seen around settlements in desert areas, nesting in houses.

IDENTIFICATION The diminutive size of the Little Swift separates it from the larger members of the family. It is also known as the House Swift.

Common Swift

FAMILY Apodidae
SPECIES *Apus apus*
LENGTH 17 cm (6½ in)
HABITAT Urban areas/open country/large lakes
CLUTCH SIZE 3

DISTRIBUTION Widely distributed in suitable habitats in summer over whole of Europe apart from extreme north, migrating south to Africa for the winter.

A FAMILIAR BIRD in summer as it wheels high over towns and cities making shrill screaming calls. The sickle-shaped outline is diagnostic and separates it from swallows and martins with which it may be feeding. Its flight is rapid and alternates between fast wingbeats and long glides. The almost all-dark plumage is relieved by a paler chin patch.

BEHAVIOUR Swifts return to the same nest site year after year and use their tiny feet to cling onto rough surfaces as they investigate potential holes and crevices.

Alpine Swift

FAMILY Apodidae

SPECIES *Apus melba*

LENGTH 22 cm (8½ in)

HABITAT Mountains/rocky coasts

CLUTCH SIZE 3

DISTRIBUTION A summer visitor to most of southern Europe and north Africa where suitable nesting sites exist. Migrates south to southern Africa for the winter.

THIS IS THE LARGEST swift, with an impressive wingspan of over 50 cm (19¾ in), but it is best identified by its white belly patch and white chin. The wingbeats are slower than in other swifts, and the voice is a long series of excited twittering notes. Alpine Swifts nest in large colonies, usually on rock faces or tall buildings, and pairs mate for life.

PLUMAGE The Alpine Swift's white throat patch is sometimes difficult to see at long range or in poor light.

Pallid Swift

FAMILY Apodidae

SPECIES *Apus pallidus*

LENGTH 17 cm (6½ in)

HABITAT Arid country/ settlements

CLUTCH SIZE 2

DISTRIBUTION A summer visitor to areas bordering the Mediterranean coastline and islands, migrating to southern Africa for the winter.

THIS IS A CONFUSINGLY similar species to the Common Swift, with a similar but lower-pitched call, but in good light the paler brown plumage may be evident. There is a large white throat patch and pale forehead, and in flight, the contrast between the dark outer primaries and pale inner wing feathers may be visible. Nesting sites are on cliff faces in small colonies, and occasionally in large buildings.

NEAR NEIGHBOURS The Pallid Swift occupies areas at the southern limit of the Common Swift's range, so the two species may overlap.

CORACIIFORMES

Kingfishers, bee-eaters, rollers, and hoopoe

This Order of perching or ground-living bird species includes some of the most colourful birds in the region. The kingfishers are medium-sized, short-legged birds adapted for diving into water in pursuit of fish. Their long bills, compact bodies, and upright posture give them a recognizable silhouette. This family also includes the Hoopoe, an entirely terrestrial bird that finds its food on the ground. Bee-eaters are very streamlined colourful birds with curved bills for catching large insects, including bees. Rollers are very colourful and conspicuous crow-like birds whose name derives from their somersaulting display flight.

Roller

FAMILY Coraciidae

SPECIES *Coracius garrulous*

LENGTH 31 cm (12 in)

HABITAT Open country/ scrubland/parkland

CLUTCH SIZE 4–5

DISTRIBUTION Summer visitor to warmer parts of southern and eastern Europe, north Africa, and the Middle East, returning to Africa for the winter.

THIS BIRD IS Jackdaw-sized but with much more colourful plumage. The overall impression is of a pale blue bird with brown wings; in flight, the wings and tail show large areas of blue. Its flight is rather powerful and direct but occasionally the bird veers off and changes course. Tree holes are the favourite nesting sites, but ruined buildings may also be used.

FEEDING HABITS The Roller's bill is large and powerful and used to catch large ground-dwelling insects such as beetles and grasshoppers.

Hoopoe

FAMILY Upupidae

SPECIES *Upupa epops*

LENGTH 28 cm (11 in)

HABITAT Cultivated land/grassy areas with trees

CLUTCH SIZE 5–8

DISTRIBUTION Summer visitor to much of southern and central Europe and the Middle East, wintering in Africa; resident on western Mediterranean coast.

A VERY DISTINCTIVE, although rather wary, bird with strikingly barred wings, giving it the appearance of a very large moth in flight. The enormous crest is raised briefly from time to time, but usually lies back over the head. The long, curved slender bill is used to catch worms and insects. Nest sites are usually tree holes. It can be wary of humans and tricky to see.

WARY When searching for food on the ground, the Hoopoe keeps its crest lowered; its markings make it quite difficult to see until it flies.

European Bee-eater

FAMILY Meropidae
SPECIES *Merops apiaster*
LENGTH 28 cm (11 in)
HABITAT Open country, often near large rivers
CLUTCH SIZE 4–7

DISTRIBUTION Summer visitor to warmer regions of southern and eastern Europe, north Africa, the Middle East, and Caucasus, wintering in Africa.

BEE-EATERS ARE bright, multicoloured birds with long tails and long curved bills. The vivid yellow throat and blue underside separate this from other species. Gregarious in habit, bee-eaters are usually found in colonies near sandy riverbanks where they can excavate nesting holes. Insects like bees and dragonflies are caught on the wing. A bubbling call is heard when they are flying.

LIVING SPACE A pair of European Bee-eaters arrive at their nesting hole in a sandy bank where a 1–2 m (3–7 ft) long tunnel will lead to a bare nesting chamber.

Blue-cheeked Bee-eater

FAMILY Meropidae
SPECIES *Merops superciliosus*
LENGTH 31 cm (12 in)
HABITAT Arid, open country
CLUTCH SIZE 4–5

DISTRIBUTION A rare visitor to Europe from its wintering grounds in Africa, but a scarce breeding species in north Africa and the Middle East.

PREDOMINANTLY GREEN plumage with a chestnut-and-yellow throat and blue cheeks with a black eye stripe distinguish this rarer bee-eater, which is slightly larger and longer-tailed than the common species. Its insect-catching habits are the same, and it also nests in sandy river banks or tunnels in the ground in dunes. Its calls are rather quieter and less melodious.

CONSPICUOUS The Blue-cheeked Bee-eater's striking facial pattern is obvious at close range. It often spots its prey from the vantage point of a perch.

Common Kingfisher

FAMILY Alcedinidae

SPECIES *Alcedo atthis*

LENGTH 17 cm (6½ in)

HABITAT Rivers/estuaries/
coasts

CLUTCH SIZE 6–7

DISTRIBUTION Resident in suitable habitats across most of western Europe, moving further east in summer, but absent from northern areas.

DESPITE ITS SMALL SIZE this is one of the most easily recognized birds in Europe. Its brilliant blue-green upperparts contrast with the chestnut breast, but when the bird is flying rapidly low over water, the blue coloration is what is most striking. The bill is long and black, with a reddish base in females. Short legs and tiny feet enable kingfishers to perch on thin branches overhanging the water, from which they make rapid vertical dives to catch small fish. If no branches are available, they will hover briefly. Nesting tunnels are excavated in riverbanks, and the eggs are laid in a chamber at the end lined with fish bones.

PATIENT HUNTER The Kingfisher can remain motionless for long periods on its perch over the water, judging the exact moment to make a dive for its prey.

White-throated Kingfisher

FAMILY Alcedinidae
SPECIES *Halcyon smyrnensis*
LENGTH 27 cm (10½ in)
HABITAT Waterways/open woodland
CLUTCH SIZE 5–6

DISTRIBUTION Resident, but not common, in suitable habitats near the eastern Mediterranean coastline, Turkey, and the Middle East.

ADAPTABLE BILL The massive red bill of the White-throated Kingfisher enables it to capture a variety of prey, both on land and in the water.

THE COMBINATION OF chestnut, vivid blue, and the large white patch on the throat makes this bird really stand out when it is perched out in the open. The sexes are similar, but juveniles have duller plumage and slight brown markings on the white throat. The largest kingfisher in the region is not tied to watery habitats, and may be encountered in forest glades, palm groves, or orchards hunting lizards and large insects, but it is also capable of diving for fish when near rivers or on the coast. It is a very noisy bird with loud, repetitive 'ti-ti-tu-tu-tu-tu' calls delivered incessantly from a high perch, and several grating alarm calls delivered in flight. Nesting sites are usually holes excavated in steep banks.

Pied Kingfisher

FAMILY Alcedinidae
SPECIES *Ceryle rudis*
LENGTH 25 cm (10 in)
HABITAT Rivers/lakes/canals/coasts
CLUTCH SIZE 4

DISTRIBUTION Resident in suitable habitats in eastern Mediterranean area, Middle East, and Red Sea, some moving south and west in winter.

A TYPICAL KINGFISHER shape and stance, and all-over black-and-white plumage make this an unmistakeable species. Always spotted near water, the Pied Kingfisher may be seen perched on a branch, or quite frequently hovering as much as 20 m (67 ft) above the water before going into a steep dive. It may also be seen out to sea, hovering over breaking waves.

WAITING GAME The Pied Kingfisher has a longer tail than other species, as an aid to hovering, but it often uses a strategic perch over the water in order to spot prey.

COMMON KINGFISHER DIVING (*see* p 226) Having caught its fishy prey, the Kingfisher must propel itself from the water, using powerful wingbeats, before flying to a perch where the prey can be killed and then swallowed.

PICIFORMES

Woodpeckers

The woodpeckers are a family of birds highly specialized for moving around in trees and seeking out invertebrate food from rotten wood and bark crevices. Stout bills for excavating holes and long tongues for drawing out the food are important adaptations. The feet have two toes pointing forwards and two pointing backwards to aid in clinging onto vertical surfaces; the squared-off tail gives support against the tree trunk in all species except the Wryneck. On the ground, they tend to hop, but in flight they are fast-moving with an undulating series of swoops. Most species produce the typical drumming sound in spring.

Lesser Spotted Woodpecker

FAMILY Picidae

SPECIES *Dendrocopos minor*

LENGTH 15 cm (5¾ in)

HABITAT Mixed woodland/
orchard/parkland

CLUTCH SIZE 4–6

COLORATION The black-and-white barred plumage of the tiny Lesser Spotted Woodpecker is its most distinctive feature.

DISTRIBUTION Widespread across most lowland regions of Europe, but absent from extreme northern regions and Scotland, Ireland, and Iceland.

THE SMALLEST OF the woodpeckers is a diminutive sparrow-sized bird, often rather difficult to locate in the treetops. The barred plumage of both adults and juveniles is distinctive, and males can be identified by their red heads. In spring, the drumming can be heard, and although quieter than other species, it lasts longer. There may be two bursts of two-second bouts of drumming, unlike the single bursts from the Great Spotted Woodpecker. There is also a shrill and repetitive 'pee pee pee pee' call, rather like a distant raptor alarm call. Areas of old trees with many rotting branches are their preferred habitat.

Great Spotted Woodpecker

FAMILY Picidae

SPECIES *Dendrocopos major*

LENGTH 23 cm (9 in)

HABITAT Woodland/parkland/ orchards

CLUTCH SIZE 4–7

DISTRIBUTION Widespread and common across most of Europe in suitable habitats, but absent from the extreme north and not present in Ireland or Iceland.

THE COMMONEST black-and-white woodpecker is best recognized by its large white wing patches and the red area underneath the tail. Both males and females have a black crown, but only the males have the small red nape patch; juveniles have an all-red crown. Although inhabitants of the treetops, they will visit bird feeders in gardens, and may be seen in a characteristic swooping flight between trees. A harsh 'tchick' call is often heard, sometimes followed by a scolding chatter, and in spring the staccato, one-second bursts of drumming ring through the woods as the woodpeckers stake out their territories from a high branch. Nest holes are excavated high in tree trunks, and the young's 'churring' calls will be heard later in the summer as they beg for food.

PRACTICAL ADAPTATIONS The sharp claws, backward-pointing toes, and stiff tail enable the Great Spotted Woodpecker to hold itself steady on vertical surfaces.

Middle Spotted Woodpecker

FAMILY Picidae

SPECIES *Dendrocopos medius*

LENGTH 22 cm (8½ in)

HABITAT Mixed, mainly deciduous woodland

CLUTCH SIZE 4–8

DISTRIBUTION Confined to mature deciduous woodlands in warmer, lowland areas of central and eastern Europe, the Iberian Peninsula, and Middle East.

CONSPICUOUS WHITE wing patches and a red crown separate this species from the other black-and-white spotted woodpeckers. The wings also have black-and-white bars, which show well in flight. An active feeder in the high canopy, making repeated 'kik' calls, this woodpecker is the least likely to be heard drumming. Rotting branches are usually chosen for nest sites.

PREFERRED HABITAT Middle Spotted Woodpeckers are often seen feeding along horizontal branches, and choose decayed areas for their nest sites.

GREAT SPOTTED WOODPECKER All woodpeckers have a remarkable ability to anchor themselves to a vertical surface with sufficient strength to be able hammer their beaks into the bark to excavate nesting holes or find food.

Grey-headed Woodpecker

FAMILY Picidae

SPECIES *Picus canus*

LENGTH 25 cm (10 in)

HABITAT Woodland/parkland/tree-lined river banks

CLUTCH SIZE 4–5

DISTRIBUTION Scattered areas of suitable habitat across a wide band of central and eastern Europe and southern Scandinavia.

THIS IS A VERY SIMILAR species to the Green Woodpecker, but much smaller, and appearing slimmer in flight. The head is mostly grey, but males have a small red forehead patch. The flanks and underside are grey, becoming paler towards the tail. Juveniles look much browner and have barred flanks. Often seen feeding on the ground, Grey-headed Woodpeckers will fly off with a fast, buoyant flight, calling loudly, if disturbed. Ants are the main prey species on the ground, but food is also obtained from rotting trees, in which large nest holes are excavated. Large old riverside trees such as alders are a favourite nesting site.

IDENTIFYING FEATURES The Grey-headed Woodpecker has very thin moustachial stripes compared with the much larger Green Woodpecker, and there is only a small patch of red on the forehead.

Three-toed Woodpecker

FAMILY Picidae

SPECIES *Picoides tridactylus*

LENGTH 22 cm (8¾ in)

HABITAT Conifer forest/willow or birch woodland

CLUTCH SIZE 4–5

DISTRIBUTION Across northern Europe, Scandinavia, and Russia in coniferous and birch woodlands, and also in mountain woodlands in southern Europe.

THE YELLOW CROWN and all black-and-white plumage separate the male Three-toed Woodpecker from all other black-and-white species; both sexes lack red coloration and the overall impression is of a very dark bird. In flight, the white rump is more obvious. Its favourite food is the larvae of spruce bark beetles, but it will also drill holes around the tree to get at the oozing sap. The calls are similar to those of Great Spotted Woodpecker (*see* p 238), but rather quiet, and the drumming is less frenzied.

PLUMAGE A complete lack of red colours, two black stripes on the face, and an almost all-dark appearance help identify this species.

Green Woodpecker

FAMILY Picidae

SPECIES *Picus viridis*

LENGTH 32 cm (12½ in)

HABITAT Forest/parkland/open
                    wooded country

CLUTCH SIZE 5–7

DISTRIBUTION Common in
suitable habitats across most
of western Europe, Middle East
and north Africa; absent from
northern areas and Ireland.

A LARGE, COLOURFUL, and conspicuous
bird, readily identified by its predominantly
green plumage, red head, and yellow rump,
seen in flight. It is very vocal with a far-
carrying, shrieking 'kyu-kyu-kyuk' flight
call that is heard when it is alarmed or
disturbed, and a ringing, laughter-like
display call heard in spring and summer.
It will occasionally make a light, rapid
drumming, but this is not often heard.
When startled, Green Woodpeckers fly
high into the tree canopy and then remain
motionless clinging to a trunk, sometimes
sidling out of sight behind a branch until it
is safe to move. Although woodland birds
adapted to life in trees, they often feed on
the ground, especially where there are many
ants, and leave characteristic droppings
resembling cigarette-ash. Nesting holes
are excavated high up in tree trunks and
piles of new wood chippings on the
ground below show where they have been
working. The young make a persistent
harsh rasping call when begging for food.

PARENTAL DUTIES Both parents work hard to care for
young Green Woodpeckers. The male can be identified
by the black edged red face stripe.

Black Woodpecker

FAMILY Picidae

SPECIES *Dryocopus martius*

LENGTH 46 cm (18 in)

HABITAT Coniferous and broad-
leaved woodland

CLUTCH SIZE 4–6

DISTRIBUTION Widespread across central and eastern Europe and most of Scandinavia, but scattered in western Europe and absent from the far west, Britain, and Ireland.

THE LARGEST AND most distinctive woodpecker has all-black plumage and a pale bill. Males have a rich red crown, but females have only a small red nape patch. Even in silhouette, the characteristic angle of holding the neck makes this woodpecker instantly recognizable. The loud fluty calls, a series of double notes, echo through the woods and the powerful machine-gun-like drumming, in longer bursts than other species, can be heard over a great distance. On the wing, the undulating flight pattern is noticeable, and the head is held slightly raised. Although a rather nervous bird, it will respond to imitations of its call.

NESTING HABITS Black Woodpeckers often nest more than 10 m (30 ft) above ground level, creating a large enough hole to accommodate their large brood, which beg noisily for food.

White-backed Woodpecker

FAMILY Picidae

SPECIES *Dendrocopos leucotos*

LENGTH 25 cm (10 in)

HABITAT Broad-leaved
woodland

CLUTCH SIZE 4–5

DISTRIBUTION Scattered in suitable woodland habitats in upland areas in central and eastern Europe and Scandinavia, Pyrenees, Turkey, Caucasus.

MORE LIKELY TO BE SEEN on the ground than the other black-and-white woodpeckers, the White-backed has broadly barred wings, a white back and rump, and reddish underparts. The bill is longer than that of the Great Spotted, and this species also appears longer necked. When drumming, the blows blur into a continuous sound resembling a creaking branch. The most favoured habitat is damp woodland with much decaying timber, but this is becoming scarce; insect food is often obtained by pecking large holes near the base of the trees.

IDENTIFICATION The longer neck and bill of the White-backed Woodpecker give it a distinctive profile compared to similar-sized woodpeckers.

Syrian Woodpecker

FAMILY Picidae

SPECIES *Dendrocopos syriacus*

LENGTH 23 cm (9 in)

HABITAT Farmland/parkland/
roadside trees

CLUTCH SIZE 5–7

DISTRIBUTION Found in a range of suitable habitats across extreme east of Europe, Balkans, Caucasus, Turkey, and the Middle East.

THIS IS A VERY SIMILAR SPECIES to the Great Spotted Woodpecker but has a whiter face, due to a shorter black cross bar and larger white patches on the wings. Where the two species occur together, the Syrian Woodpecker tends to remain in higher-altitude forests, although it seems to be spreading to new areas.

COLORATION Larger white wing patches and the greater area of white on the face help separate the Syrian Woodpecker from other similar species.

Wryneck

FAMILY Picidae

SPECIES *Jynx torquilla*

LENGTH 17 cm (6½ in)

HABITAT Open country/
farmland/parkland

CLUTCH SIZE 7–10

DISTRIBUTION Summer visitor to much of Europe, Russia, and southern Scandinavia, but now extinct in Britain. Migrates south to Africa in winter.

THE WRYNECK DIFFERS from other woodpeckers in being a long-distance migrant and a summer visitor. Its cryptic coloration gives it excellent camouflage, and together with the long tail make it look more like a large brown warbler than a woodpecker. Ants are a favourite food so Wrynecks spend much time feeding on the ground, but they nest in large tree holes and use nesting boxes. A series of 'kew kew kew' calls recall those of a nuthatch or small raptor. They are often seen in coastal areas on return migration in the autumn.

ALTERNATIVE NAME 'Snakebird' is one name sometimes used for the Wryneck because of the scaly appearance of its plumage and its ability to twist its head through 180°.

PASSERIFORMES

Perching birds

The largest of the avian Orders, the Passeriformes includes a wide range of different genera, and has a worldwide distribution. Passeriformes are often reasonably small birds, many of which tend to display shades of brown and grey in their plumage, rather than being vividly coloured. Many are quite social by nature, and live in flocks. As their name suggests, they spend most of their time perching, but they will often come down to the ground in search of food. Their diet is varied, but many feed on seeds and invertebrates. They also tend to be relatively sedentary in their habits.

Shore Lark

FAMILY Alaudidae
SPECIES *Eremophila alpestris*
LENGTH 19 cm (7½ in)
HABITAT Montane areas/coasts
CLUTCH SIZE 3–5

DISTRIBUTION Summer visitor to northern Europe from Scotland to Scandinavia northwards, and winters further south. Resident populations in the southeast.

THE ADULT COCK in summer has raised feathers on the head, resembling small horns in appearance, whereas those of the hen are much shorter. This explains their alternative name of Horned Lark. At this time of year, those in northern areas move to the far north, but will then fly south before the onset of winter.

DISTINCTIVE PLUMAGE The yellow coloration on the face of these larks aids their identification. Young birds have a spangled appearance, without these prominent yellow-and-black markings.

Dupont's Lark

FAMILY Alaudidae
SPECIES *Chersophilus duponti*
LENGTH 18 cm (7 in)
HABITAT Sandy areas/coasts
CLUTCH SIZE 3–4

DISTRIBUTION Resident in Europe largely in the eastern part of Spain; more widely distributed across North Africa in areas of suitable habitat.

THESE LARKS HAVE a striking display flight, soaring up to 150 m (500 ft) above the ground, remaining there for perhaps an hour, singing loudly. At other times, however, they are not easy to observe, although they may also be heard singing after dark. If disturbed, they seek cover on the ground rather than flying off.

APPEARANCE The dull brownish coloration of Dupont's Lark helps it to blend into the background. It has a long bill, which curves downwards towards its tip.

Crested Lark

FAMILY Alaudidae
SPECIES *Galerida cristata*
LENGTH 19 cm (7½ in)
HABITAT Grassland
CLUTCH SIZE 3–5

DISTRIBUTION Resident through most of western and central parts of Europe southwards, except the area to the north of Italy. Also absent from the British Isles.

THE LONG CREST feathers of these larks are present on the central area of the head, and the crest is pointed in shape. When held flat, the crest extends back over the rear of the head. The sexes are identical in appearance, although there are slight regional variations. There is some streaking on the breast, and the bill is quite long, and pointed at its tip. Crested Larks may be seen in a wide range of open countryside, from fields to overgrown industrial areas. They feed mainly on seeds, but the young are reared largely on invertebrates.

MUSICAL The Crested Lark has a melodious song, which often heralds the start of the breeding period.

Thekla Lark

FAMILY Alaudidae
SPECIES *Galerida theklae*
LENGTH 17 cm (6¾ in)
HABITAT Upland, arid country
CLUTCH SIZE 3–5

DISTRIBUTION Occurs mainly in Spain, although its distribution extends via Gibraltar across the Mediterranean to North Africa. Resident throughout the area of distribution.

THIS SPECIES TENDS to be found at higher altitudes than the Crested Lark in areas where their ranges overlap. The hen builds a cup-shaped nest located on the ground and sits alone, with the incubation period lasting about 15 days. The young larks may leave the nest when only eight days old, before they are able to fly properly.

DISTINGUISHING COLORATION The breast streaking is more pronounced, and the crest more fan-shaped in the Thekla Lark, compared with its Crested cousin.

Greater Short-toed Lark

FAMILY Alaudidae

SPECIES *Calandrella brachydactyla*

LENGTH 15 cm (6 in)

HABITAT Open country

CLUTCH SIZE 2–3

DISTRIBUTION Occurs across southern parts of Europe in the summer, in the vicinity of the Mediterranean, as well as the Caspian and Black Seas. Overwinters mainly in Africa.

THIS SPECIES IS more widely distributed that its Lesser cousin, and apart from its slightly larger size, it can be distinguished by the dark patch on the sides of the breast, which is essentially white rather than being striped; the sexes have similar coloration. The nest is made on the ground. Males have a rather disconcerting display, flying up singing loudly, and then abruptly halting, seeming to fall back down towards the ground, before repeating the cycle.

WIDE RANGING Greater Short-toed Larks may occasionally be seen further north, with records of sightings from the British Isles.

Lesser Short-toed Lark

FAMILY Alaudidae

SPECIES *Calandrella rufescens*

LENGTH 14 cm (5½ in)

HABITAT Arid country

CLUTCH SIZE 2–3

DISTRIBUTION Resident in parts of the Iberian Peninsula and the western Mediterranean. Summer visitor north of the Black and Caspian Seas, migrating to the Middle East.

THIS SPECIES TENDS to occur in more arid countryside than the Greater Short-toed Lark. Like other members of the family, it eats both seeds and invertebrates, and breeds on the ground, where its dull, streaked plumage helps to conceal its presence. Its patterning is similar to that of the Skylark, but its bill is much stockier in appearance, and it is also smaller in terms of its overall size. The sexes are again identical in appearance, but there are distinctive regional variations between different subspecies.

VARIATIONS Lesser Short-toed Larks from Spain are greyish-brown, with Turkish birds being greyer overall and displaying less streaking on their breasts and flanks.

Woodlark

FAMILY Alaudidae
SPECIES *Lullula arborea*
LENGTH 15 cm (6 in)
HABITAT Open forest/heathland
CLUTCH SIZE 4–6

DISTRIBUTION Resident in western and southern parts of Europe. Summer visitor further east, north to southern Scandinavia, overwintering further south.

THE SONG OF THE WOODLARK is most likely to be heard either in the early morning or at dusk, and sometimes even after dark. It can be difficult to identify the source of sound, because Woodlarks soar high in the sky before they start to sing.

ELUSIVE Except when displaying, Woodlarks spend much of their time largely concealed on the ground.

Skylark

FAMILY Alaudidae
SPECIES *Alauda arvensis*
LENGTH 18 cm (7 in)
HABITAT Open country
CLUTCH SIZE 3–5

DISTRIBUTION Resident across most of western Europe, and from the Mediterranean to the Caspian Sea. Ranges in summer from Scandinavia into the former USSR, overwintering further south.

IN SPITE OF THEIR NAME, Skylarks spend most of their time on the ground. Especially during the winter, they may form large flocks, which break up in the early spring, with pairs returning to their breeding territories. Males display by flying up and singing loudly, with pairs seemingly remaining together for life. The nest itself is hidden on the ground, often hidden by tussocks of grass. The incubation period lasts about 11 days, with the young leaving the nest after a similar interval, remaining nearby.

RAISING CHICKS
Young Skylarks will abandon the nest before they can fly. Adult pairs may rear two or three broods in a season.

Desert Lark

FAMILY Alaudidae

SPECIES *Ammomanes deserti*

LENGTH 15 cm (6 in)

HABITAT Arid, open country

CLUTCH SIZE 3–4

DISTRIBUTION Resident in the eastern Mediterranean region and further east, although the main centre of distribution of this species lies in North Africa.

IN CONTRAST TO MANY LARKS, this species is relatively quiet, although it displays the typical dipping flight pattern associated with these birds. The nest is made of vegetation, often with stones being incorporated alongside it. Chicks will fledge before they are able to fly properly.

HABITAT Desert Larks are well adapted to thrive in very dry surroundings, often being encountered well away from water.

Bimaculated Lark

FAMILY Alaudidae

SPECIES *Melanocorypha bimaculata*

LENGTH 18 cm (7 in)

HABITAT Arid, open country

CLUTCH SIZE 4–5

DISTRIBUTION Summer visitor to northeastern Mediterranean region, east and south of the Black Sea, out to the Caspian Sea; overwinters further south.

THESE RELATIVELY large larks also occur in dry country terrain, with their range overlapping in part with that of the Desert Lark. Aside from the difference in their size, however, they can be distinguished by the presence of a streak of black plumage running for a short distance from each side of the body across the chest, and streaking on the head.

BEHAVIOUR Bimaculated Larks tend to favour higher altitudes than other larks that occur within their area of distribution. They are also migratory in their habits.

Calandra Lark

FAMILY Alaudidae
SPECIES *Melanocorypha calandra*
LENGTH 20 cm (8 in)
HABITAT Open, dry country
CLUTCH SIZE 4–5

DISTRIBUTION Resident through much of Spain and the Mediterranean, and around the Black and Caspian Seas.

A MORE DISTINCTIVE black patch above the wings and black coloration under the wing, with white edging to the rear of the flight feathers, serve to identify this species. The tail feathers are also relatively short and edged with white. Pairs nest on the ground, and following the breeding season, Calandra Larks join up to form flocks.

PLUMAGE Like most larks, the Calandra is mainly brown in colour, but the black patch above the wings is variable in shape and size.

White-winged Lark

FAMILY Alaudidae
SPECIES *Melanocorypha leucoptera*
LENGTH 19 cm (7½ in)
HABITAT Open country
CLUTCH SIZE 3–6

DISTRIBUTION Winters in the area between the Black Sea and Caspian Sea. Resident around the north of the Caspian Sea.

THE WHITE-WINGED Lark is a relatively colourful species, with a clear distinction in appearance between the sexes. Cock birds have a reddish-brown head and ear coverts, with similar coloration on the upper part of the wings too. Hens have streaked heads, along with the white wing patches, which are most apparent in flight.

HOLDING ON Like many larks, loss of their grassland habitat to agriculture has resulted in a decline in their numbers in some areas, but they are not threatened.

Sand Martin

FAMILY Hirundinidae
SPECIES *Riparia riparia*
LENGTH 13 cm (5¼ in)
HABITAT Gravel pits/rivers
CLUTCH SIZE 4–5

DISTRIBUTION Summer visitor across almost the entire area of Europe, although not seen in Iceland or the extreme north of Scandinavia. Overwinters in western parts of Africa.

A PROMINENT BROWN band running across the breast helps to distinguish the Sand Martin from related species. It is often associated with river banks, where it nests in large colonies. Instead of building a nest, these martins tunnel into the soft earth, and construct a burrow that enlarges into a nesting chamber at its end. This chamber is lined with feathers and vegetation. The chicks spend approximately three weeks in the nest, and when they first emerge, they can be identified by the buff markings on the wings, and the greyish-buff rather than white coloration of the throat.

RIVERSIDE HOME Adult Sand Martins at their nesting burrow. This may extend back over 1 m (3 ft) into the bank.

Red-rumped Swallow

FAMILY Hirundinidae
SPECIES *Hirundo daurica*
LENGTH 19 cm (7½ in)
HABITAT Montane areas/cliffs
CLUTCH SIZE 3–6

DISTRIBUTION Summer visitor to the Mediterranean region, extending from the Iberian Peninsula through this region, including islands, influenced by habitat. Overwinters in Africa.

THIS PARTICULAR SPECIES is most likely to be seen in mountain ranges and may be encountered on coastal cliffs as well. They may also nest on man-made structures, such as bridges, creating a closed nest made of damp mud, which hardens as it dries, rather like concrete. As their name suggests, these swallows can be identified by the presence of rusty-red feathering on the rump area.

PLUMAGE These swallows have a rusty-brown marking around the nape of the neck, and relatively short tail streamers.

Crag Martin

FAMILY Hirundinidae
SPECIES *Ptyonoprogne rupestris*
LENGTH 15 cm (6 in)
HABITAT Cliffs/caves
CLUTCH SIZE 4–5

DISTRIBUTION Resident in Spain, Italy, and other areas of the Mediterranean, and to the southeast of the Black Sea. Summer visitor further north.

A RELATIVELY EVEN brownish body coloration helps to characterize these martins, although when seen from below, their underwing coverts are a darker shade of brown. The sexes are similar in appearance. As their name suggests, they favour rocky crags and may be found at relatively high altitude in some parts of their range. On occasion, Crag Martins can be seen soaring high into the skies, seeking midges and similar flying insects, with which they rear their young. The nest is made of mud, and depending on the locality, it may be built on a bridge or a tall building.

SOLITARY Crag Martins usually build their nests beneath the overhang of a cliff. They do not occur in large colonies.

Barn Swallow

FAMILY Hirundinidae
SPECIES *Hirundo rustica*
LENGTH 20 cm (8 in)
HABITAT Open country/ farmland
CLUTCH SIZE 3–5

DISTRIBUTION Summer visitor throughout Europe, only absent from Iceland and northeastern parts of Scandinavia. A small resident population in Spain. Most birds overwinter in Africa.

AS ITS NAME SUGGESTS, the Barn Swallow is often seen in agricultural areas, and may attach its nest to the wall of a building such as a barn. These birds possess remarkably strong homing instincts, with pairs returning to the same site annually, assuming that they survive the perilous journey back and forth to their African wintering grounds. These swallows tend to breed in small colonies, with the sexes being similar in appearance. The young spend about 20 days in the nest.

DIFFERENCES These are two different subspecies of swallow. The red-bodied individual originates from the Middle East, with a European bird on the right.

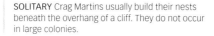

NESTING INDOORS Barn Swallows nest in buildings, which ensures that their young have some security and protection from the elements. Thanks to their flying abilities, feeding time creates no problems.

House Martin

FAMILY Hirundinidae

SPECIES *Delichon urbica*

LENGTH 15 cm (6 in)

HABITAT Open country/urban areas

CLUTCH SIZE 4–5

DISTRIBUTION Occurs throughout Europe during the summer, only absent from Iceland, the far northeast of Scandinavia, and areas south of the Black Sea. Overwinters in Africa.

A GLOSSY BLUE-BLACK BACK AND HEAD, combined with clear white underparts, serves to identify this species, which has white feathering extending to the rump. This is particularly conspicuous, contrasting with the colour of the wings and tail. Through the centuries, these members of the swallow family have adapted to increasing urbanization by adopting man-made structures as nesting sites, although in more remote areas of the continent, they still breed in caves. The nest is laboriously constructed using damp mud, with pairs nesting communally.

NEST BUILDING A House Martin gathering mud to construct its nest. The entrance is kept deliberately small, so as to prevent House Sparrows from displacing the martins.

Pied Wagtail

FAMILY Motacillidae

SPECIES *Motacilla alba*

LENGTH 18 cm (7 in)

HABITAT Open country/urban areas

CLUTCH SIZE 4–6

DISTRIBUTION Resident throughout western parts of Europe and the Mediterranean. Summer visitor elsewhere; winters in Africa and Middle East.

THE COLORATION OF the cock Pied Wagtail varies dramatically through its range, with those occurring in the British Isles being black on the wings, rather than having grey plumage on this part of the body as is typical of those occurring on mainland Europe. Hens in both cases have grey backs, again lighter in the case of European birds, with the head and back coloration merging together, rather than being clearly defined. Pied Wagtails have a very jaunty way of walking, sometimes combing city pavements in search of insects.

QUICK MOVER A cock Pied Wagtail from Britain, seen on a fence post. These nimble birds can run surprisingly quickly along the ground.

Grey Wagtail

FAMILY Motacillidae
SPECIES *Motacilla cinerea*
LENGTH 20 cm (8 in)
HABITAT Around rivers/lakes
CLUTCH SIZE 4–6

THESE WAGTAILS OCCUR in the vicinity of shallow, fast-flowing streams where there are plenty of rocks and boulders. They use these as vantage points from where they can grab their invertebrate prey. Pairs nest in rocky crevices nearby, not uncommonly in the vicinity of watermills.

GENDER DIFFERENCES Less yellow on the underparts and a grey rather than black throat distinguish the hen Grey Wagtail from her mate.

DISTRIBUTION Resident right across western Europe. Absent from Scandinavia to the Black Sea, but summer visitor further northwest. Overwinters in Africa and the Middle East.

Yellow Wagtail

FAMILY Motacillidae
SPECIES *Motacilla flava*
LENGTH 15 cm (6 in)
HABITAT Marshland/meadows
CLUTCH SIZE 4–6

THERE MAY BE anywhere from 8–20 distinctive subspecies of this particular wagtail occurring across Europe and into Asia. They differ primarily on the basis of the head coloration of the cock bird, which may be a yellowish shade, in the case of the British subspecies, through to the blackish head plumage that is a feature of the Turkish race. Yellow Wagtails are all similar in their habits, and hens in general are paler and less brightly coloured than their mates.

DISTRIBUTION Summer visitor across much of Europe, but absent from Scotland and Ireland. Resident population between the Black and Caspian Seas. Overwinters in Africa.

APPEARANCE An example of a cock Yellow Wagtail belonging to the British subspecies, known scientifically as *Motacilla flava flavissima*. These birds occur near water.

Rock Pipit

FAMILY Motacillidae

SPECIES *Anthus petrosus*

LENGTH 17 cm (6¾ in)

HABITAT Rocky areas

CLUTCH SIZE 4–5

DISTRIBUTION Resident on British coasts and neighbouring parts of France. Summer visitor to the Scandinavia; overwinters southwards along the coast.

THE COLORATION OF these pipits can vary quite significantly through their range, with this feature being most conspicuous over the winter period, when these birds migrate from their breeding grounds to the coast of western Europe. Some have pinkish underparts in the summer period, becoming darker over the winter. They nest on the ground in rocky areas and feed mainly on invertebrates. Rock Pipits tend to be quite approachable, being less nervous than other pipits, and generally will only fly off a short distance if disturbed, staying relatively close to the ground. They often hop, jump, and walk amongst boulders.

PLUMAGE A typical Rock Pipit, displaying the relatively dark brown plumage, which is streaked on the underparts. The markings here will vary according to the individual concerned.

Tawny Pipit

FAMILY Motacillidae

SPECIES *Anthus campestris*

LENGTH 18 cm (7 in)

HABITAT Sandy areas/ gravel pits

CLUTCH SIZE 4–6

DISTRIBUTION Summer visitor seen typically as far north as Denmark, but less common in northwestern parts and absent from the British Isles. Overwinters in Africa.

ADULT BIRDS OF this species can be distinguished quite easily by their underparts, which are essentially white, apart from some light streaking on the sides of the chest. The plumage over the back is also largely unmarked. Pairs return to their nesting grounds in Europe during April, with cock birds then engaging in spectacular courtship flights, soaring almost vertically to heights of about 30 m (100 ft), and then plummeting back down again while singing loudly. The hen will build the nest by herself on the ground.

CHICKS The incubation period of the Tawny Pipit lasts two weeks, with the young then leaving the nest after a similar interval.

Red-throated Pipit

FAMILY Motacillidae
SPECIES *Anthus cervinus*
LENGTH 15 cm (6 in)
HABITAT Mountains/tundra
CLUTCH SIZE 4–6

DISTRIBUTION Summer visitor restricted entirely to northeastern Scandinavia and further northeast up into the former USSR. May be seen further south on passage, overwintering in Africa.

THESE PIPITS FAVOUR swampy areas when breeding, and feed on invertebrates. They may occasionally be seen further west of their typical breeding range, and have even been seen as vagrants in the British Isles, often during the autumn period. Hens have red on the throat.

DISTINCTIVE Red-throated Pipits are the most colourful member of the family, often being observed as here on the ground.

Meadow Pipit

FAMILY Motacillidae
SPECIES *Anthus pratensis*
LENGTH 15 cm (6 in)
HABITAT Open country/ moorland
CLUTCH SIZE 4–6

DISTRIBUTION Resident in the British Isles and northwestern Europe. Summer visitor to the north, overwintering throughout southern Europe and in Africa.

THIS SPECIES CAN be confused with the Tree Pipit (*see* p 252), but usually the different habitats where they occur indicate a bird's identity. Even so, there may be areas such as wooded pastureland, or times when the pipits are migrating, when recognizing an individual becomes more problematic. The Meadow Pipit usually displays more heavy streaking on its upperparts, however, and lacks the pinkish hue evident at the base of the Tree Pipit's lower bill. Young birds have no streaking on the flanks.

TYPICAL POSE Meadow Pipits prefer to rest quite near to the ground, using rocks and fence posts for this purpose.

Tree Pipit

FAMILY Motacillidae
SPECIES *Anthus trivialis*
LENGTH 16 cm (6¼ in)
HABITAT Woodland
CLUTCH SIZE 4–5

DISTRIBUTION Summer visitor across most of northern Europe, up to Scandinavia; less common in south, especially in the Iberian Peninsula. Winters in Africa.

THESE PIPITS favour open woodland, occurring in both coniferous and deciduous areas, seeking food on the ground. The streaking on their flanks is relatively fine, more so than the thicker markings apparent on the breast. They are typically present in Europe between April and September, and may spend the winter down in southern parts of Africa.

STANCE Tree Pipits tend to perch more than related species, and cocks will launch into their flight display from a branch. They feed on invertebrates.

Bohemian Waxwing

FAMILY Bombycillidae
SPECIES *Bombycilla garrulus*
LENGTH 21 cm (8¼ in)
HABITAT Woodland
CLUTCH SIZE 4–6

DISTRIBUTION Resident in parts of Scandinavia eastwards into the former USSR, and breeds further north in summer. Winter visitor over a much wider area of Europe.

THE CREST FEATHERS of this sleek bird are carried low, only being raised when the bird is alert. Pairs may rear their chicks in nests built up to 15 m (50 ft) up, often in a conifer, using a horizontal branch for support. The nest itself is constructed from twigs, with the interior being lined with softer material such as moss.

DISTINCTIVE FEATURE The Waxwing is so called because of the red markings, resembling sealing wax, that are present on each wing.

Dipper

FAMILY Cinclidae
SPECIES *Cinclus cinclus*
LENGTH 20 cm (8 in)
HABITAT Upland streams
CLUTCH SIZE 3–6

DISTRIBUTION Resident through much of southern and western Europe, as well as up into Scandinavia and also parts of the former USSR, in areas of suitable habitat.

THE DIPPER IS only likely to be seen in the vicinity of fast-flowing upland streams, usually surrounded by forest. Its name comes from the way in which it moves in and out of the water, hopping from one partially submerged rock to another. Dippers can also swim underwater in search of food, as well as at the surface. Pairs only come together to breed in spring. Their nest is well hidden, sometimes being built under a man-made structure such as a bridge. Incubation lasts for two weeks, and the young fledge at three weeks old.

SONGSTER Dippers will sing even on a cold winter's day, being audible above the sound of the rushing water.

Wren

FAMILY Troglodytidae
SPECIES *Troglodytes troglodytes*
LENGTH 10 cm (4 in)
HABITAT Woodland
CLUTCH SIZE 4–7

DISTRIBUTION Resident throughout western Europe and much of central Europe. Also ranges further north in summer, up to Scandinavia.

WRENS HAVE AN unmistakeably jaunty profile, and although small in size, they have a loud voice that is very audible, revealing their presence in undergrowth where they often hide away. Their coloration varies somewhat through their range, but their basic coloration is reddish-brown over the wings, with barring on the flanks, which extends across the wings and tail.

BILL SHAPE The short, pointed bill of the Wren is used to catch invertebrates. Spiders often feature in their diet, being found in old walls.

BOHEMIAN WAXWING (*see* p 252) These distinctive birds range widely across Europe over the winter months. Local weather conditions and availability of food influence their precise distribution from year to year.

Rufous Bush Chat

FAMILY Turdidae

SPECIES *Cercotrichas galactotes*

LENGTH 17 cm (6¾ in)

HABITAT Arid, open country

CLUTCH SIZE 3–5

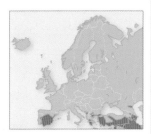

DISTRIBUTION Breeding visitor to various parts of southern Europe, notably the Iberian Peninsula and from Greece to the eastern end of the Mediterranean. Overwinters in Africa.

THIS SPECIES IS ALSO known as the Rufous Bush Robin and the Rufous-tailed Scrub Robin. The sexes are similar in appearance, and young birds resemble adults when they fledge. They have a very distinctive movement, flicking their long tail feathers vertically at regular intervals, and open these long feathers to create a fan, revealing their white tips, bordered by a black band above. Rufous Bush Chats are seen in Europe from mid-May until September.

VARIED APPEARANCE The different races vary quite widely in appearance, with those from western areas having lighter upperparts than those that are found further east.

European Robin

FAMILY Turdidae

SPECIES *Erithacus rubecula*

LENGTH 14 cm (5½ in)

HABITAT Woodland/gardens

CLUTCH SIZE 5–7

DISTRIBUTION Resident throughout western Europe and the Mediterranean. Summer visitor to central and eastern parts, up into Scandinavia. May overwinter around the Black Sea.

THE ROBIN RANKS as one of the best-known birds in the British Isles, where it has become indelibly linked with Christmas. The sexes are identical in appearance. Robins are highly territorial birds, but their bold nature means that they are also one of the easiest garden birds to tame. They will be the first to come and inspect food put out on a bird table, or accompany a gardener digging the soil, darting down to seize worms as they are uncovered.

COLORATION Only adult Robins have a red breast. Their offspring are mainly brown in colour, with speckling here and on the head.

Bluethroat

FAMILY Turdidae
SPECIES *Luscinia svecica*
LENGTH 14 cm (5½ in)
HABITAT Wet areas with woods
CLUTCH SIZE 4–7

DISTRIBUTION Summer visitor to northern and central Europe, up into Scandinavia; resident in Spain and southeast of the Black Sea. Overwinters in Africa.

THERE ARE A NUMBER of distinctive races of Bluethroat that can be seen across Europe, differing in terms of the blue plumage on the throat. In the case of the northern European form, there is a reddish area at the centre, while southern and central European Bluethroats have a white area here instead. Hens, in comparison, are much paler, usually lacking any blue plumage here. The throat area is white, with black spotting along its lower edge. Like many thrushes, not only are Bluethroats talented songsters, but they can also prove to be remarkably good mimics. In spite of only being summer visitors to the far north, they have been known to mimic the sounds of reindeer bells on their breeding grounds. Pairs start nesting in June, with the hen building the nest on her own. Incubation and fledging both take approximately two weeks.

DIET Bluethroats feed mainly on the ground, searching for worms and other larger invertebrates, including snails. They may also eat berries.

Red-flanked Bluetail

FAMILY Turdidae
SPECIES *Tarsiger cyanurus*
LENGTH 14 cm (5½ in)
HABITAT Sparse forest
CLUTCH SIZE 4–5

DISTRIBUTION Summer visitor, restricted only to areas of southern Scandinavia and further eastwards, into the former USSR. Wintering grounds in this case are in southeastern Asia.

CONTRARY TO WHAT its name suggests, the flanks of this small member of the thrush family are actually more yellowish-orange than red. Cock birds are easily distinguished by their blue upperparts. Red-flanked Bluetails twitch both their wings and tail on a regular basis.

IDENTIFICATION This is either a hen or a young cock Red-flanked Bluetail, recognizable by its olive-grey upperparts.

White-throated Robin

FAMILY Turdidae
SPECIES *Irania gutturalis*
LENGTH 18 cm (7 in)
HABITAT Arid country with bush
CLUTCH SIZE 4–6

DISTRIBUTION A summer visitor, occurring in the extreme southeast, being seen to the south of the Black Sea at this stage. Overwinters in eastern Africa.

DISTINGUISHING THE sexes is quite straightforward, in the case of adult birds, with cocks being more colourful than their mates. They have deep orange-brown underparts, contrasting with their grey upperparts. Hens are duller, with the orange-brown plumage restricted to their flanks, and they lack the black areas that extend down from the eyes over the cheeks in the cock.

ELUSIVE White-throated Robins nest in bushes. They can be hard to spot, except when the cock bird is singing in the open.

Thrush Nightingale

FAMILY Turdidae
SPECIES *Luscinia luscinia*
LENGTH 17 cm (6¾ in)
HABITAT Woodland
CLUTCH SIZE 4–5

DISTRIBUTION Summer visitor occurring northwards as far as southern Scandinavia. Also central parts of Europe eastwards into the former USSR. Overwinters in Africa.

THE BREAST OF the Thrush Nightingale is a mottled shade of greyish-brown, helping to distinguish it from the Nightingale itself, with its back and wings generally being a more greyish shade too. The upper surface of the tail is a further point of distinction, being browner, and their song is not as musical.

CONFUSION Both species can overlap at times, with Thrush Nightingales having been recorded in England, for example, where they are not normally found.

Nightingale

FAMILY Turdidae
SPECIES *Luscinia megarhynchos*
LENGTH 16 cm (6¼ in)
HABITAT Woodland
CLUTCH SIZE 4–5

DISTRIBUTION Summer visitor across western Europe, as far as southern parts of England. Extends through Mediterranean, around the Black Sea.

A LIGHT SANDY-BROWN band across the breast, and similar brown coloration over the back and wings help to identify the Nightingale. It may have a fairly nondescript appearance, but it is the song of this bird that has proved to be an inspiration for poets and other writers. In Europe, Nightingales arrive quite early in April, with their song traditionally heralding the return of spring.

PARENTING A Nightingale feeds her brood on insects. By September, these thrushes will have left their breeding grounds, flying to Africa for the winter.

Black Redstart

FAMILY Turdidae

SPECIES *Phoenicurus ochruros*

LENGTH 14 cm (5½ in)

HABITAT Upland areas/cities

CLUTCH SIZE 5–6

DISTRIBUTION Resident in western parts of Europe and along the Mediterranean. Summer visitor up into southern Scandinavia. Birds overwinter further south and in Africa.

AS THEIR NAME SUGGESTS, the coloration of these redstarts, and especially the European subspecies, is subdued. These birds have no reddish plumage on their underparts, aside from the vent area and along the tail, with the rump being similarly coloured. Pairs may breed on tall buildings, replicating the mountains where they nest more commonly.

GENDER DIFFERENCES This is a cock Black Redstart. Hens are much greyer in appearance, rather than being black, as are young birds of both sexes.

Güldenstädt's Redstart

FAMILY Turdidae

SPECIES *Phoenicurus erythrogaster*

LENGTH 16 cm (6¼ in)

HABITAT Mountians

CLUTCH SIZE 5–6

DISTRIBUTION Restricted to two small areas at high altitude in the region that lies between the Black and Caspian Seas, being resident here throughout the year.

GÜLDENSTÄDT'S REDSTART can be sighted up to altitudes of nearly 5,000 m (15,000 ft) in summer, but descending down to as low as 900 m (2,400 ft) in winter. The sexes vary widely in appearance. Hens are greyish-brown overall, while cock birds have a white top to the head, and a prominent white wing patch, with the chest and underparts, as well as the rump and tail feathers being rusty-red.

MOBILE These redstarts have a very localized distribution, and undergo seasonal movement, depending on the prevailing weather conditions, which influence the availability of food.

Common Redstart

FAMILY Turdidae

SPECIES *Phoenicurus phoenicurus*

LENGTH 15 cm (6 in)

HABITAT Woodland

CLUTCH SIZE 5–7

DISTRIBUTION A summer visitor across virtually the entire European continent, although absent from Iceland and Ireland. Overwinters in Africa.

THIS SPECIES IS the most widely occurring redstart species in Europe, and perhaps unsurprisingly, there are regional variations in its appearance. Cocks have a black face, with a white cap, and deep orange plumage on the chest, becoming white on the lower abdomen. The upperparts are grey. Hens are not as brightly coloured, having paler, buff-orange plumage on the breast, and are greyish-brown elsewhere, with young birds of both sexes resembling hens. They breed in woodland, often preferring mature trees such as oaks, which offer hollows that can be used as nesting sites. Males arrive back in Europe ahead of females, usually being sighted here from March onwards, with the aim of establishing a breeding territory.

They will sing quite loudly at this stage with the aim of attracting a mate. Common Redstarts are reasonably adaptable in terms of seeking a suitable nest site, providing it offers seclusion. They will even use abandoned buildings on occasion, and sometimes abandoned underground burrows. The hen will incubate the eggs on her own, with hatching usually occurring after 14 days. The young Redstarts will grow quickly, and should fledge after a similar interval. Their parents may then rear a second brood, before migrating south again.

PLUMAGE This is the most widely seen form of the Common Redstart in Europe. Unlike birds originating from the vicinity of Turkey, there is no white wing patch.

COMMON REDSTARTS A pair of Common Redstarts, with the cock bird on the right. They are essentially insectivorous in their feeding habits, particularly when rearing their young. When not feeding on the ground, they prefer to perch.

Winchat

FAMILY Turdidae
SPECIES *Saxicola rubetra*
LENGTH 14 cm (5½ in)
HABITAT Open country
CLUTCH SIZE 5–6

DISTRIBUTION Summer visitor from Africa across most of Europe, but restricted to northern parts of the Iberian Peninsula, and absent from southern England and eastern Mediterranean.

WHINCHATS CAN BE found in a range of different terrain, from rough grazing ground through to water meadows, but not normally within ploughed agricultural areas. These birds can be sexed quite easily, as cock birds having more brightly coloured breasts than hens, and a white rather than buff-coloured stripe above each eye. They are insectivorous in their feeding habits, catching insects largely in flight, but sometimes when they are on the ground.

GENDER ROLES A male Whinchat perches on a wire fence. Nest building and incubation are carried out by the hen alone, although both parents feed the resulting brood.

Stonechat

FAMILY Turdidae
SPECIES *Saxicola torquata*
LENGTH 13 cm (5 in)
HABITAT Open country
CLUTCH SIZE 5–6

DISTRIBUTION Resident in most of western mainland Europe, seen more sporadically in the British Isles. Summer visitor to Scandinavia and the former USSR. Overwinters in Africa.

HEATHLAND IS a popular haunt of the Stonechat, and it may often choose to nest in among clumps of gorse, with the sharp spines of this plant offering protection against would-be predators. They may also be seen in coastal areas, frequenting dunes here. Sexing is again straightforward: cock birds have black heads, with a prominent white half-collar on each side of the head, whereas hens have streaky brown patterning on the head, and paler underparts. These birds are now sometimes regarded as flycatchers, rather than thrushes.

CALLS The Stonechat's unusual name originates from its calls: these sound like stones being hit together.

Cyprus Wheatear

FAMILY Turdidae

SPECIES *Oenanthe cypriaca*

LENGTH 15 cm (6 in)

HABITAT Arid, rocky areas

CLUTCH SIZE 3–5

DISTRIBUTION Restricted to the island of Cyprus in the eastern Mediterranean. Overwinters in East Africa, in areas of Ethiopia and southern Sudan, flying here via the Middle East.

THESE WHEATEARS UNDERGO quite a dramatic change in coloration in the spring, with the male becoming predominantly black, with white plumage extending from the bill to the nape of the neck. This area is mottled in hens. The underparts are whitish, with a pale orange suffusion.

VISITOR The Cyprus Wheatear is commonly seen on this island between the months of March and October each year.

Desert Wheatear

FAMILY Turdidae
SPECIES *Oenanthe deserti*
LENGTH 15 cm (6 in)
HABITAT Arid country
CLUTCH SIZE 3–5

DISTRIBUTION Restricted to southeastern parts of Europe, where it is a summer visitor from Africa, occurring in the eastern Mediterranean and around the Caspian Sea.

SANDY SURROUNDINGS with sparse vegetation is home to the Desert Wheatear, rather than true desert. The difference between the sexes in terms of their coloration is quite pronounced, with cock birds having black facial colouring, which extends down over the shoulders onto the wings. There is a narrow white stripe above the eye, with the top of the head and back being buff-brown. In contrast, hens lack the black plumage on the face, but have rufous-tinged ear coverts instead, with their underparts being white.

Pairs establish distinct territories, and feed on invertebrates, which they may catch by swooping down from above. The nest is built by the hen in a secluded spot, using dry vegetation.

KEEPING GUARD A watchful cock Desert Wheatear. The incubation period for this species lasts for a fortnight, with the young fledging after a similar interval.

Finsch's Wheatear

FAMILY Turdidae
SPECIES *Oenanthe finschii*
LENGTH 15 cm (6 in)
HABITAT Upland areas
CLUTCH SIZE 3–5

DISTRIBUTION Occurs in the area south of the Black Sea and in a northeasterly direction, being seen around the shore of the Caspian Sea in summer.

THE COCK BIRD in this case is predominantly black and white, whereas the hen is greyer, with brownish ear coverts. Finsch's Wheatear is found in bare mountainous areas, where there is little vegetation to provide cover. Pairs nest in crevices or hollows in the rocks.

BEHAVIOUR Highly territorial by nature, Finsch's Wheatear feeds mainly on invertebrates but these birds may also eat seeds occasionally.

Black-eared Wheatear

FAMILY Turdidac
SPECIES *Oenanthe hispanica*
LENGTH 15 cm (6 in)
HABITAT Open country
CLUTCH SIZE 3–5

DISTRIBUTION Summer visitor to southern Europe, present throughout the Mediterranean region, from the Iberian Peninsula eastwards, via the Black Sea. Overwinters in Africa.

IN SPITE OF ITS NAME, there are a number of other wheatears with similar black facial patterning extending behind the eyes of the cock bird. In this species, however, the black plumage here is not continuous down onto the wings. Hens are brownish with white plumage on the abdomen. Black-eared Wheatears breed in Europe in fairly isolated arid areas, sometimes close to mountain streams. The hen disguises the location of the nest by placing it near a boulder.

COLORATION This is the 'pale-throated' form of the Black-eared Wheatear, which also has white rather than brownish plumage on the head.

Isabelline Wheatear

FAMILY Turdidae
SPECIES *Oenanthe isabellina*
LENGTH 16 cm (6¼ in)
HABITAT Grassland
CLUTCH SIZE 3–8

DISTRIBUTION Summer visitor to the eastern Mediterranean, extending east and north of the Black Sea. Overwinters south, in the Middle East and Africa.

THE NAME OF this wheatear reflects its coloration, with 'isabelline' being an old term for a greyish-brown shade. The sexes are almost identical in appearance, although it may be possible to distinguish them on the basis that the lores of the cock bird, in front of the eyes, are blacker in colour than in hens.

UPRIGHT STANCE The Isabelline Wheatear has a characteristic vertical pose, as seen here. Pairs often nest underground, rearing their chicks in the disused burrows of rodents.

Mourning Wheatear

FAMILY Turdidae
SPECIES *Oenanthe lugens*
LENGTH 16 cm (6¼ in)
HABITAT Montane areas
CLUTCH SIZE 3–5

DISTRIBUTION Resident in the eastern Mediterranean region, down into parts of Africa and the Middle East, but does not occur elsewhere in Europe.

COCK BIRDS OF this species are essentially black and white in colour, with buff undertail coverts. Mourning Wheatears occur in an upland region where vegetation is sparse, and they often frequent steep, rocky slopes. Pairs seek cover among the rocks where they can rear their chicks hidden from potential predators.

PLUMAGE The sexes are similar in appearance during the summer, but hens are slightly duller in colour at this stage. During the winter, however, they are greyer.

Common Wheatear

FAMILY Turdidae
SPECIES *Oenanthe oenanthe*
LENGTH 15 cm (6 in)
HABITAT Open country
CLUTCH SIZE 3–5

DISTRIBUTION Breeds in summer across almost the entire continent, from Iceland southwards. Absent from some localities in western Europe, including parts of southern England. Overwinters in Africa.

AS ITS NAME SUGGESTS, this is the most common European species of wheatear. It can be observed in a range of different habitats, from grassland to coastal shingle. Cock birds in breeding plumage have a characteristic black stripe running back from the bill on each side of the head, widening as it passes through the eyes. Hens have just a faint greyer loral stripe, between the eyes and bill, with the area at the back of the head being streaked.

Invertebrates feature prominently in their diet, but they will eat seeds, too. The nest is most likely to be concealed on the ground, although it can be hidden in a suitable crevice in a wall. Pairs may rear two rounds of chicks over the course of the summer, particularly in southern parts of Europe. Remarkably, these young Wheatears are likely to head even further south than their parents, overwintering in South Africa.

VOCALIZATION The word 'wheatear' is said to reflect the sound of the calls of this group of birds.

Pied Wheatear

FAMILY Turdidae
SPECIES *Oenanthe pleschanka*
LENGTH 16 cm (6¼ in)
HABITAT Montane areas
CLUTCH SIZE 3–5

DISTRIBUTION Summer visitor seen from the northern coast of the Black Sea in a northeasterly direction, being present on both sides of the Caspian Sea.

CONTRARY TO ITS NAME, the cock Pied Wheatear is not simply black and white, as there is a slight brownish-orange suffusion to the white plumage on the breast. Hens can be easily distinguished by their much duller appearance, being predominately grey overall, with streaking on the lower breast, merging into pale grey on the abdomen. The Pied Wheatear occurs in mountainous countryside, at a higher altitude than the Black-eared Wheatear where their range overlaps.

MIGRANTS Pied Wheatears overwinter in East Africa, passing over the Middle East on their annual migration to and from southeastern Europe where they breed.

Rock Thrush

FAMILY Turdidae
SPECIES *Monticola saxatilis*
LENGTH 20 cm (8 in)
HABITAT Open rocky country
CLUTCH SIZE 3–6

DISTRIBUTION Occurs through southern parts of Europe during the summer months, extending right across to the Caspian Sea. Overwinters in Africa.

OUTSIDE THE breeding period, the sexes are similar in appearance, but when these thrushes return to their European breeding grounds in the spring, the cock bird has moulted to become far more colourful than the hen. She is relatively dark in colour with barring on her body. Rock Thrushes are encountered at high altitudes, typically above 1,500 m (4,500 ft), and will nest in holes in the cliff face, or even use buildings for this purpose.

APPEARANCE A cock Rock Thrush in breeding plumage, shown by the blue head plumage, and the orange underparts.

Blue Rock Thrush

FAMILY Turdidae
SPECIES *Monticola solitarius*
LENGTH 23 cm (9 in)
HABITAT Open rocky country
CLUTCH SIZE 3–6

DISTRIBUTION Resident through much of the Mediterranean from the Iberian Peninsula eastwards. More of a summer visitor in the far east, heading up to the Caspian Sea.

ALTHOUGH OCCURRING at lower altitudes than the Rock Thrush itself, this species will breed in a similar way, nesting among rocky outcrops or deserted buildings. The male Blue Rock Thrush does not undergo a seasonal change in appearance at the start of the breeding period, however, and these particular birds are also resident through most of their range. Only the cock bird displays the characteristic blue plumage, with hens being brownish, lighter on the underparts with fine streaking evident here. Their bill is long, and helps these thrushes to probe for invertebrates, which make up the bulk of their diet, although they will also eat berries and even small vertebrates such as young lizards. Blue Rock Thrushes are quite shy, and occur in largely treeless areas, so they tend to hide away if disturbed. When in the open, they may often be seen perching on rocks, which explains their common name.

ON THE LOOKOUT Ever alert, a male Blue Rock Thrush adopts a vertical stance looking for signs of danger. They may betray their presence by their loud song.

Redwing

FAMILY Turdidae
SPECIES *Turdus iliacus*
LENGTH 23 cm (9 in)
HABITAT Coniferous forest
CLUTCH SIZE 4–5

DISTRIBUTION Summer visitor to northeastern parts of Europe, including Iceland, Scandinavia, and further east. Overwinters throughout western parts of Europe, down through the Mediterranean.

REDWINGS HAVE PROMINENT whitish stripes above the eyes, combined with evident thrush-like markings on the underparts. There is no means of distinguishing between the sexes. They are commonly seen in the British Isles and western Europe over the winter months, when flocks may descend into gardens in large numbers in search of food, especially during harsh winters.

FEEDING Redwings will eat various berries including holly in winter. The rusty-red patches on their flanks are more evident here than those under the wing.

Blackbird

FAMILY Turdidae
SPECIES *Turdus merula*
LENGTH 29 cm (11½ in)
HABITAT Woodland/gardens
CLUTCH SIZE 3–5

DISTRIBUTION Resident from southwestern Scandinavia and the British Isles across Europe to the Mediterranean. Summer visitor further north and east.

THE BLACKBIRD has become a common garden bird over the course of the last century or so, although before this period, it used to be seen more commonly in rural areas. They are talented songsters, with males singing loudly during the breeding period, which extends from spring through until late summer. Although they will readily feed on bird table fare, blackbirds will also comb the lawn and other areas of soil seeking worms just below the surface.

PLUMAGE This is a cock Blackbird. Hens are browner, while unusual piebald individuals can crop up.

Song Thrush

FAMILY Turdidae
SPECIES *Turdus philomelos*
LENGTH 22 cm (8½ in)
HABITAT Woodland/gardens
CLUTCH SIZE 5–6

DISTRIBUTION Resident in the British Isles and western Europe, down via Italy to the Mediterranean. Overwinters in Spain and this region. Summer visitor to Scandinavia and eastern Europe.

AS THEIR NAME IMPLIES, Song Thrushes are talented songsters. Male birds usually adopt a fairly prominent position on a particular branch, for example, when they are singing. They are very welcome birds in the garden environment, because they will help to control invertebrate pests. These thrushes have developed a particular way of breaking open snails, by repeatedly

WIDESPREAD The Song Thrush is resident in many parts of Europe throughout the year. Pairs may rear up to three clutches of chicks during the summer months.

smashing the rather fragile shell of the snail down onto a hard surface, typically the edge of a path or a stone, which is described as the anvil. Aside from invertebrates, however, these thrushes also eat berries and fruit in season, pecking at fallen apples and the like. When nesting, the hen constructs a typical cup-shaped nest out of vegetation, usually hidden in a hedge, but occasionally, this may be within a building. The incubation period lasts approximately 15 days, with the young thrushes then leaving the nest after a similar interval.

Fieldfare

FAMILY Turdidae
SPECIES *Turdus piliaris*
LENGTH 25 cm (10 in)
HABITAT Woodland/gardens
CLUTCH SIZE 5–6

DISTRIBUTION Resident in woods in northern Europe and Scandinavia, and a summer visitor to more northern areas, with most birds migrating south and west in winter.

THE FIELDFARE IS one of the larger thrushes, with pale grey upperparts and white underwings, which show well in flight; the dark tail then appears relatively long. The underparts are heavily spotted, and the upper chest has a yellowish-orange tinge. The sexes are similar, but juveniles have pale spots on the wings.

Fieldfares are familiar birds in gardens in winter, when they feed on fallen fruit and red berries, but in the breeding season they are more scattered, nesting in woods and parks, sometimes in small colonies.

BERRY LOVERS Fieldfares feed voraciously on berries in winter, often invading feeding areas in large flocks.

Ring Ousel

FAMILY Turdidae
SPECIES *Turdus torquatus*
LENGTH 24 cm (9½ in)
HABITAT Rocky moorland
CLUTCH SIZE 4–5

DISTRIBUTION A summer visitor to rocky uplands in western and northern Europe. Most birds overwinter in south Europe and North Africa.

RING OUSELS INHABIT remote rocky upland areas, and are rather shy birds, so they are easily overlooked. On migration they may be observed feeding on coastal grassland, but when they are on their breeding sites they are far more secretive. The sexes are similar, but females have more brown in the plumage and the white throat crescent is less distinct. Snatches of their rather mournful song can sometimes be heard, and sharp 'chack' alarm notes may be given if danger threatens.

COLLAR The male's bold white collar distinguishes it from the similar male Blackbird (*see* p 272).

Mistle Thrush

FAMILY Turdidae
SPECIES *Turdus viscivorous*
LENGTH 27 cm (10½ in)
HABITAT Woodland/parkland
CLUTCH SIZE 4–5

DISTRIBUTION A widespread and sometimes common resident across most of Europe, Turkey, and the Middle East, and a summer visitor to more northern areas.

THE LARGEST of the common thrushes has mostly grey-brown upperparts and boldly spotted underparts. In flight, large white patches can be seen under the wings. The Mistle Thrush is one of the first birds to start singing early in the year, and will often sing in stormy weather when other birds have ceased, usually choosing a very high perch as a song post. The short snatches of song sound quite melancholy by comparison with the Song Thrush (*see* p 273); there are also some churring alarm calls and harsh 'cheek' sounds. Favourite foods include worms, insects, and berries.

FEEDING YOUNG A Mistle Thrush brings food to its young in their grass-lined nest built high in the fork of a tree.

Blackcap

FAMILY Sylviidae
SPECIES *Sylvia atricapilla*
LENGTH 14 cm (5½ in)
HABITAT Woodland/scrubland
CLUTCH SIZE 5

DISTRIBUTION A common summer visitor to Europe, apart from the far north; resident in much of southwest Europe and the Mediterranean islands.

THIS IS A MOSTLY grey warbler with a distinctive black cap in the male and red-brown cap in the female. Juvenile males at first resemble females, but by autumn they have a black cap flecked with brown. The shade of the grey coloration in the male is slightly darker than that of the female. Blackcaps have a pleasant warbling song, usually delivered from deep cover, and they also make various chattering and clicking call notes. The song is very similar to that of the Garden Warbler, but usually delivered in shorter phrases. Blackcaps feed on insects and spiders, but also take fruits, especially in the winter when they may feed on windfall apples. Some overwinter in Britain in mild winters.

IN TUNE The male Blackcap is one of the best songsters of the spring, delivering his tuneful, liquid song from perches within his territory.

Garden Warbler

FAMILY Sylviidae
SPECIES *Sylvia borin*
LENGTH 14 cm (5½ in)
HABITAT Woodland/parkland
CLUTCH SIZE 4–5

DISTRIBUTION A common summer visitor to Europe; absent from Iceland, the far north of Scandinavia, Russia, and Mediterranean fringes.

A VERY PLAIN grey-brown and rather plump bird, the Garden Warbler has no distinctive plumage features. There is sometimes a hint of grey on the sides of the neck and the underside is paler than the upperparts. The bill is fairly thick and dark grey. The sexes are identical, but juveniles have paler tips to the wing feathers. Garden Warblers are very furtive in their habits and so difficult to observe.

HIDDEN SINGER The Garden Warbler normally remains in deep cover, but will sometimes visit drinking pools. Its song is pleasant and musical.

Subalpine Warbler

FAMILY Sylviidae
SPECIES *Sylvia cantillans*
LENGTH 12 cm (4¾ in)
HABITAT Scrubland/maquis
CLUTCH SIZE 3–4

DISTRIBUTION A summer visitor to the Mediterranean coast, Iberia, and North Africa, occasionally turning up further north during migration.

THE SUBALPINE WARBLER is rather slender and short-tailed with grey upperparts, a white moustachial stripe, a brick-red eye ring, and a red throat and flanks. The female is much paler than the male with a pale eye ring surrounding a bright red eye ring. Both the calls and the song are a series of scratchy sounding notes usually delivered from a dense bush, but occasionally males sit out in the open when responding to a rival's call.

UNDERCOVER This warbler prefers dense cover, but on migration may be seen in more open habitats.

Common Whitethroat

FAMILY Sylviidae
SPECIES *Sylvia communis*
LENGTH 14 cm (5½ in)
HABITAT Hedgerows/scrubland
CLUTCH SIZE 4–5

DISTRIBUTION A common summer visitor to Europe, but not Iceland and the far north of Scandinavia and Russia; spends winters in sub-Saharan Africa.

THE WHITETHROAT IS a brownish-grey, rather long-tailed warbler with a very appropriate name; when sitting prominently on a bush in full song the gleaming white throat is a very obvious feature. The wings look slightly reddish-brown by comparison with the greyer head and back. The staccato, rather hoarse song is sometimes delivered from a short fluttering flight above a favourite patch of scrub. Nests are usually constructed deep inside thick cover, and feeding birds moving through the undergrowth occasionally utter sharp alarm calls.

SONG PERCH A male Common Whitethroat sits on an open perch on a hedgerow to pour out his rapid, rather scratchy song.

Spectacled Warbler

FAMILY Sylviidae
SPECIES *Sylvia conspicillata*
LENGTH 13 cm (5 in)
HABITAT Garrigue
CLUTCH SIZE 4–5

DISTRIBUTION A summer visitor to open, bushy areas of the western Mediterranean coastal area, and a more permanent resident in the coastal areas of North Africa.

AT A GLANCE, the Spectacled Warbler resembles a dark-headed Common Whitethroat (*see* p 277), but in good light the pale eye ring may be visible. Males are pink-grey below and both sexes show rusty-red wing coverts. The song is similar to the Whitethroat, but usually starts with clearer whistling notes, and is often delivered from a short, fluttering flight. There is also a dry, rattling alarm call.

HIDDEN NEST Spectacled Warblers nest in dry, scrubby habitats, and both parents help care for the young.

Lesser Whitethroat

FAMILY Sylviidae
SPECIES *Sylvia curruca*
LENGTH 13 cm (5¼ in)
HABITAT Scrubland/open country
CLUTCH SIZE 4–6

DISTRIBUTION A common summer visitor from northeast Africa to Europe, Turkey, and the Caucasus, but absent from southwest Europe, Ireland, and the far north.

THE RATHER SHY and retiring Lesser Whitethroat is only slightly smaller than the Common Whitethroat (*see* p 277), but the best distinction between them is the greyer plumage and more skulking habits. The ear coverts are dark grey, giving a slight masked effect in certain lights, and some birds have a very pale supercilium. The dry rattling song is usually delivered from a concealed perch in a shrub, and short clicking calls are also made from cover when birds are alarmed.

GREY BIRD By comparison with the Common Whitethroat, this a much greyer bird, lacking any red-brown tones.

Orphean Warbler

FAMILY Sylviidae
SPECIES *Sylvia hortensis*
LENGTH 15 cm (6 in)
HABITAT Maquis
CLUTCH SIZE 4–5

DISTRIBUTION A summer visitor from sub-Saharan Africa to Mediterranean coastal areas, Iberia, Turkey, the Caucasus, and North Africa.

THE ORPHEAN WARBLER is the largest of the *Sylvia* warblers but one of the most difficult to see because of its retiring habits; it often keeps to the treetops and the only clue to its presence is its pleasant Song Thrush-like song (*see* p 273). When glimpsed among foliage, the contrasting black head and white throat and overall grey coloration are diagnostic.

STRIKING HEAD The male Orphean Warbler's gleaming pale yellow eye makes a striking contrast with its sooty black cheeks and crown.

Desert Warbler

FAMILY Sylviidae
SPECIES *Sylvia nana*
LENGTH 12 cm (4¾ in)
HABITAT Desert/scrubland
CLUTCH SIZE 4–5

DISTRIBUTION Resident in North Africa and Asia, and thought to be two separate races, very occasionally turning up in northern Europe on autumn migration.

THIS IS THE SMALLEST OF the scrub warblers. It can sometimes be one of the easiest to see as it has the habit of feeding in the open, often running on the ground from bush to bush. The African race is very pale buff above and white below, while the Asian race is grey-brown above with slightly darker flanks. It is the Asian race that is more likely to wander as far as Europe. In its home range it is sometimes seen feeding alongside Desert Wheatears (*see* p 266).

DISTINCTIVE FEATURES This diminutive bird can be identified by its yellow eye with its white eye ring, yellow legs, and dark-tipped, yellow bill.

Barred Warbler

FAMILY Sylviidae
SPECIES *Sylvia nisoria*
LENGTH 15 cm (6 in)
HABITAT Hedgerows/scrubland
CLUTCH SIZE 5

DISTRIBUTION A widespread and common visitor from East Africa to central and eastern Europe; immature birds may be seen further west on migration.

THE BARRED WARBLER is one of the largest and most heavily built of the scrub warblers, appearing mostly grey from a distance. The pale underparts are barred and the eye is bright yellow; adult males have a rather fierce shrike-like expression. Females have far less striking markings and juveniles are much plainer. The song is very similar to the Garden Warbler's (*see* p 276), but harsher.

VOCAL The Barred Warbler has a loud call sounding rather like a rattle. It is not an easy bird to spot, however, hiding away in undergrowth.

Marmora's Warbler

FAMILY Sylviidae
SPECIES *Sylvia sarda*
LENGTH 12 cm (4¾ in)
HABITAT Maquis
CLUTCH SIZE 3–4

DISTRIBUTION A locally common resident on Mallorca, Corsica, and Sardinia; some birds winter in North Africa or on the Mediterranean coast.

THIS IS A MOSTLY grey and rather small scrub warbler with a bright red eye ring, black-tipped red bill, and orange-brown legs. The long tail is frequently cocked up as the bird perches on top of a low bush. The song is a typical scrub warbler's burst of scratchy notes. Marmora's Warblers in Mallorca inhabit coastal areas, but in Corsica and Sardinia they are present in more upland areas; they avoid woodland.

FEEDING THE YOUNG A Marmora's Warbler brings food to its young in their nest, which is concealed in the base of a thorny shrub.

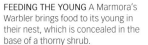

Dartford Warbler

FAMILY Sylviidae
SPECIES *Sylvia undata*
LENGTH 13 cm (5 in)
HABITAT Scrubland/heathland
CLUTCH SIZE 3–4

DISTRIBUTION Resident in suitable habitats in southwest Europe, including southern Britain; some birds migrate to North Africa in harsh winters.

THE MALE DARTFORD WARBLER often sits out in the open, tail cocked, delivering his high-speed scratchy song. At other times they flit through scrub, occasionally making harsh alarm calls. The upperparts are grey and the underparts deep wine-red. Males have a bright red eye ring and a yellowish bill. Females are very similar but with less intense coloration. Juvenile birds have more brown tones in the autumn.

SPRING SONG A familiar sound of spring on the gorse-covered heaths of southern England is the song of the male Dartford Warbler.

Scrub Warbler

FAMILY Sylviidae
SPECIES *Scotocerca inquieta*
LENGTH 10 cm (4 in)
HABITAT Arid country
CLUTCH SIZE 6–8

DISTRIBUTION Resident in deserts and stony steppe habitats in North Africa, the Middle East, and the eastern Caspian Sea region.

THE SCRUB WARBLER APPEARS slightly unbalanced as it feeds on the ground because its long legs are set rather far back and the long tail is usually held erect as it moves around. As well as harsh alarm notes, there is also a wader-like whistling call. There are two races with subtle differences in the plumage: birds from North Africa appear paler, with more buff tones, while birds from Egypt eastwards are greyer above.

DARK TAIL The Scrub Warbler's long tail is darker than the rest of the body, but it has a paler central band.

Paddyfield Warbler

FAMILY Sylviidae
SPECIES *Acrocephalus agricola*
LENGTH 13 cm (5 in)
HABITAT Scrubland/swamps
CLUTCH SIZE 4–5

DISTRIBUTION A summer visitor from India to the Caspian and Black Sea regions, with occasional sightings further west during migration.

A VERY SIMILAR SPECIES to the more common Reed Warbler, the Paddyfield Warbler is a fraction smaller, with a dark-bordered, pale supercilium and a dark tip to the pale bill. The best distinction is probably the song: it lacks the grating sounds of the Reed Warbler (*see* p 287), but includes lots of mimicry, with some phrases repeated a few times. Soft, clicking alarm calls and contact notes are frequently heard.

PALE EYEBROW The Paddyfield Warbler's pale supercilium often has a darker lower margin and the bill has a darker tip, but these features are not always clearly visible.

Great Reed Warbler

FAMILY Sylviidae
SPECIES *Acrocephalus arundinaceus*
LENGTH 19 cm (7½ in)
HABITAT Reedbeds
CLUTCH SIZE 4–6

DISTRIBUTION A widespread, sometimes common, summer visitor from tropical Africa to Europe apart from northern regions; a rare vagrant in Britain.

THE GREAT REED WARBLER is the largest warbler to occur in Europe: it is almost the size of a small thrush, but still has the agility to move through reed stems with ease. The overall coloration is grey-brown above with a paler underside; the flanks show a yellowish tinge and there is a hint of light grey streaking on the throat. The Great Reed Warbler has a voice to match its size and its loud, erratic, and croaking song is far carrying and not to be confused with the quieter songs of any of the other reedbed songsters.

SONG POST Certain phrases in the male Great Reed Warbler's song vocabulary sound similar to the calls of large frogs.

Blyth's Reed Warbler

FAMILY Sylviidae

SPECIES *Acrocephalus dumetorium*

LENGTH 13 cm (5 in)

HABITAT Scrubland

CLUTCH SIZE 4–5

DISTRIBUTION A summer visitor from India to Finland, the eastern Baltic, and Russia. An occasional visitor to western Europe.

THIS IS A RATHER PLAIN reed warbler with few distinctive plumage features. Blyth's Reed Warbler is most like the Marsh Warbler (*see* p 286) in appearance, but has dark legs, a longer bill, and shorter wings. It is also more at home in drier habitats, often turning up in forest clearings or open scrubby areas. The song, which is heard mostly at night, contains lots of skilled mimicry, with most of the phrases being repeated several times over.

DRY HABITAT Blyth's Reed Warbler is more likely to be seen in dry, bushy areas than in reedbeds.

Moustached Warbler

FAMILY Sylviidae

SPECIES *Acrocephalus melanopogon*

LENGTH 13 cm (5 in)

HABITAT Reedbeds

CLUTCH SIZE 3–4

DISTRIBUTION A scarce visitor to widely scattered locations across southern Europe, with some birds remaining on their territories throughout the year.

A CONTRASTINGLY patterned head and rich brownish-red upperparts marked with darker streaks separate this warbler from other reedbed warblers. The most similar is the Sedge Warbler (*see* p 287), but the Moustached Warbler's darker crown and square-cut white supercilium are the identifying features. This species is also more likely to be seen hopping along at the base of a reedbed. The song is similar to the Reed Warbler's (*see* p 287), and it makes many harsh, trilling scolding calls, often accompanied by tail flicking.

VERSATILE This warbler is very agile among the reed stems, but is also quite likely to be seen hopping on the ground.

GREAT REED WARBLER (*see* p 282) In common with all reed warblers, the Great Reed Warbler is a skilled nest builder, making a neat cup of woven shreds of reed leaves, well above the water to avoid flooding.

Aquatic Warbler

FAMILY Sylviidae

SPECIES *Acrocephalus paludicola*

LENGTH 13 cm (5 in)

HABITAT Reedbeds

CLUTCH SIZE 5–6

DISTRIBUTION A scarce summer visitor from West Africa to eastern Europe, especially the marshes of Poland; may occasionally appear in Britain on return autumn migration.

THE AQUATIC WARBLER is rather secretive and difficult to see in its preferred dense reedbed habitat, but the pale buff-and-brown head stripes and streaked mantle make it unmistakeable when it is spotted, and quite different from the Sedge Warbler. The song is rather a monotonous series of two scratchy notes, and there are also some clicking alarm calls.

INSECT MEAL Aquatic Warblers find plenty of insect food in the reedbeds and wet meadows and are rarely seen away from this habitat.

Marsh Warbler

FAMILY Sylviidae

SPECIES *Acrocephalus palustris*

LENGTH 13 cm (5 in)

HABITAT Bushy areas

CLUTCH SIZE 4–5

DISTRIBUTION A summer visitor from tropical Africa to central and eastern Europe, southern Scandinavia, and Russia; a very small population reaches southern Britain.

THE MARSH WARBLER is at first sight a very similar bird to the Reed Warbler, but its song and choice of habitat help to separate it. The upperparts are mostly grey-brown, lacking any rufous tones, and the bill is a fraction shorter and less pointed, but these features are very difficult to see in the field. Marsh Warblers are more likely to be encountered away from reedbeds, preferring ditches and rank vegetation. The song is a frenzied series of mimetic calls, often poured out through the night.

SHY BIRD Marsh Warblers are often found in stands of cow parsley or meadowsweet on the fringes of wetter areas, but can be secretive in their habits.

Sedge Warbler

FAMILY Sylviidae

SPECIES *Acrocephalus schoenobaenus*

LENGTH 13 cm (5 in)

HABITAT Marshland

CLUTCH SIZE 5–6

DISTRIBUTION A common summer visitor from sub-Saharan Africa to Europe and Scandinavia, but a passage migrant only in southern Europe and the Mediterranean.

THE FIRST CLUE TO the presence of a Sedge Warbler is the strange medley of grating and sweet notes, mingled with snatches of mimicry. Spells of silence may be punctuated by harsh churring and scolding sounds. The most distinctive feature of the Sedge Warbler's appearance is the bold buff eye stripe contrasting with darker cheeks and crown. The rest of the plumage is olive-brown with some darker streaking.

MIMIC The Sedge Warbler's repertoire includes mimicry of other birds plus rapid trills and whistles, and may be delivered from a brief song flight.

Reed Warbler

FAMILY Sylviidae

SPECIES *Acrocephalus scirpaceus*

LENGTH 13 cm (5 in)

HABITAT Reedbeds

CLUTCH SIZE 4

DISTRIBUTION A common and widespread summer visitor from tropical Africa across Europe; absent from northern areas, Ireland, and Iceland.

ALTHOUGH RATHER plain in appearance, the Reed Warbler is easily identified by its choice of habitat and behaviour. The plumage is mostly brown above and pale buff below, although eastern races tend to look greyer. There is a pale supercilium and the bill has a lighter lower mandible. Reed Warblers are very agile among the reeds and are often very visible as they jerk the reed stems around. The song is a series of staccato and harsh trilling notes interspersed with whistles and snatches of mimicry.

BASKET NEST Reed Warblers build a basket-like nest among the reed stems, securing it with thick leaves and lining the interior with fine leaves and cobwebs.

River Warbler

FAMILY Sylviidae
SPECIES *Locustella fluviatilis*
LENGTH 13 cm (5 in)
HABITAT Bushy swamps
CLUTCH SIZE 5–6

DISTRIBUTION A summer visitor from East Africa to river margins and swamps in eastern Europe and Russia; a very rare vagrant further west.

THE RIVER WARBLER is a very shy and elusive small bird with plain olive-brown plumage that helps it blend with the vegetation in the shady, damp forests and thickets it lives in. The undertail coverts have pale tips creating a spotted appearance. The incessant, reeling call, sounding like a sewing machine running non-stop, is often the only clue to the whereabouts of this very secretive bird.

LONG SONG The elusive River Warbler often chooses a high perch from which to deliver its song, which may last for hours, but at other times it keeps well hidden.

Lanceolated Warbler

FAMILY Sylviidae
SPECIES *Locustella lanceolata*
LENGTH 11 cm (4½ in)
HABITAT Swampy forest
CLUTCH SIZE 5

DISTRIBUTION A summer visitor from southeast Asia to taiga areas of northern Russia and Siberia; a very occasional visitor to western Europe.

THIS WARBLER is a very scarce in western Europe, where its counterpart is the Grasshopper Warbler. Its plumage is mostly greyish-brown with darker streaks above, paler below with variable streaking. It is a very furtive bird, creeping about in dense cover and quite difficult to see, but is sometimes located by the 'chick' alarm calls and the reeling song delivered in bouts of up to a minute.

WELL HIDDEN The Lanceolated Warbler may be glimpsed as it skulks in dense cover, but it is reluctant to emerge into the open.

Savi's Warbler

FAMILY Sylviidae
SPECIES *Locustella luscinioides*
LENGTH 14 cm (5½ in)
HABITAT Reedbeds
CLUTCH SIZE 4–5

DISTRIBUTION A summer visitor from sub-Saharan Africa to a wide area of Europe where suitable habitats exist. Very localized in southern England, and absent from Scandinavia.

SAVI'S WARBLER IS VERY SIMILAR in appearance to the Reed Warbler (*see* p 287), but differs in being slightly larger and having pale tips to the undertail coverts and a pale edge to the wing. The reeling, insect-like song is quite distinctive and usually delivered from a high perch in a reedbed.

REED NEST The cup-shaped nest of the Savi's Warbler is concealed in the base of the reedbed, just above the water level.

Grasshopper Warbler

FAMILY Sylviidae
SPECIES *Locustella naevia*
LENGTH 13 cm (5 in)
HABITAT Dense grassland
CLUTCH SIZE 6

DISTRIBUTION A summer visitor from Africa to western and central Europe, southern Scandinavia, and Russia, and a common passage migrant in southern Europe and Turkey.

SECRETIVE HABITS and olive-brown, streaked plumage make the Grasshopper Warbler a very difficult bird to see in its tussocky grassland habitat. It rarely emerges above the vegetation, moving around low down. The high-pitched reeling call is heard at dusk and through the night, and as the bird turns its head, it changes in volume and direction. Although similar to the Sedge Warbler (*see* p 287), it lacks the bold head markings.

MOUSE-LIKE The well-camouflaged Grasshopper Warbler is at home in dense vegetation, preferring to move around in a mouse-like manner, close to the ground.

Zitting Cisticola

FAMILY Sylviidae
SPECIES *Cisticola juncidis*
LENGTH 10 cm (4 in)
HABITAT Marshland/grassland
CLUTCH SIZE 4–6

DISTRIBUTION A common resident over southern Europe, mainly in coastal regions, but more widespread in Iberia, the Mediterranean and North Africa.,

THE ZITTING CISTICOLA'S name is derived from its song, which is an endlessly repeated 'dzip dzip dzip' that is uttered during its yo-yo-like song flight, making this a very easy bird to locate and identify. Its former name of Fan-tailed Warbler comes from the fanned-out appearance of the short tail just before landing. The plumage is mostly brown above with darker streaks, and plain buff below, and the tail is tipped with white spots.

FANNED TAIL The Zitting Cisticola's short, rounded tail is fanned out in flight, revealing dark and white-tipped tail feathers. It will often perch in the open, avoiding dense tree cover.

Cetti's Warbler

FAMILY Sylviidae
SPECIES *Cettia cetti*
LENGTH 14 cm (5½ in)
HABITAT Reeds/bushes
CLUTCH SIZE 4

DISTRIBUTION A widespread resident across much of western and southern Europe, Turkey, and North Africa, and a summer visitor further east.

AN EXPLOSIVE BURST of bubbling calls from bushes adjacent to a reedbed signal the presence of the otherwise secretive and skulking Cetti's Warbler; sometimes rendered as 'chuppi chuppi chuppi…', the call is unmistakeable and is sometimes started off by the close presence of observers. If the bird is glimpsed, it appears mostly brown above with a longish tail, usually cocked up, and short rounded wings. It spends much of its time low down and often feeds on the ground.

TAIL UP A Cetti's Warbler offers a rare view as it perches in the open, its tail raised in the posture of an alert bird.

Graceful Prinia

FAMILY Sylviidae
SPECIES *Prinia gracilis*
LENGTH 10 cm (4 in)
HABITAT Shrubland
CLUTCH SIZE 5–6

DISTRIBUTION Resident in southern Turkey and the Middle East, often in coastal regions, in areas of dense undergrowth in both arid and wet habitats.

THE GRACEFUL PRINIA IS one of the smallest warblers, with a compact body and a proportionately long, graduated tail. The tail has banded markings on the underside and is tipped black and white; it is often held erect and is sometimes twitched from side to side. The plumage is mostly grey-brown above and pale below, and the head has darker streaks. In summer the bill is black, but in winter the lower mandible becomes paler. The song is a long series of hoarse 'zer-wit' notes followed by a metallic-sounding trill, and there are also several sharp alarm notes. Occasionally males will perform a display flight around their territories, producing curious triple wing-snapping sounds as they fly around. Graceful Prinias often move around in small noisy groups but rarely stay in one place for long, constantly searching for food. The nests are built close to the ground in thick cover.

LONG TAIL The tiny Graceful Prinia has a tail more the half the total length of the bird. The plumage often has a rather scruffy, fluffed-up appearance.

Booted Warbler

FAMILY Sylviidae
SPECIES *Hippolais caligata*
LENGTH 11 cm (4½ in)
HABITAT Bushy areas
CLUTCH SIZE 5–6

DISTRIBUTION A summer visitor from India to Russia, Kazakhstan, the Caspian Sea, and the Middle East, sometimes wandering further west.

RARE CAPTIVE A very rare visitor to western Europe, this warbler may sometimes be caught in mist nets, when it is studied more closely.

SIMILAR IN APPEARANCE to a small leaf warbler (*see* pp 295–99), the Booted Warbler is a small and fairly compact warbler with plain grey-brown plumage above and pale buff colours below. The legs are a dark pink with contrasting darker toes. This is a very difficult bird to observe in the field, as its preferred habitat is dense and shrubby. An alarm call, sounding like stones knocking together, may be heard.

Icterine Warbler

FAMILY Sylviidae
SPECIES *Hippolais icterina*
LENGTH 13 cm (5¼ in)
HABITAT Forest margins
CLUTCH SIZE 4–5

DISTRIBUTION A summer visitor from tropical Africa to eastern and northern Europe; a passage migrant in southern Europe. A few stray to Britain.

RESEMBLING A RATHER bulky leaf warbler, the Icterine Warbler has grey-green upperparts, a yellow underside, a pinkish bill, and blue-grey legs. In profile, it has a slightly peaked crown. It keeps to the high treetops, making it a very difficult bird to see, but the typical tri-syllabic 'di-der-oid' call is a good clue to its presence. The song is a very complex torrent of musical and discordant notes with much mimicry of other species.

IDENTIFIABLE The large bill, blue-grey legs, and a peaked crown are key features of the Icterine Warbler.

Upcher's Warbler

FAMILY Sylviidae
SPECIES *Hippolais languida*
LENGTH 14 cm (5½ in)
HABITAT Scrubland/gardens
CLUTCH SIZE 4–5

DISTRIBUTION A summer visitor from East Africa to Israel, Syria, the Caspian Sea region, and the Middle East in areas below 2,000 m (6,500 ft).

THIS IS A MOSTLY grey warbler with pale buff underparts. The wings have slightly darker primaries, and the tail is darker than the mantle. Upcher's Warbler has a habit of gliding on outstretched wings just before alighting, and when perched it often sways its tail from side to side and fans it out slightly. The slightly smaller Olivaceous Warbler (*see* p 294) is very similar.

STOUT BILL The bill of the Upcher's Warbler is quite stout and has a pale lower mandible. There is also a thin, pale eye stripe.

Olive-tree Warbler

FAMILY Sylviidae
SPECIES *Hippolais olivetorum*
LENGTH 15 cm (6 in)
HABITAT Open woodland
CLUTCH SIZE 4

DISTRIBUTION A summer visitor from tropical Africa to the eastern Mediterranean, including the Balkans, Turkey, and Israel, and larger islands.

DESPITE ITS LARGE SIZE, the Olive-tree Warbler is a very tricky bird to see in its thorn-scrub and woodland habitats, usually spending its time in dense cover. The plumage is grey above and pale greyish-white below with some darker streaking, and there is the impression of a pale wing panel and a white supercilium. The legs are dark and rather thick. It makes harsh alarm notes and has a coarse song of 'chak chi chi chak chuk' calls.

LARGE BIRD This is one of the largest warblers with relatively long wings; immature birds have browner plumage.

Olivaceous Warbler

FAMILY Sylviidae
SPECIES *Hippolais pallida*
LENGTH 13 cm (5¼ in)
HABITAT Bushy areas
CLUTCH SIZE 3–4

DISTRIBUTION A widespread summer visitor from sub-Saharan Africa to Iberia, the eastern Mediterranean, Turkey, the Middle East, and North Africa.

PLAIN GREY plumage and rather secretive habits lead to the Olivaceous Warbler being overlooked in its favourite dense, bushy habitats, which may include gardens and cultivated land. Its monotonous calls, resembling a hoarse Melodious Warbler, can be heard coming from dense cover, as can the harsh 'tak tak' alarm notes; the tail is repeatedly dipped downwards, especially when the bird is giving the alarm call. The upperparts are grey with an olive tinge, but this only shows in good light, and birds from the west of the range in Iberia are rather browner above. The bill is long and relatively broad for a warbler.

PLAIN PLUMAGE Pale outer edges to the tail feathers, pale-tipped secondary wing feathers, and a pale supercilium are the only distinctive features on the upperparts of this bird.

Melodious Warbler

FAMILY Sylviidae
SPECIES *Hippolais polyglotta*
LENGTH 13 cm (5 in)
HABITAT Woodland/scrubland
CLUTCH SIZE 3–5

DISTRIBUTION A summer visitor to southwest Europe and North Africa, occasionally straying further and reaching Britain. Most birds spend the winter in West Africa.

THIS IS A FAIRLY PLUMP warbler with yellowish-brown underparts and grey-green, plain upperparts with no conspicuous wing bars or eye stripes, although when seen at close range there is a hint of a yellow supercilium. The bill is relatively large for a warbler. The legs are dark brown, differing from the almost black legs of the Icterine Warbler (*see* p 292). The common name is apt, for the Melodious Warbler has a liquid, musical song with snatches of other bird songs interspersed with its chirping call notes.

DIFFERENT SONG The Melodious Warbler appears rather short-winged by comparison with the similar Icterine Warbler, but the best distinction is the difference in their songs.

Bonelli's Warbler

FAMILY Sylviidae
SPECIES *Phylloscopus bonelli*
LENGTH 11 cm (4½ in)
HABITAT Upland woodland
CLUTCH SIZE 4–6

DISTRIBUTION A widespread summer visitor to southern Europe, the Balkans, Turkey, and North Africa, returning to tropical Africa in winter.

SMALL AND RATHER PALE, this leaf warbler has a yellowish rump, yellow patches on the wings, and white underparts. Birds from eastern parts of the range have a greyer tinge to the plumage and a monosyllabic 'chipp' call, whereas in western Europe they tend to be slightly browner on the mantle and make a disyllabic 'hu-if' call.

INSECT MEAL A Bonelli's Warbler brings food to its chicks in their nest, which is concealed in a hollow on the ground.

Arctic Warbler

FAMILY Sylviidae
SPECIES *Phylloscopus borealis*
LENGTH 12 cm (4¾ in)
HABITAT Forest/scrubland
CLUTCH SIZE 5–6

DISTRIBUTION A summer visitor to birch forests in Siberia and parts of northern Russia, occasionally in northern Scandinavia. Most birds spend winter in southeast Asia.

A BOLD SUPERCILIUM and dark stripe through the eye plus mottled ear coverts make the Arctic Warbler stand out from the rather similar, but more streamlined Willow Warbler (*see* p 299). It also has a rather monotonous stuttering song, unlike the more tuneful song of the Willow Warbler. The ranges of these species may overlap in the far north, but the Arctic Warbler is usually a very late arrival on the breeding grounds.

PALE COLOURING The Arctic Warbler has overall greenish-grey colouring, dusky flanks, and a hint of a wing bar; some birds show a second faint wing bar.

Chiffchaff

FAMILY Sylviidae

SPECIES *Phylloscopus collybita*

LENGTH 11 cm (4¼ in)

HABITAT Woodland/scrubland

CLUTCH SIZE 4–9

DISTRIBUTION A common and widespread summer visitor to Europe, absent only from the far north. Many overwinter in southwest Europe, but large numbers migrate to Africa.

ONE OF THE FIRST signs of spring in much of Europe is the incessant 'chiff chaff' or 'zip zap' calls, interspersed with some harsher notes and sharp whistles, which emanate from scrub patches and woodland edges in fine weather. The Chiffchaff looks very similar to the Willow Warbler (*see* p 299); the best distinction between them is their quite different song. At close range, the Chiffchaff is seen to have dark legs and rather greyer tones than the Willow Warbler, but young

Chiffchaffs can have yellowish tints in the plumage. Chiffchaffs occur across a wide area of Europe, and different races, with slightly varying colours and different calls, have been identified.

HIDDEN HOME Chiffchaffs conceal their nests close to the ground in thick vegetation, and in good years often manage to raise two broods of young.

Caucasian Chiffchaff

FAMILY Sylviidae

SPECIES *Phylloscopus lorenzii*

LENGTH 11 cm (4¼ in)

HABITAT Mountain slopes

CLUTCH SIZE 4–6

DISTRIBUTION A summer visitor to willow scrub or spruce forests on the slopes of mountains in the Caucasus, usually at an altitude of 1,700–2,500 m (5,500–8,200 ft).

THE CAUCASIAN CHIFFCHAFF is similar in many respects to the other chiffchaffs, and is sometimes considered to be only a distinctive race, geographically isolated high in the Caucasus mountains, rather than a separate species. The plumage colourings are very similar to that of the more eastern races, but lack any green or yellow tones, so the first impression is of a greyish-brown bird with an off-white underside. There is a buff-coloured supercilium contrasting with the brownish head. The legs are very dark, as with all races of chiffchaff. The song is very similar to the Chiffchaff's familiar disyllabic 'chiff chaff' but is slightly shorter in duration and a little harsher. Pairs of birds will also make a rather mournful sounding contact note from deep cover. Chiffchaffs are usually early arrivals on their breeding territories.

MOUNTAIN DWELLER The Caucasian Chiffchaff is very similar to the more widespread species but lives at higher altitudes in the mountains.

Green Warbler

FAMILY Sylviidae

SPECIES *Phylloscopus nitidus*

LENGTH 11 cm (4¼ in)

HABITAT Mountain woodland

CLUTCH SIZE 4–6

DISTRIBUTION A summer visitor from southern India to mountain slopes in northeast Turkey, the Caucasus, and Iran.

THIS APTLY NAMED leaf warbler has bright green upperparts and clear yellow underparts. There is also a bold sulphur-yellow eye stripe and yellow wing bar, which show up well in the dappled light of a woodland. The song is similar to the descending scale of the Willow Warbler (*see* p 299), but with slightly harsher Wren-like notes, and there is also a penetrating 'chee-wee' call, often heard as the birds forage. The habits and song are similar to the Greenish Warbler (*see* p 298), which lives in a different area and may be a different species.

SIMILAR BUT DIFFERENT The Green Warbler is very similar to the Greenish Warbler, but its plumage shows much more green coloration.

Wood Warbler

FAMILY Sylviidae

SPECIES *Phylloscopus sibilatrix*

LENGTH 13 cm (5 in)

HABITAT Beech woodland

CLUTCH SIZE 6–7

DISTRIBUTION A common summer visitor over western and central Europe, but absent from Iberia and the far north of Scandinavia.

WOOD WARBLERS often nest in lofty beech woods with sparse ground vegetation, and can be observed hunting insects in the canopy; they look very white below, and compared with the Willow Warbler are plumper and shorter-tailed. The upperparts are greenish and the throat and eye stripe are bright lemon-yellow. During breeding, the accelerating trilling call, likened to a coin spinning on a plate, is heard; there is also a plaintive call.

GROUND NESTER Wood Warblers often feed high up in the canopy of beech trees, but they always nest close to the ground, usually building a domed nest in the undergrowth.

Greenish Warbler

FAMILY Sylviidae

SPECIES *Phylloscopus trochiloides*

LENGTH 11 cm (4¼ in)

HABITAT Open woodland

CLUTCH SIZE 4–6

DISTRIBUTION A summer visitor from India to mixed woodlands in northeastern Europe and Russia, arriving late May and leaving early autumn.

THIS IS NOT by any means the greenest of the leaf warblers, but the plumage of its upperparts does have a distinct green tinge in certain lights. Superficially similar to the slightly larger Willow Warbler, the Greenish Warbler has a more pronounced eye stripe, and an off-white wing bar; there is sometimes a hint of a second wing bar. It is quite an active bird, constantly moving through vegetation in short hops and rapid flights. Its song is similar to the Wren's (*see* p 253) and it is also makes a sharp disyllabic call.

TRAVELLER The Greenish Warbler is a long-distance migrant from India, occasionally straying into Britain in the late summer.

Willow Warbler

FAMILY Sylviidae

SPECIES *Phylloscopus trochilus*

LENGTH 11 cm (4¼ in)

HABITAT Woodland/scrubland

CLUTCH SIZE 6–7

DISTRIBUTION A very common and widespread summer visitor to northern Europe, Scandinavia, and Russia; a passage migrant and winter visitor in southern and western areas.

A VERY COMMON leaf warbler in northern Europe, the Willow Warbler is often seen during the summer in woodland and shrubby areas foraging actively among the leaves for insects, and occasionally making little forays into the open to chase a larger flying insect. It is very similar in appearance to the Chiffchaff (*see* p 296), although a fraction longer, overlapping in range and habitat in many areas. However, the Willow Warbler can be distinguished immediately by its pleasant, liquid song, and if observed in good light, by its paler legs. Birds from the north of the range have greyer plumage than those breeding further south. In autumn, young birds have richer, more yellow tones on the underside and browner upperparts. The Willow Warbler is one of the most common birds in northern Europe, with a population numbering many millions, but it is largely overlooked in many of its habitats.

SPRING SONG The Willow Warbler sings its descending scale of slightly melancholy notes, a welcome sign of spring in many northern areas of Europe.

WILLOW WARBLER FAMILY A Willow Warbler feeds its chicks in their well-concealed nest. Its plain plumage provides excellent camouflage as it moves quietly around in the dappled light of woodland areas.

Firecrest

FAMILY Sylviidae
SPECIES *Regulus ignicapillus*
LENGTH 9 cm (3½ in)
HABITAT Woodland
CLUTCH SIZE 7–11

DISTRIBUTION Resident in southern and western Europe, and a summer visitor to central and northern Europe. A rare breeder and passage migrant in southern Britain.

EUROPE'S SMALLEST BIRD, along with the Goldcrest, is a tiny, restless warbler with a narrow pointed bill. The most obvious features are the black and white eye stripes and black-bordered crest, yellow in females, orange in males. Thin, high-pitched 'peep' calls are run together into a short, barely audible song.

CUP NEST Firecrests often nest in conifers, making a tiny cup of lichens, mosses, and cobwebs, which is often suspended from slender twigs.

Goldcrest

FAMILY Sylviidae
SPECIES *Regulus regulus*
LENGTH 9 cm (3½ in)
HABITAT Woodland
CLUTCH SIZE 7–10

DISTRIBUTION A common and widespread resident across western and northern Europe; some birds migrate south in winter and there are occasional influxes westwards into Britain.

SHRILL 'SEE SEE SEE' calls and a longer high-pitched song are the clues to the presence of this diminutive warbler, which often feeds high in the canopy in mixed woodlands. If they do move to lower levels, Goldcrests seem indifferent to the presence of humans. During the breeding season they are often found in conifer woods, but in winter they may join mixed flocks of tits in deciduous woods.

BRIGHT CREST The male's crest has bright orange feather bases, but it may look yellow, like the female's, when the feathers are not raised.

Spotted Flycatcher

FAMILY Muscicapidae
SPECIES *Muscicapa striata*
LENGTH 14 cm (5½ in)
HABITAT Gardens/glades
CLUTCH SIZE 4–5

DISTRIBUTION A summer visitor from Africa to Europe, Scandinavia, North Africa, and the Middle East, and absent only from the extreme north.

ALTHOUGH THERE are few distinguishing features on its grey-brown plumage, the Spotted Flycatcher has a very distinctive way of catching its food: short flights from an exposed perch in pursuit of insects and occasional bouts of hovering draw attention to this otherwise quiet bird. Nests are often located on ledges on buildings or in ivy-covered trees.

PERCH Spotted Flycatchers often sit on a prominent perch to watch out for passing insects and to deliver their short, scratchy songs.

Collared Flycatcher

FAMILY Muscicapidae
SPECIES *Ficedula albicollis*
LENGTH 13 cm (5 in)
HABITAT Woodland/parkland
CLUTCH SIZE 6–7

DISTRIBUTION A summer visitor from Africa to eastern Europe and Russia, sometimes overlapping in range with the Pied Flycatcher (*see* p 304).

THE MALE Collared Flycatcher is a boldly marked black-and-white bird with a distinct broad white collar and white forehead patch. The rump is pale grey. Females are mostly grey above with black-and-white wings and a very indistinct white collar. Males usually sit on a high perch to deliver their soft song.

NATURAL HOME Although they naturally use tree holes for their nests, Collared Flycatchers take to nest boxes when they are provided.

European Pied Flycatcher

FAMILY Muscicapidae
SPECIES *Ficedula hypoleuca*
LENGTH 13 cm (5 in)
HABITAT Woodland
CLUTCH SIZE 4–7

DISTRIBUTION A summer visitor from West Africa especially to mature oak woods and parks over a wide area of western and northern Europe and Scandinavia.

THIS IS THE ONLY small black-and-white bird that has the regular habit of catching insects in flight. Arriving in late spring from Africa, male Pied Flycatchers quickly establish a territory, choosing a prominent song perch to display from, while the females build a nest in a natural tree hole or nest box. Both parents contribute to the feeding of the young, and after the breeding season they become rather furtive while they moult. In winter, and on autumn migration, the sexes are difficult to distinguish as they both have much greyer plumage. The song has been rendered phonetically as 'tree tree tree, once more I come to thee'.

WAITING FOR FOOD An alert male Pied Flycatcher looks for insects from its regular perch; it is often seen to cock its tail while waiting for prey.

Red-breasted Flycatcher

FAMILY Muscicapidae
SPECIES *Ficedula parva*
LENGTH 11 cm (4½ in)
HABITAT Woodland
CLUTCH SIZE 5–6

DISTRIBUTION A summer visitor from western Asia to mature forests in eastern Europe, with occasional stray birds turning up as far west as Britain, usually in autumn.

SOFT SONG The song of the Red-breasted Flycatcher is usually delivered from an open perch, but it is quiet and often confused with the songs of other woodland birds.

THIS IS A SMALL but lively flycatcher with the habit of flicking its tail, sometimes revealing its black-and-white wheatear-like tail pattern. Male Red-breasted Flycatchers may at a glance be confused with larger Robins (*see* p 256), having a grey head and orange-red bib, although this feature is not fully developed in young birds. Females and juveniles are much plainer with brown upperparts and a pale buff-yellow underside. In the breeding season, the Red-breasted Flycatcher can be a difficult bird to observe as it spends much of its time high in the canopy, constantly on the move in search of insects. The nests are often built lower down the tree under a piece of peeling bark or in a crevice; the female does most of the building, and while she is incubating the eggs, the male brings her food.

Semi-collared Flycatcher

FAMILY Muscicapidae
SPECIES *Ficedula semitorquata*
LENGTH 13 cm (5 in)
HABITAT Mountain woodland
CLUTCH SIZE 5–6

DISTRIBUTION A summer visitor from Africa to mixed woodland in the Balkans, Turkey, the Caucasus, and Asia Minor.

THIS BIRD IS intermediate in appearance between the Pied and Collared Flycatchers. The male has a partial white collar on the neck, a small white patch on the forehead, and a second smaller white wing bar. Females are very difficult to distinguish from females of the other species, but do show a second indistinct white wing bar. The calls and song are most similar to those of the Collared Flycatcher. These species have separate breeding ranges; it is only on migration that they may be seen together, allowing a comparison of the plumages.

NECK RING The partial white neck ring is a variable feature and not always easy to differentiate when viewed from certain angles.

Coal Tit

FAMILY Paridae
SPECIES *Periparus ater*
LENGTH 11 cm (4½ in)
HABITAT Conifer woodland
CLUTCH SIZE 7–9

DISTRIBUTION Widespread over most of Europe; absent from Iceland and the far north of Scandinavia and Siberia. Some migrate south in winter.

VARIED DIET The Coal Tit is frequently found in conifer woods where it feeds on seeds, insects, and spiders, often searching energetically in the treetops and outermost branches.

THE COAL TIT is the smallest member of this family and, apart from its small size, is easily recognized by its black cap, white cheeks, and white nape patch. The rest of the plumage is mainly olive-grey with buff tones, especially in birds from Britain and Iberia, although this varies with birds from different parts of Europe, with some races being quite dark. The sexes are very similar, and juveniles resemble adults. In the breeding, season males make a high-pitched slightly grating call and a thin 'ticha ticha' call. Sometimes, when calling at another bird or mobbing an owl, a tiny crest can be raised on the head. At other times, when they join mixed flocks of other tits to forage more widely, they make thin 'tsee' calls. In some years, northern birds are forced to migrate when the spruce seeds fail.

Blue Tit

FAMILY Paridae
SPECIES *Cyanistes caeruleus*
LENGTH 11 cm (4½ in)
HABITAT Woodland/parkland
CLUTCH SIZE 7–12

DISTRIBUTION Common and widely distributed across Europe apart from Iceland and the far north of Scandinavia, Russia, and Siberia.

A FAMILIAR VISITOR to garden bird feeders, the Blue Tit is the only small bird to have a combination of blue and yellow plumage; when seen closely the blue cap is especially distinctive. There is some variation in the colourings in different areas of Europe, with some races being much darker. Although primarily woodland birds, Blue Tits forage with great agility in many other habitats, especially gardens, taking a variety of insect and plant food. Nests are built in natural tree holes, but these small birds readily take to nest boxes.

GOING SOUTH Blue Tits may migrate in great numbers to escape harsh northern winters and seek food in more sheltered areas.

Siberian Tit

FAMILY Paridae
SPECIES *Poecile cinctus*
LENGTH 13 cm (5¼ in)
HABITAT Conifer forest
CLUTCH SIZE 6–10

DISTRIBUTION Resident in birch and conifer forests in northern Scandinavia, Russia, and Siberia. Harsh winters may lead to a migration south in some years.

THIS IS A LARGE and rather plain-plumaged member of the tit family with a grey-brown cap, white cheeks and neck, and a black bib. The flanks have a rusty-brown tinge and the plumage always looks warmer and more fluffed up than that of the similar but smaller and greyer Willow Tit (*see* p 312), which may also occur in the same northern conifer forests. The calls are very similar to those of the Willow Tit with nasal 'tstee tstee – tah tah tah' sounds, and in the breeding season, males sing a series of slightly chirping 'chi-urr' notes. Females excavate a nest hole in rotten wood or use an abandoned woodpecker hole.

TWIGGY PERCH The Siberian Tit is often observed searching for food on lichen-covered twigs in mature conifer forests.

GROUP OF TITS ON GARDEN FEEDER A Long-tailed Tit (*see* p 314) prepares to alight on a garden feeder. Peanuts are popular with many members of the tit family in winter, and they find it easy to land on and cling to such feeders.

Crested Tit

FAMILY Paridae

SPECIES *Lophophanes cristatus*

LENGTH 11 cm (4½ in)

HABITAT Conifer woodland

CLUTCH SIZE 4–8

DISTRIBUTION Widespread in coniferous forests across most of Europe, but absent from the extreme north, and in Britain confined to Caledonian pine forests of Scotland.

THE SOFT TRILLING call of the Crested Tit is quite distinctive and is often the best clue to the presence of this small bird as it moves acrobatically through the upper branches of pines and spruces searching for insects, spiders, and seeds. Once spotted, the crest is unmistakeable, but the rest of the plumage is a rather drab grey. Although a largely sedentary species, harsh weather will sometimes drive Crested Tits out of the coniferous forests to feed in other areas. When food is plentiful, seeds are stored in bark crevices and then relocated in the winter. Female Crested Tits excavate a nesting hole in a rotten tree stump, lining it with moss, cobwebs, and strands of hair.

DISTINCTIVE HEAD No other small bird has a prominent crest as obvious as that of the Crested Tit, making it an easily identified member of this family.

Azure Tit

FAMILY Paridae
SPECIES *Cyanistes cyanus*
LENGTH 13 cm (5¼ in)
HABITAT Birch woodland/
scrubland
CLUTCH SIZE 9–11

DISTRIBUTION A common resident on the plains of Russia, very rarely occurring further to the west.

LOOKING RATHER like a washed-out version of the slightly smaller Blue Tit (*see* p 306), this species replaces it in Asia, its range extending no further west than Russia as a breeding species. Most of the plumage is white, but the long tail, wings, and nape are dark blue-grey and the upper mantle is pale blue-grey. The tail has a white tip and there is also a broad white wing bar. The plumage has a rather fluffy appearance, especially in winter. The calls and feeding habits are very similar to those of the Blue Tit, but there is unlikely to be any confusion because of the size and colour differences. Nests are built in natural tree holes, and when the young emerge both parents help look after them and they remain as a family group for some time.

MAINLY WHITE The Azure Tit has very distinctive white plumage, but occasionally hybrids between this species and the Blue Tit occur, giving rise to pale young with blue heads.

Sombre Tit

FAMILY Paridae
SPECIES *Poecile lugubris*
LENGTH 14 cm (5½ in)
HABITAT Rocky country
CLUTCH SIZE 5–7

DISTRIBUTION Resident in wooded and rocky areas in southeast Europe, particularly in the Balkans, some of the eastern Mediterranean islands, Turkey, and the Middle East.

THIS LARGE MEMBER of the tit family has rather drab greyish-brown plumage and fairly quiet habits, so it is often overlooked. At a glance, the plumage resembles that of the Marsh and Willow Tits (*see* pp 313 and 312), but apart from the larger size, the bib is also much larger and the cheeks are whiter. The calls are very similar to those of the Great Tit (*see* p 312) and a single 'chrrr' call is also uttered quite frequently. Nests are built in holes in trees or stone walls. In winter, Sombre Tits may join mixed flocks of other tit species.

WEDGE The conspicuous white cheek of the Sombre Tit forms a characteristic wedge shape, contrasting with the dark head and bib.

Great Tit

FAMILY Paridae
SPECIES *Parus major*
LENGTH 14 cm (5½ in)
HABITAT Woodland/gardens
CLUTCH SIZE 8–13

DISTRIBUTION A common and widespread resident across Europe, absent only from Iceland and the extreme north of Scandinavia and Russia.

ONE OF THE COMMONEST and most familiar of all birds to be found in woodlands and gardens, the Great Tit is adept at feeding on bird feeders and is a regular user of nesting boxes. The black-and-white head and broad central band on the yellow underparts create a striking pattern. The sexes are similar, but males have brighter colours and bolder markings. Calls range from a sharp 'pink' to the spring song, rendered as a grating 'teacher teacher', although there are many other sounds in the repertoire. Harsh winters drive birds from northern Europe further west.

EARLY SONG The male Great Tit is one of the first birds to start singing in the springtime, and quickly establishes a territory near a suitable nest site.

Willow Tit

FAMILY Paridae
SPECIES *Poecile montana*
LENGTH 11 cm (4½)
HABITAT Woodland
CLUTCH SIZE 6–9

DISTRIBUTION A widespread, but scattered resident across western and northern Europe; absent from Iberia, the extreme north of Scandinavia, and Russia.

SHOWING NO preference for willows, the Willow Tit can be found in a range of woodland habitats, especially in wetter areas, and where there are rotten stumps in which it can excavate its nest holes. Best identified by its nasal 'chay chay chay' calls, it is confusingly similar to the Marsh Tit. If seen in good light, however, the dark crown appears sooty, rather than glossy, and the bib is larger. Willow Tits are rather timid, and do not visit bird tables in winter.

DISTINGUISHABLE Pale wing panels and a larger head and neck separate the Willow Tit from the similar Marsh Tit.

Marsh Tit

FAMILY Paridae
SPECIES *Poecile palustris*
LENGTH 11 cm (4½ in)
HABITAT Mixed woodland
CLUTCH SIZE 6–9

DISTRIBUTION A widespread, and sometimes common, resident in western Europe and southern Scandinavia, but absent from Ireland and Iberia.

A WOODLAND rather than a marshland resident, the Marsh Tit can be found in a range of woodland habitats, although there does seem to be a preference for damper areas of broad-leaved woodlands with plenty of old trees and rotten wood. Where the range overlaps with the almost identical Willow Tit, Marsh Tits dominate and outcompete them for nest sites and food. Marsh Tits will use nesting boxes and visit gardens in winter, often mingling with other tit species. Despite their small size, they appear to be quite fearless. A good distinction from the Willow Tit is the glossy, rather than sooty, black crown, and the smaller, more sharply defined black bib, but these features are often difficult to see clearly in a woodland habitat when the birds are constantly on the move. The

calls and songs are very distinctive and are usually the best way to separate the species. Marsh Tits regularly make a loud 'pitchou' call and a repetitive, whistling 'chiu chiu chiu'; the song is very similar and is a series of repeated 'chip chip chip' notes, although it tends to get lost among the louder calls of other woodland birds. The sexes are identical, and juveniles resemble adults, but there are slight differences in plumage in birds from the northern part of the range, which appear slightly browner above.

BIB AND CROWN The Marsh Tit's neat black bib and glossy crown are useful identification features.

Long-tailed Tit

FAMILY Aegithalidae

SPECIES *Aegithalos caudatus*

LENGTH 14 cm (5½ in)

HABITAT Woodland

CLUTCH SIZE 8–12

DISTRIBUTION A widespread resident across most of Europe apart from Iceland, northern Scandinavia, and Russia, and some Mediterranean islands.

THIS IS AN UNMISTAKEABLE small bird with a tail longer than the rest of the body. Looking like tiny balls of feathers, small flocks of Long-tailed Tits are often spotted in swooping flight as they move in line from tree to tree. They show remarkable agility when feeding in trees and often visit garden feeding stations in winter. Most birds are a combination of pink, white, and black plumage, but the Scandinavian race has an all-white head and southern races have darker pink streaking on the underside. The sexes are very similar, but juveniles lack the pink tones. Both sexes co-operate to build elaborate domed nests of mosses, lichens, and feathers, bound together by cobwebs. Small flocks moving through the trees chatter to each other with quiet, rattling 'tsirrup' calls, and sharper 'sri-sri-sri' sounds; there is also a very quiet and rarely heard trilling song.

SHORT BILL The Long-tailed Tit has a very short bill, used for feeding on insects and tiny seeds.

Bearded Reedling

FAMILY Timaliidae
SPECIES *Panurus biarmicus*
LENGTH 17 cm (6½ in)
HABITAT Reedbeds
CLUTCH SIZE 5–7

DISTRIBUTION A resident in scattered areas of suitable habitat across Europe, and a winter visitor to parts of Britain and southern Scandinavia.

REEDBEDS OFFER perfect cover for the Bearded Reedling, which rarely emerges into the open apart from making rapid flights across wide channels. The overall colouring, blending perfectly with dead reed stems, is warm buff-brown with paler colours below, but males have grey heads and broad black moustache-like stripes on the sides of the head. Small feeding flocks call to each other with metallic 'ping' calls and they may sometimes be seen holding onto swaying reed stems. Nests of shredded leaves are skilfully woven between stems, and in some years three broods are raised. Occasionally a large flock will gather and fly high above the reeds to another lake in search of a better feeding area.

STEM PERCH The Bearded Reedling is very skilled at holding on to swaying stems where it searches for food such as reed seeds, insects, and spiders.

Penduline Tit

FAMILY Remizidae
SPECIES *Remiz pendulina*
LENGTH 11 cm (4¼ in)
HABITAT Marshland/fenland
CLUTCH SIZE 6–8

DISTRIBUTION Resident in suitable habitats across much of southern Europe but a summer visitor to a much wider area of western and central Europe and apparently spreading westwards.

THE PENDULINE TIT is a small, pale, tit-like bird with a prominent black mask, usually found in marshy areas with willow trees scattered around. The sexes are alike, but the female's mask is smaller, and juveniles have no mask. Both sexes co-operate in building their elaborate, suspended, flask-shaped nest that has an entrance tunnel and is composed mainly of the down from reedmace seedheads. The nest is usually at the end of a twig, hanging over water, and is therefore safe from most predators. Penduline Tits make a variety of thin, whistling, 'tsi-tsi-tsi' calls.

HOME BIRD The Penduline Tit is one of the most skilled of all nest-builders, constructing its distinctive suspended nest over a period of about two weeks.

Nuthatch

FAMILY Sittidae
SPECIES *Sitta europaea*
LENGTH 14 cm (5½ in)
HABITAT Woodland
CLUTCH SIZE 6–9

DISTRIBUTION A widespread resident across most of Europe where suitable wooded habitats occur. Absent from Ireland, Iceland, and northern Scandinavia, and some smaller Mediterranean islands.

THE NUTHATCH is the only small bird likely to be seen climbing in all directions on tree trunks and large branches. The slate-grey upperparts and rusty-buff underside are found in birds in Britain and western Europe, but those from the north and east of the range can be much paler beneath. The long straight bill is used to probe bark for food and is capable of cracking open hazelnut shells. Nesting holes in trees are usually plastered up with mud to reduce their size. Shrill, penetrating 'peeu peeu peeu' calls can be heard all year round.

SPECIALISM Nuthatches wedge seeds in bark crevice in order to hammer them open with their sharp bills.

Kruper's Nuthatch

FAMILY Sittidae
SPECIES *Sitta kruperi*
LENGTH 13 cm (5 in)
HABITAT Coniferous forest
CLUTCH SIZE 5–6

DISTRIBUTION Resident in mature coniferous forests in Turkey and some nearby Mediterranean Islands, and eastwards to the Caucasus.

THIS IS A VERY ACTIVE nuthatch that, when seen from below, has a pale underside with a rusty-red patch on the breast. There is a narrow black eye-stripe with a white supercilium. Kruper's Nuthatches forage at all levels in the trees, searching for food on the bark, amongst the needles and cones high up in the canopy and even sometimes on the ground below. Nests are usually built in an old woodpecker hole and the entrance is not plastered with mud.

PLUMAGE The rusty-red breast patch of Kruper's Nuthatch is clearly visible from below and is present in both males and females.

Rock Nuthatch

FAMILY Sittidae
SPECIES *Sitta neumayer*
LENGTH 14 cm (5½ in)
HABITAT Cliffs/gorges
CLUTCH SIZE 6–10

DISTRIBUTION Resident in rocky areas from Greece and the Balkans, eastwards through Turkey to the Middle East, sometimes reaching altitudes up to 2,500 m (8,200 ft).

THIS LARGE NUTHATCH has pale grey upperparts and a very pale buff underside. The bill and legs are longer in proportion than in the common Nuthatch, and this species is much more likely to be seen hopping on the ground and among rocks than feeding in trees. A very lively bird at times, it is nevertheless quite adept at hiding behind a rock if danger threatens. The nest is a chamber constructed of mud pellets built up on a rock and has a narrow tunnel entrance. The song and alarm calls are composed of loud and clear ringing tones.

EXPERT CLIMBER The Rock Nuthatch is as much at home on rock faces as the other Nuthatches are on tree trunks.

Eastern Rock Nuthatch

FAMILY Sittidae
SPECIES *Sitta tephronota*
LENGTH 15 cm (6 in)
HABITAT Mountains/ravines
CLUTCH SIZE 4–7

DISTRIBUTION Resident in high mountains, rarely descending below 1,000 m (3,280 ft), in eastern Turkey and Middle East, preferring rocky areas with scattered deciduous trees.

THE LARGE SIZE of the Eastern Rock Nuthatch gives it its alternative name of Great Rock Nuthatch, as it is the largest species in this family. Similar in many respects to the smaller Rock Nuthatch, there are a few areas where their ranges overlap, but the larger size and louder calls help to separate them, and this species is usually found at far higher altitudes. Nests are constructed from mud and lined with hair and feathers.

STRIKING All features seem to be larger in the Eastern Rock Nuthatch, especially the head, bill, and bold black eye-stripe.

Corsican Nuthatch

FAMILY Sittidae
SPECIES *Sitta whiteheadi*
LENGTH 12 cm (4¾ in)
HABITAT Pine forest
CLUTCH SIZE 5–6

DISTRIBUTION A scarce resident of pine forests on Corsica, usually above 1,000 m (3,280 ft), but descending to lower altitudes in winter. Endemic to Corsica.

THIS IS A SMALL NUTHATCH with a black crown and broad white supercilium. Females have a grey crown and both sexes have very pale undersides. Recognition should not be a problem here as no other species of nuthatch occurs on Corsica. The total world population of this rare bird may be as few as 2,000 pairs. Nests are usually constructed in holes in old pine trees, and may be as high as 30 m (98 ft) above the ground; the entrance is not plastered. In the breeding season, the quiet, nasal 'dew dew dew dew di di' song may be heard and there are also some harsh alarm calls.

HABITAT Corsican Nuthatches spend most of their time feeding in the forests of Corsican Pines where they seek insects and pine seeds.

Short-toed Treecreeper

FAMILY Certhiidae
SPECIES *Certhia brachydactyla*
LENGTH 13 cm (5 in)
HABITAT Woodland/parkland
CLUTCH SIZE 6–7

DISTRIBUTION A widespread resident in suitable wooded habitats across most of western and central Europe, many Mediterranean Islands, and coastal areas of Turkey and North Africa.

TREECREEPERS look rather like mice as they work their way up a tree trunk, probing crevices in the bark to find small invertebrates. Having reached the top, they fly down to the base of another tree and start again. The Short-toed Treecreeper is a difficult species to separate from the Treecreeper where their ranges overlap, but its song is louder and lower in tone, and the call-notes are more penetrating. The pale flanks are slightly duskier and the bill may be a little longer.

SIMILAR APPEARANCE Short-toed Treecreepers have subtle differences in the wing pattern and coloration from Treecreepers, but these features are very hard to distinguish in the field.

Treecreeper

FAMILY Certhiidae
SPECIES *Certhia familiaris*
LENGTH 13 cm (5 in)
HABITAT Woodland/parkland
CLUTCH SIZE 6

DISTRIBUTION A widespread resident in mixed woodlands and parks in Britain, Ireland, and much of northern and eastern Europe, overlapping with the Short-toed Treecreeper in central Europe.

DISTINGUISHING FEATURES
Clean white flanks and a white supercilium can be detected in the Treecreeper in good light.

THIS IS A VERY SIMILAR SPECIES to the Short-toed Treecreeper, but is the only species to occur in Britain, Ireland, and Scandinavia, where there should be no confusion. Where the species do overlap, the Treecreeper's brighter white flanks, more contrasted plumage, and purer white supercilium may be visible, but with birds in poor light in woodland shade this is very difficult to see. A very high-pitched, thin 'sreeit' call may be heard as birds forage over tree trunks. Nests are usually built behind a flap of bark or in a split branch.

Wallcreeper

FAMILY Tichodromadidae

SPECIES *Trichodroma muraria*

LENGTH 17 cm (6½ in)

HABITAT Precipices/ravines

CLUTCH SIZE 4

DISTRIBUTION A scarce resident of sheer cliffs and ravines in mountainous areas of Europe from the Pyrenees to the Caucasus. Occasionally seen on sea cliffs in western Europe.

THIS DISTINCTIVE small bird of precipitous mountain cliffs and ravines resembles a treecreeper, but with all-grey plumage and red wing patches. Wallcreepers constantly flick their wings as they creep around on the rocks, revealing the red patches and spotted white primaries. The sexes are similar, but males have a black throat in summer. Females build their nests in crevices and incubate the eggs, but the male returns to help feed the young.

HIDDEN ENTRANCE A female Wallcreeper perches on a rock before entering the nest that is concealed in a crevice on a sheer cliff.

Red-backed Shrike

FAMILY Laniidae

SPECIES *Lanius collurio*

LENGTH 17 cm (6¾ in)

HABITAT Open country

CLUTCH SIZE 5–6

DISTRIBUTION A summer visitor to a wide area of Europe and Russia, but now very scarce in the west and usually only seen as a passage migrant in Britain.

ALL SHRIKES have a habit of sitting out in the open on a prominent perch, making them easy to identify. The male Red-backed Shrike has a reddish-brown back, a pale grey head, and a broad 'highwayman's mask' black eye-stripe. Females and juveniles have browner plumage with a scaly look to the undersides. Shrikes prey on large beetles and other insects and will also take small lizards and frogs, which may be seen impaled on thorns in their 'larder' if food is plentiful.

FEEDING Red-backed Shrikes have powerful bills and sharp claws, which they use to help tear up their prey; they may also impale it on thorns to secure it.

Great Grey Shrike

FAMILY Laniidae

SPECIES *Lanius excubitor*

LENGTH 24 cm (9½ ins)

HABITAT Open country

CLUTCH SIZE 5–7

DISTRIBUTION A widespread but thinly scattered resident across most of Europe, spreading north in summer to Scandinavia and Russia. Some birds move south and west in autumn, a small number over-wintering in Britain.

THE LARGEST of the shrikes often sits boldly on top of a thorny bush or on overhead wires, its contrasting black, grey, and white plumage standing out well against the background. Large enough to prey on small birds and voles, the Great Grey Shrike will also take large insects and create a larder of food impaled on thorns.

PLUMAGE Across its wide geographical range there is some variation in the markings of the Great Grey Shrike, but they all show the bold black eye-stripe and white wing patches.

Isabelline Shrike

FAMILY Laniidae
SPECIES *Lanius isabellinus*
LENGTH 18 cm (7 in)
HABITAT Open country
CLUTCH SIZE 4–6

DISTRIBUTION A summer visitor to eastern Siberia and Central Asian steppes, but occasionally strays further west into Europe, usually on autumn migration, and has reached Britain a few times.

IN MANY RESPECTS, this is a very similar species to the Red-backed Shrike (*see* p 320), but its colouring is much plainer with a faded appearance. The male still has the black mask and the tail is rusty-red, but the upperparts are mostly grey-brown. Its habits are the same as those of other shrikes, with the birds spending much time perched in the open looking for insect prey.

IDENTIFICATION Female and immature Isabelline Shrikes have a scaly appearance on the underside and a dark brown eye-stripe, and are very similar to young Red-backed Shrikes.

Lesser Grey Shrike

FAMILY Laniidae
SPECIES *Lanius minor*
LENGTH 20 cm (8 in)
HABITAT Open country
CLUTCH SIZE 5–6

DISTRIBUTION A summer visitor to sunny lowland areas of southern and eastern Europe, Turkey, and the Middle East; heads south and east in winter.

IN SOME WAYS, this is a very similar bird to the larger Great Grey Shrike (*see* p 321), but with relatively long wings and a shorter tail. The black mask extends across the face to give a bold black forehead, and the underside of the male in the breeding season is flushed with pink. Lesser Grey Shrikes prefer warmer, drier lowland areas and so are more likely to be seen in the Mediterranean region in summer.

STANCE This bird often adopts a very upright posture when perched. Its head and bill look large in comparison with those of the Great Grey Shrike.

Masked Shrike

FAMILY Laniidae
SPECIES *Lanius nubicus*
LENGTH 17 cm (6¾ in)
HABITAT Open woodland
CLUTCH SIZE 4–6

DISTRIBUTION A scarce summer visitor to the eastern Mediterranean region, usually arriving later than other migrants and leaving for Africa by the end of August.

THE MASKED SHRIKE is the most shy and retiring of the shrike family, spending more time concealed in bushes than sitting out in the open. Its favourite habitat is woodland glades and dense thorny scrub, although it is sometimes seen perched on wires in the open. The adult's black-and-white upperparts, a white forehead, deep orange flanks, and white underparts are distinctive; the juveniles are pale brown above and white below with light brown worm-like patterns. The song is usually given from deep cover and is similar to the Reed Warbler's stuttering medley. Harsh scolding calls are also heard, usually when birds have just taken off. Their favourite food is large insects, especially dung beetles.

DISTINCTIVE BEHAVIOUR The Masked Shrike usually sits partly concealed in a bush, rather than out in the open like other shrikes. Females have paler orange flanks than males.

Woodchat Shrike

FAMILY Laniidae
SPECIES *Lanius senator*
LENGTH 17 cm (6¾ in)
HABITAT Maquis/gardens
CLUTCH SIZE 5–6

DISTRIBUTION A summer visitor from Africa to dry, sunny areas of southwest Europe, North Africa, Turkey, and the Mediterranean area, occasionally wandering further north.

THE WOODCHAT SHRIKE prefers cultivated areas and especially orchards, and can often be seen sitting in a fig tree watching for insects below. The rich chestnut crown is unmistakeable and the black-and-white pattern seen in flight differs from the Masked Shrike in having a prominent white rump and broad tail. The Woodchat has the most melodious song of all the shrikes, but it produces harsh, chattering notes in alarm.

GENDER DIFFERENCES Male and female Woodchat Shrikes have very similar plumage, but the female's colours are paler and there is more white at the base of the bill and over the eye.

Azure-winged Magpie

FAMILY Corvidae
SPECIES *Cyanopica cyanus*
LENGTH 34 cm (13½ in)
HABITAT Open woodland
CLUTCH SIZE 5–7

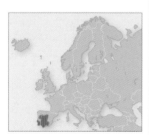

DISTRIBUTION A resident of southwest Spain and Portugal, in woodlands of Stone Pine and mixed deciduous trees. Not seen outside this area anywhere else in Europe, but also occurs in the Far East.

THIS VERY DISTINCTIVE and colourful bird has a long blue tail, blue wings, and a sooty-black head and nape. In bright sunlight, they are very conspicuous, but within woodland, the colours are more subdued. The very gregarious Azure-winged Magpies draw attention to themselves by flying over woodlands in noisy flocks, although if approached they can be very shy and soon disappear. Flying birds frequently make dry rattling and trilling calls.

ATTRACTING BIRDS Like all members of the Crow family, Azure-winged Magpies can be tempted with a wide range of foods, and will cautiously visit garden feeders.

Magpie

FAMILY Corvidae

SPECIES *Pica pica*

LENGTH 46 cm (18 in)

HABITAT Farmland/urban areas

CLUTCH SIZE 5–8

DISTRIBUTION A common and widespread resident across almost all of Europe, apart from the extreme north, and found in a wide range of habitats

THIS VERY FAMILIAR, long-tailed bird appears to be all black-and-white from a distance, but in good light is seen to have a green gloss on the tail and a dark blue gloss on the wings. In flight, the outer wings show a large area of white. Magpies almost always occur in association with human habitation, being adept at scavenging, but also suffer much persecution. The diet varies through the year and may include some live food. Very wary at all times, Magpies are quick to scold with their familiar chattering calls if cats or other predators appear. Large, twiggy, domed nests are constructed high in trees; these are lined with mud and then finished off with softer material. Magpies pair for life and usually return to the same nest each year.

UNMISTAKEABLE LOOKS One of the most instantly recognizable of all birds, the Magpie is a familiar species, even in parks in the centre of large cities.

Alpine Chough

FAMILY Corvidae
SPECIES *Pyrrhocorax graculus*
LENGTH 38 cm (15 in)
HABITAT Montane areas
CLUTCH SIZE 4

DISTRIBUTION Resident in high mountains, above 1,500 m (4,920 ft), across Europe, Turkey and the Middle East, descending to lower altitudes in severe winters.

REVELLING IN the up-draughts from precipices and mountain tops, flocks of Alpine Choughs can often be seen tumbling through the air, calling to each other with a slightly metallic 'zirrrr' or 'prreee' sound. If an eagle appears in their territory, flocks will soon gather to mob it noisily until it retreats. These birds seem equally at home around ski resorts and cafes, where they will eagerly scavenge for food scraps. Alpine Choughs always live in small flocks.

DISTINCTIVE The Alpine Chough is the only all-black bird with red legs and a short yellow bill to be seen high in the mountains.

Red-billed Chough

FAMILY Corvidae
SPECIES *Pyrrhocorax pyrrhocorax*
LENGTH 39 cm (15 in)
HABITAT Sea cliffs/mountains
CLUTCH SIZE 3–4

DISTRIBUTION A widespread resident on sea cliffs, ravines, and mountainous areas across a wide area of western and southern Europe, sometimes occurring in the same areas as Alpine Choughs.

THE CHOUGH'S bright red bill contrasts with its glossy black plumage and is used to probe grassland for invertebrates, especially ants. In flight, Choughs look very broad-winged and the outer wings are distinctly 'fingered'. They often perform aerial acrobatics and can make steep, plunging dives with their wings folded back. In the breeding season, they tend to be more solitary, nesting in caves or ruins, but in winter small flocks form to forage in fields.

NESTING BEHAVIOUR Choughs build untidy twiggy nests in caves and line them with sheep's wool. The young do not develop the red bill colour until they are fully mature.

Jay

FAMILY Corvidae
SPECIES *Garrulus glandarius*
LENGTH 34 cm (13½ in)
HABITAT Woodland/farmland
CLUTCH SIZE 5–7

DISTRIBUTION A widespread resident across most of Europe, apart from the extreme north, and usually found near woodland areas where oak trees are present.

THIS IS A COLOURFUL, lively, and sometimes noisy bird with bright blue wing patches, a black tail, and a white rump, which are conspicuous features as it flies screeching through a woodland. The overall body colouring is pinkish-grey above and pinkish-brown below. Although a very obvious bird when out in the open, Jays are nervous of humans and will hide in the tree canopy if disturbed. Fond of acorns, they collect large numbers in the autumn and create caches in the ground for the winter. Twiggy nests lined with mud and feathers are built in dense cover, or sometimes high in a tree fork. Many calls are made and some mimic other birds like buzzards.

FEEDING A Jay collects a rose hip in autumn, which may be added to its food store to help it survive the winter.

HEAD FOR HEIGHTS Alpine Choughs (*see* p 326) survey the slopes from their lofty perch high in the Alps. Perfectly at home in this harsh environment, they rarely wander far from the rocky peaks where they nest and feed.

Siberian Jay

FAMILY Corvidae

SPECIES *Perisoreus infaustus*

LENGTH 31 cm (12 in)

HABITAT Spruce forest

CLUTCH SIZE 4

DISTRIBUTION A resident of the dense spruce forests of northern Scandinavia, Russia, and Siberia. Harsh weather sometimes drives them closer to human habitation in winter.

THE SIBERIAN JAY is most at home in remote northern spruce forests, where small family groups forage for a wide range of plant and animal foods. In autumn, nuts, berries, and seeds are collected and put into caches under pine needles or in bark crevices. Siberian Jays may sometimes be seen at the tip of conifer branches reaching out to feed on cones. Although generally silent, they will make a variety of curious mewing and screeching sounds, and there is also a rarely heard quiet sub-song. Adept at remaining concealed in the foliage, they will occasionally make sudden appearances to investigate human activity and can be quite bold around habitations where they feed on scraps. The overall coloration is grey-brown, with a dark brown cap and pale orange-buff underparts. The long tail is rusty-red at the edges and the rump and wings show rusty-red patches in flight. The sexes are identical.

ADAPTATION TO COLD
The Siberian Jay fluffs out its feathers in winter to provide good insulation against the extremely cold conditions.

Nutcracker

FAMILY Corvidae

SPECIES *Nucifraga caryocatactes*

LENGTH 32 cm (12½ in)

HABITAT Conifer forest

CLUTCH SIZE 3–4

DISTRIBUTION A resident of coniferous and mixed woodlands in southern Scandinavia, central Europe, Russia, and Siberia, sometimes irrupting south and west when nut crops fail.

THE GREY-BROWN plumage densely spotted with white and white patches on the tail and undertail coverts are unique features to this distinctive member of the crow family. The powerful bill is used for breaking open nutshells and for extracting seeds from pine cones, but Nutcrackers will also take some animal food in summer. They inhabit spruce forests but seek out nearby hazel woods in autumn to collect the nuts.

REMEMBERED LARDER Nutcrackers create hoards of food in the ground for the winter and have a remarkable ability to relocate them at any time.

Raven

FAMILY Corvidae

SPECIES *Corvus corax*

LENGTH 64 cm (25 in)

HABITAT Hilly country/coasts

CLUTCH SIZE 4–6

DISTRIBUTION A widespread resident of hilly country, coastal cliffs, moors, and uplands across most of Europe, including Iceland, but very scarce in lowland areas of western Europe.

THE DEEP CROAKING call of the Raven is heard as it flies over its territory. In spring, Ravens engage in remarkable aerobatic displays, tumbling and twisting through the air. Although large and powerful birds, Ravens are very wary of humans and difficult to approach. On the ground, they walk with an unsteady side-to-side gait. Large nests of sticks lined with sheep's wool are built on cliffs, large trees, or even pylons. They scavenge, but also take young birds and mammals.

IMPOSING The Raven is the largest member of the crow family and has all-black, glossy plumage, a wedge-shaped tail, and a powerful bill.

Carrion Crow

FAMILY Corvidae
SPECIES *Corvus corone*
LENGTH 47 cm (18½ in)
HABITAT Farmland/parkland
CLUTCH SIZE 4–6

DISTRIBUTION A widespread resident in Britain and western and southwestern Europe, but absent from Ireland and northern Scotland. Hybrids with Hooded Crows occur in overlap areas.

A FAMILIAR BIRD seen in habitats ranging from open farmland and woods to urban parks and gardens. In good light, the all-black plumage is seen to have a dark green gloss. Crows are usually solitary or seen in pairs, but occasionally roost in flocks. Large nests of twigs are built high in a tree with a good view all around. Crows take a variety of foods from carrion to young birds and mammals, and also feed on the sea shore.

UNGAINLY In flight, Carrion Crows look rather heavy, and on the ground they often walk or hop sideways.

Hooded Crow

FAMILY Corvidae
SPECIES *Corvus cornix*
LENGTH 47 cm (18½ in)
HABITAT Farmland/parkland
CLUTCH SIZE 4–6

DISTRIBUTION Resident across most of Europe but absent from areas where the Carrion Crow occurs. A partial migrant in the north of its range in Scandinavia and Russia.

WARY Hooded Crows are always on the alert for danger, as they are heavily persecuted by man wherever they occur.

SIMILAR IN almost every respect to the Carrion Crow, the Hooded Crow differs in having a grey, flecked body with a dark head, wings, and tail. In flight, the wings and underside show large areas of grey. This is a common and easily identified species in many areas of Europe, but near areas where Carrion Crows occur, hybrids with intermediate markings are sometimes seen; true Hooded Crows have a black bib, but hybrids may have much more black on the underside. The most common call is a deep 'kraak', repeated several times.

Rook

FAMILY Corvidae
SPECIES *Corvus frugilegus*
LENGTH 46 cm (18 in)
HABITAT Farmland
CLUTCH SIZE 3–5

DISTRIBUTION A common resident across most of Europe, but a summer visitor to northern Europe and a winter visitor to southern areas. Absent from Scandinavia and Iceland.

ADULT ROOKS can be distinguished from crows by their bare faces, longer bills, purple-glossed plumage, and 'baggy trousers' formed by bushy feathers on the legs. Young rooks are very difficult to separate from crows unless seen in good light, as they do not have the bare faces. In flight, Rooks show broad, fingered wings with narrow wing bases. Rooks are highly social birds, always living in large colonies, nesting communally high in treetops, and feeding together in large flocks, usually on open fields. The nests are large, untidy, and twiggy, and built as high as possible in the trees in traditional sites used year after year. They take a variety of plant and animal foods, mostly found on the ground, and will sometimes forage on the strand line on the coast. The commonest call is a harsh 'kaaaw', but many other croaking sounds are produced, some confusingly similar to those of other corvids.

DIET Rooks often feed in grassland, using their long beaks to probe the soil for earthworms and leatherjackets. The bare face prevents feathers from becoming grubby in the soil.

Jackdaw

FAMILY Corvidae
SPECIES *Corvus monedula*
LENGTH 33 cm (13 in)
HABITAT Urban areas/cliffs
CLUTCH SIZE 4–6

DISTRIBUTION A common and widespread resident of most of Europe, but absent from much of Scandinavia and the far north, and a summer visitor to parts of Russia.

THE SMALLEST of the black crows, the Jackdaw is the only all-black bird to have a grey nape. On closer examination, the plumage is seen to be very dark grey; the eye is white. The bill is smaller than in the other crows and the Jackdaw is generally lighter and more agile in its movements. The most frequently heard call is a metallic, repetitive 'chack'. Jackdaws live in colonies, often nesting in ruined buildings or holes in cliffs, and sometimes in city centres where they inhabit cathedrals and castles. They pair for life and even within a flock are rarely separated. In the open countryside Jackdaws sometimes form mixed flocks with other corvids, feeding on a variety of food items.

QUICK LEARNERS Jackdaws are lively, inquisitive birds and when not persecuted soon become quite confiding, learning to follow humans in search of food scraps.

Fan-tailed Raven

FAMILY Corvidae
SPECIES *Corvus rhipidurus*
LENGTH 47 cm (18½ in)
HABITAT Desert/cliffs
CLUTCH SIZE 3–5

DISTRIBUTION Resident in mountainous and desert areas around the Red Sea, Israel, and Jordan and often found near remote habitations or steep cliffs.

IN ITS REMOTE desert location, the Fan-tailed Raven is often seen soaring on outstretched wings, and then the short tail and broad wings are obvious features; at certain angles the fanned-out tail seems no longer than the inner wing, giving it a curious bat-like outline against the sky. A gregarious bird, fond of group aerobatics, Fan-tailed Ravens also scavenge on the ground, visiting refuse tips or cultivated areas. Groups will mob birds of prey, making deep rolling calls.

PLUMAGE The short length of tail makes the Fan-tailed Raven appear long-winged by comparison with other large crows.

House Crow

FAMILY Corvidae
SPECIES *Corvus splendens*
LENGTH 43 cm (17½ in)
HABITAT Urban areas
CLUTCH SIZE 4–5

DISTRIBUTION Resident in a very localized area around the northern Red Sea, almost always occurring near ports and docks. Introduced, deliberately or accidentally, from India.

INTERMEDIATE IN SIZE between the Jackdaw and Hooded Crow, both of which also have areas of grey plumage, the House Crow is a more streamlined and elegant bird than either of these, being slightly longer winged and slimmer. Lively, sociable birds, House Crows are usually found scavenging for scraps around docks and rubbish tips. Twiggy nests are built in tree tops in parks or gardens.

VARIETY The degree of paleness in the nape of the House Crow varies between individuals, but all birds have a dark face and glossy plumage.

Tristram's Starling

FAMILY Sturnidae

SPECIES *Onychognathus tristramii*

LENGTH 25 cm (10 in)

HABITAT Ravines/montane areas

CLUTCH SIZE 3–5

DISTRIBUTION Resident in wild, rocky areas of Jordan, Israel, and around the Red Sea, favouring ravines, wadis, dry valleys, and sometimes also cultivated land in dry lowland.

THIS IS A LARGE, almost all-black starling with chestnut-orange wing patches that show up very well in flight, but are more difficult to detect on the folded wings. Males are mostly glossy black with a hint of a blue tint in good light. Females are similar but have greyer heads and necks with darker spots. Gregarious in habit and quite noisy at times, Tristram's Starlings can often be seen in flocks of up to 50 birds tumbling around in the sky over a rock face making strange whistling calls and harsh screeching alarm notes. Their large twiggy nests are usually built in holes in rock faces.

VARIED DIET Tristram's Starlings are lively, inquisitive birds, with a strong bill that allows them to feed on foods as varied as insects, fruits, and berries.

Rose-coloured Starling

FAMILY Sturnidae

SPECIES *Sturnus roseus*

LENGTH 22 cm (8½ in)

HABITAT Grassy plains

CLUTCH SIZE 5–6

DISTRIBUTION Widespread summer visitor to dry, grassy steppes and farmland around the Black Sea, Turkey, and the Middle East. Some stray further into Europe in late summer.

AN UNMISTAKEABLE bird in the breeding season, the Rose-coloured Starling has bright pink and black plumage, a yellow-pink bill, and a short crest. Juveniles have more mottled grey-brown plumage with a black head, wings, and tail. Fond of large insects, Rose-coloured Starlings will often follow locust swarms, and in some years vast flocks will gather when the feeding is good. Irruptions into new areas usually follow this.

LINE UP A small flock of Rose-coloured Starlings gather on telephone wires to rest and preen, here showing off their unique breeding plumage.

Spotless Starling

FAMILY Sturnidae
SPECIES *Sturnus unicolor*
LENGTH 21 cm (8¼ in)
HABITAT Farmland/cliffs
CLUTCH SIZE 4

DISTRIBUTION This is a fairly common resident in farmland, olive groves, open country, and rocky areas in the Iberian Peninsula and coastal northwest Africa; also present in Corsica, Sardinia, and Sicily.

AT FIRST GLANCE the Spotless Starling appears very similar to the Common Starling, but it always appears blacker. Birds in breeding plumage have a glossy blue tinge in good light, and no spots, but in winter they have very light spots. Their legs are always light pink. Spotless Starlings often nest colonially in cliffs or among ruined buildings.

CLEAR VOICE The Spotless Starling has a loud, clear song, heard frequently during the breeding season. Flocks make chattering calls.

Common Starling

FAMILY Sturnidae
SPECIES *Sturnus vulgaris*
LENGTH 22 cm (8½ in)
HABITAT Farmland/urban areas
CLUTCH SIZE 5–7

DISTRIBUTION A widespread and common resident across Europe, spreading north and east to breed, and sometimes moving south to overwinter.

A VERY FAMILIAR BIRD of a huge range of habitats, sometimes found in enormous numbers. Breeding birds have dark, glossy green-tinged plumage with pale spots, which become more conspicuous in winter. The yellow bill becomes brown in winter. Juveniles are much plainer grey-brown with dark bills and no spots. Many habitats support Starlings and they can be found in city centres, coastlines, farmland, and woodland. They have a huge range of chattering and whistling calls, many of them skilfully mimicking other birds.

STRIKING PLUMAGE The glossy green, spotted plumage of the Common Starling is at its most striking in winter after the autumn moult.

Golden Oriole

FAMILY Oriolidae
SPECIES *Oriolus oriolus*
LENGTH 24 cm (9½ in)
HABITAT Woodland/parkland
CLUTCH SIZE 3–4

DISTRIBUTION A widespread summer visitor to most of Europe, apart from the far north and Scandinavia. A rare breeder in southeast England.

MELODIOUS, fluty calls ringing from high in a woodland canopy in spring announce the arrival of the brightly coloured Golden Orioles. Harsh alarm calls are also produced. Despite the vivid black-and-yellow plumage of the male, so striking in the open, this shy and nervous bird is not easy to detect in dappled sunlight, and the greenish colours of the females make them even harder to spot among the leaves. The nest is suspended in a fork between branches.

BRILLIANT GOLD The male Golden Oriole is unmistakeable, but this colourful bird can be surprisingly furtive during the breeding season.

House Sparrow

FAMILY Passeridae
SPECIES *Passer domesticus*
LENGTH 15 cm (5¾ in)
HABITAT Urban areas
CLUTCH SIZE 3–5

DISTRIBUTION A widespread resident across most of Europe, apart from the extreme north and very high altitudes.

ONE OF THE MOST familiar of all birds, but not the most common, the House Sparrow is found in even the most extreme urban areas. Although at first glance House Sparrows appear to be rather plain, males have bold black bibs, grey crowns, and barred chestnut upperparts. Females are plainer greyish-brown, and in winter, males lose the black bib and become drabber. They feed mainly on seeds but readily take food scraps. The untidy nests are often built in buildings.

PLAIN CLOTHES An urban female House Sparrow. Calls are mainly a series of 'chip churp' sounds.

Spanish Sparrow

FAMILY Passeridae

SPECIES *Passer hispaniolensis*

LENGTH 15 cm (5¾ in)

HABITAT Scrubland/olive groves

CLUTCH SIZE 5–6

DISTRIBUTION Resident in southwest Iberia, North Africa, Canaries, Sardinia, and Sicily; more migratory in the eastern Mediterranean, Balkans, and Turkey, moving south in large flocks for the winter.

SPANISH SPARROWS are often found in large, noisy colonies in trees near rivers or in farm buildings, occasionally building their nests in the larger nests of other birds such as White Storks (*see* p 50). Markings vary, and Spanish Sparrows sometimes hybridize with House Sparrows. In winter, the colours are paler.

BREEDING PLUMAGE This male Spanish Sparrow shows the white cheeks, spotted flanks, and chestnut crown of the breeding season plumage.

Dead Sea Sparrow

FAMILY Passeridae

SPECIES *Passer moabiticus*

LENGTH 12 cm (4¾ in)

HABITAT Tamarisk scrub

CLUTCH SIZE 4–6

DISTRIBUTION Resident in scattered lowland locations in the eastern Mediterranean, eastern Turkey, and the Dead Sea area, with some migrating south in winter.

NOT TIED TO man in the way the other sparrows are, and more nomadic in its habits, the diminutive Dead Sea Sparrow is usually found in areas of tamarisk scrub not far from open water. Superficially similar to the larger House Sparrow, males have paler grey heads with a yellow patch on either side of the chin, and lack the white wing bar. Females are also much paler than other sparrows. Usually shy and wary, Dead Sea Sparrows can sometimes be found in mixed flocks with Spanish Sparrows.

DESERT HABITAT The shy Dead Sea Sparrow has a smaller bill than the other sparrows, enabling it to cope with the tiny seeds of the desert plants it feeds on.

Tree Sparrow

FAMILY Passeridae
SPECIES *Passer montanus*
LENGTH 14 cm (5½ in)
HABITAT Woodland/farmland
CLUTCH SIZE 4–6

DISTRIBUTION Widespread resident in lowland areas across much of Europe, but absent from extreme northern regions. Some migrate into these areas in good summers.

LESS LIKELY to be seen in urban areas than House Sparrows, Tree Sparrows are mainly encountered in rural areas of habitation and near cultivated land. Tree hollows, farm buildings, and nest boxes will be used for nesting sites, and large flocks will gather on winter stubble and in hedgerows that contain abundant seeds and berries. The calls are similar to those of the House Sparrow, but higher pitched and more incisive. Changes in farming practices have wiped out this species in some areas.

FACIAL MARKINGS The Tree Sparrow's brown crown, white cheeks, and dark cheek patches are distinctive features shared by both males and females. Juveniles have darker faces.

Rock Sparrow

FAMILY Passeridae
SPECIES *Petronia petronia*
LENGTH 14 cm (5½ in)
HABITAT Ravines/ruins
CLUTCH SIZE 5–6

DISTRIBUTION Resident in deserts, rocky areas, and mountains in southern Europe, North Africa, Turkey, and the Middle East; some migrate to overwinter in the Middle East.

BOTH MALE and female Rock Sparrows are similar to a pale female House Sparrow (*see* p 338), but have a more boldly patterned head and a pale yellow spot below the throat, although the spot is not always visible if the birds are hunched up. The tail shows white spots at the tip, a feature best seen in flight, and there are very indistinct wing bars. Juveniles are very similar but lack the yellow throat patch. Rock Sparrows are usually encountered in rocky habitats, which may include ruins where nesting holes are located.

LARGE BILL A very large bill with an orange-pink lower mandible is a useful feature for identifying the otherwise rather plain-looking Rock Sparrow.

Snowfinch

FAMILY Passeridae
SPECIES *Montifringilla nivalis*
LENGTH 18 cm (7 in)
HABITAT Mountain slopes
CLUTCH SIZE 4–5

DISTRIBUTION Resident in the higher mountains of Europe and the Caucasus with some migration to lower altitudes in severe winter weather.

A RESIDENT of the high mountain tops, usually at well over 1,500 m (5,000 ft), and often difficult to see when feeding in low vegetation, the Snowfinch's dull chestnut upperparts provide good camouflage. In flight, the wings show a bold black-and-white pattern and its chattering alarm call may be heard. The bill is black in summer, yellow in winter when the black bib also fades.

FOOD SEARCH In winter, Snow Finches often descend to lower altitudes and occasionally feed around mountain huts and ski lifts.

Chaffinch

FAMILY Fringillidae
SPECIES *Fringilla coelebs*
LENGTH 15 cm (6 in)
HABITAT Woodland/parkland
CLUTCH SIZE 4–5

DISTRIBUTION A very common and widespread resident across Europe, migrating north and east in the summer to Scandinavia, northern Europe, and Russia.

THE CHAFFINCH IS a very common bird in much of Europe and found in a range of habitats where trees occur, including city parks. Its nests are usually built of moss and lichens and sited in a high fork of a dense tree. Both sexes have a white shoulder patch, white wing bar, and a pale green rump, but only the males have a pinkish-brown underside and a slate blue head and neck; the females are more uniformly grey-brown. The cheerful rattling song is heard in the breeding season, but the metallic 'pink pink' call is heard more often. Chaffinches often gather in mixed flocks in winter, feeding in stubble fields or visiting gardens.

MALE CHAFFINCH The male Chaffinch's bill changes from pale brown in winter to grey-blue in the breeding season when his plumage colourings become much richer, too.

Brambling

FAMILY Fringillidae

SPECIES *Fringilla montifringilla*

LENGTH 15 cm (5¾ in)

HABITAT Birch and beech woodland

CLUTCH SIZE 5–7

DISTRIBUTION Resident in summer in Scandinavia, northern Europe, and Russia; overwinters in southern and western Europe.

THE WHITE RUMP of the Brambling is a feature that can distinguish it from other finches when mixed flocks are observed in winter; it shows well as flocks fly across open fields. Similar in structure to a Chaffinch, the Brambling can also be identified by its orange breast, white underside with spotted flanks, and darker head. The black head and bill of the male in summer plumage are sometimes seen before winter migrants leave for their breeding sites in the north. Bramblings feed on beech mast, but will readily visit garden feeding stations.

PLUMAGE In winter, the male has rather faded plumage and a yellowish bill with a black tip; the colours become more intense prior to migration.

Linnet

FAMILY Fringillidae
SPECIES *Carduelis cannabina*
LENGTH 13 cm (5¼ in)
HABITAT Heathland/shrubland areas
CLUTCH SIZE 4–6

DISTRIBUTION A widespread and common resident across western and southern Europe, and a summer visitor to lowland areas of Scandinavia, eastern Europe, and Russia.

THE OVERALL brown plumage of the Linnet is relieved by the grey head, red crown, and red breast of the male, and the white wing patches. Females lack red colours and are more boldly spotted. In summer, Linnets breed in areas of scattered bushes, but in winter, they may gather in small flocks on coastal marshes or stubble fields.

PRICKLY SITE A male Linnet sings from the top of a gorse bush, often chosen as a safe nesting place.

Redpoll

FAMILY Fringillidae
SPECIES *Acanthis flammea*
LENGTH 13–15 cm (5¼–6 in)
HABITAT Mixed forest
CLUTCH SIZE 4–5

DISTRIBUTION Breeds in birch, willow, and coniferous forests of western Europe, northern Scandinavia, and Russia, migrating over wide area of Europe in winter.

A RED CROWN, black chin, and small, sharply pointed, yellow bill are key features for identifying Redpolls, which may be confused with the rather similar Linnet. The underside is pale with darker streaking, while the rest of the plumage is a mottled dark brown. Juveniles lack red colours. Redpolls often feed in waterside birch and alder trees, extracting seeds from cones with their pointed bills, but they will also visit garden feeders in mixed flocks in winter.

SPRING PLUMAGE The male in breeding plumage has a red crown and a rosy-pink breast, seen at its most colourful in springtime.

CHAFFINCH (*see* p 342) This bird frequents wooded areas and gardens. Its numbers increase significantly in the British Isles over the winter period, when there is an additional influx of these finches here from northern parts of Europe.

Twite

FAMILY Fringillidae
SPECIES *Carduelis flavirostris*
LENGTH 13 cm (5¼ in)
HABITAT Moorland/heathland
CLUTCH SIZE 5–6

DISTRIBUTION Resident in Britain and Scandinavia; many overwinter on the shores of the North Sea and Baltic. Also present in similar habitats in Turkey and the Caucasus.

THE TWITE is a very similar bird to the Linnet (*see* p 343), but is found in wilder, more open, upland habitats, and more coastal areas in winter. The Twite is also much plainer than the Linnet, with few distinctive features on its mottled brown plumage. The best feature to look for is the male's pink rump, seen in flight, and the grey bill, which turns yellow in winter. Both sexes show pale greyish wing bars. The song is similar to the Linnet's, but small flocks make a very distinctive, slightly wheezy, 'twa-it' call. In winter, birds may gather in large flocks on saltmarshes, vanishing as they feed low down and then restlessly moving off to settle in a new area.

WELL HIDDEN The rather dull brown, mottled plumage of the Twite offers it perfect camouflage when feeding in low vegetation, where its favourite food is small seeds.

Arctic Redpoll

FAMILY Fringillidae
SPECIES *Carduelis hornemanni*
LENGTH 13 cm (5 in)
HABITAT Tundra/willow trees
CLUTCH SIZE 5

DISTRIBUTION Resident in the extreme north on tundra with scattered willows and birches, overwintering in Scandinavia.

A VERY SIMILAR BIRD to the Common Redpoll, the Arctic Redpoll is sometimes difficult to distinguish with certainty. It is usually rather paler than the Redpoll, and always has a plain white, unstreaked rump: it stands out if seen in a mixed flock. There is sometimes a narrow dark streak on the undertail coverts. The yellow bill is very finely pointed. Arctic Redpolls usually remain in their far northern haunts feeding in willow and birch scrub, and only venture south when driven there by harsh winter weather.

SUGAR LUMP Look for a plain white rump 'as large as a lump of sugar' when identifying the Arctic Redpoll in winter or summer plumage.

European Goldfinch

FAMILY Fringillidae
SPECIES *Carduelis carduelis*
LENGTH 12 cm (4¾ in)
HABITAT Woodland/gardens
CLUTCH SIZE 4–6

DISTRIBUTION A common and widespread resident in western Europe, North Africa, and Turkey, and a summer visitor to eastern areas. Many migrate south and west in winter.

THIS IS A SMALL, COLOURFUL finch with a red face, black-and-white head, and broad yellow wing bars; in flight the white rump and black tail with white spots show well. The sexes are alike, but juveniles are more spotted and lack the red face.

SEED EATER The sharply pointed bill of the Goldfinch is used to extract small seeds from teasel heads.

European Greenfinch

FAMILY Fringillidae
SPECIES *Carduelis chloris*
LENGTH 14 cm (5¾ in)
HABITAT Woodland/ hedgerow
CLUTCH SIZE 4–6

DISTRIBUTION A common and widespread resident across most of lowland Europe; a summer visitor to northern areas; absent from the far north.

THE EUROPEAN GREENFINCH is a large, yellowish-green finch with bright yellow wing patches, a yellow rump, and yellow patches on either side of the tail. The males have the brightest colours; females are greyish with a green tinge and juveniles are streaked below. The large conical bill is flesh coloured. Loud, nasal 'dzwheee' calls are heard in the breeding season.

YELLOW PATCHES The greenish plumage of the male is brightened by large patches of yellow, which become much more intense during breeding.

Siskin

FAMILY Fringillidae
SPECIES *Carduelis spinus*
LENGTH 12 cm (4¾ in)
HABITAT Conifer woodland
CLUTCH SIZE 3–5

DISTRIBUTION Resident in western and central Europe, migrating north to Scandinavia and Russia in summer; may make mass migrations southwest in harsh winters.

THE SISKIN IS A SMALL yellowish-green finch with a slender, seed-eating bill. The plumage has darker streaks, and in flight the dark wings show yellow patches and the yellow rump can be clearly seen. Females and juveniles are plainer with no black on the head. Siskins nest high in the tops of spruce trees, but regularly come down to garden bird feeders when they may gather in large flocks, mingling with other finches.

BLACK CAP In winter, the male Siskin's black cap and bib show grey fringes, but these colours become more striking in the breeding season.

Citril Finch

FAMILY Fringillidae
SPECIES *Serinus citrinella*
LENGTH 12 cm (4¾ in)
HABITAT Mountain forests
CLUTCH SIZE 4–5

DISTRIBUTION Resident in spruce forests of the Pyrenees, Alps, Corsica, and Sardinia, usually above 700 m (2,300 ft) and sometimes above the tree-line in shrubs.

ALTHOUGH RATHER similar to the Serin and Siskin, Citril Finches are plainer and have greyer heads and necks with no black markings. The face is yellowish-green and there are two yellow wing bars. The sexes are similar, although males have more bright yellow on the underside and face. Juveniles are browner with buff wing bars. In Corsica and Sardinia, Citril Finches have much browner mantles. Stands of mature spruce trees near open alpine meadows are a favourite habitat. The quiet, twittering song is similar to that of the European Goldfinch (*see* p 347).

SEED EATER The Citril Finch has a quite long, pointed bill to enable it to feed on seeds in cones, but it will also eat on the ground.

Red-fronted Serin

FAMILY Fringillidae
SPECIES *Serinus pusillus*
LENGTH 12 cm (4¾ in)
HABITAT Alpine woodland
CLUTCH SIZE 3–5

DISTRIBUTION Resident in forests and scrub, often near streams, mountainous areas of Turkey, Caucasus, and the Middle East, moving to lower altitudes in winter.

A VERY DISTINCTIVE small finch, the Red-fronted Serin has a black head and deep red forehead. Most of the plumage is brown and streaked, but the underside is paler and the rump looks yellowish in flight. The sexes are very similar; juveniles lack the black-and-red head markings.

GROUND FEEDER The Red-fronted Serin has a very short, but stout, dark-coloured bill, ideal for feeding on small seeds; they often seek this food on the ground.

European Serin

FAMILY Fringillidae
SPECIES *Serinus serinus*
LENGTH 11 cm (4½ in)
HABITAT Woodland/gardens
CLUTCH SIZE 4

DISTRIBUTION Resident in southwest Europe and around the Mediterranean; summer visitor to central Europe and Turkey. Some spend winter in the eastern Mediterranean.

THE EUROPEAN SERIN IS the smallest of the finches. It has mottled brown plumage with a yellow rump; males have a bright yellow head with darker cheeks and crown. Lively behaviour, fluttering flight, and a buzzing trill-like call draw attention to Serins, which are often found in areas with conifers, high in the treetops.

WATER BIRD Serins are attracted to water, and small flocks will regularly visit garden ponds and sprinklers in summer to drink and bathe.

Eurasian Bullfinch

FAMILY Fringillidae
SPECIES *Pyrrhula pyrrhula*
LENGTH 14–16 cm (5¾–6¼ in)
HABITAT Woodland/gardens
CLUTCH SIZE 4–5

DISTRIBUTION A widespread resident across Europe, Scandinavia, and Russia, but migratory in the north of its range; a winter visitor to southern Europe and absent from southern Iberia.

THE MALE BULLFINCH is a most distinctive bird with a black bib and crown and bright red underparts; the less colourful female has light brown underparts, but both sexes have broad white wing bars and a white rump. In profile, the Bullfinch seems to have no neck and looks rather plump. Juveniles are browner and lack the black cap and bib. Although brightly coloured, Bullfinches can be difficult to spot as they move through the trees making quiet, nasal 'phu-phu' calls to each other. They are usually found in pairs, but small flocks may gather near good food sources. Birds from the north of the range are larger.

SHORT BILL The stubby, black bill of the Bullfinch is ideally suited to cracking open hard seed cases, but in summer these birds will also eat some insects.

Pine Grosbeak

FAMILY Fringillidae
SPECIES *Pinicola enucleator*
LENGTH 20 cm (8 in)
HABITAT Conifer and birch forest
CLUTCH SIZE 4

DISTRIBUTION Resident in the Taiga region of northern Scandinavia and Russia, but mass irruptions occur further south in some years.

THE PINE GROSBEAK, the largest of the finch family, is confined to northern pine forests and scrub, where it feeds on seeds, berries, and shoots. Males are mostly bright red with white wing bars, and females and juveniles are a dull yellowish green, providing them with excellent camouflage. Although similar in appearance to crossbills (*see* pp 352–53), the stout bill is not twisted. During the breeding season, these large birds are fairly secretive, but in harsh winters they migrate south and feed fearlessly on berries in town parks and gardens.

HIGH SITE The male Pine Grosbeak chooses a high perch as a post to deliver his far-carrying, tuneful song when the breeding season begins.

Hawfinch

FAMILY Fringillidae

SPECIES *Coccothraustes coccothraustes*

LENGTH 18 cm (7 in)

HABITAT Mixed woodland

CLUTCH SIZE 5

DISTRIBUTION Resident across much of western Europe; a summer visitor to eastern Europe; some migrate south in harsh winters.

THE HAWFINCH is one of the largest finches, with a massive, powerful bill used to crack open tough seeds. In winter, the bill is yellow, but in summer, it becomes steely grey. The body appears plump and short-necked with a disproportionately large head and bill, and in flight shows a very short tail. The sexes are very similar with light brown plumage, bold white wing bars, and broad white tips to the tail feathers. Males have rather richer colours in the summer, but this can be difficult to pick out in the tree canopy. Hawfinches have a very quiet song, not often heard, but they make a sharp 'pix' contact note as they move through the treetops. Small flocks are often overlooked as they feed quietly on fruits and seeds high in a forest, but in winter they may be more visible. They will often gather in small groups at dusk, sitting out in the open on prominent treetops, calling quietly to each other, before going to roost.

NUTCRACKER The incredibly strong, conical bill of the Hawfinch can crack open the toughest cherry stones and hardest seed cases.

Common Crossbill

FAMILY Fringillidae
SPECIES *Loxia curvirostra*
LENGTH 17 cm (6½ in)
HABITAT Coniferous forest
CLUTCH SIZE 3–4

DISTRIBUTION A widespread resident across Europe; absent from the extreme north and an occasional migrant during irruption years in other areas.

THIS IS A BULKY, colourful finch, looking large-headed in profile, with crossed mandibles, enabling it to extract seeds from pine cones. From a distance, the strange shape of the bill may not be obvious, but the size and characteristic feeding motion, and the metallic 'jip jip' flight calls are identifiable features. Males are usually bright red, although this can be indistinct, and females are usually olive-brown or greyish. Crossbills breed very early, often in February, to coincide with the ripening of the pine cones.

DRINKING A male Crossbill, usually in the treetops feeding on cones, lands to drink from a puddle.

Two-barred Crossbill

FAMILY Fringillidae
SPECIES *Loxia leucoptera*
LENGTH 14 cm (5¾ in)
HABITAT Larch woodland
CLUTCH SIZE 3–4

DISTRIBUTION Resident in northern Scandinavia and Russia; occasionally irrupts westwards in large flocks when some may remain to nest.

FORMERLY KNOWN AS the White-winged Crossbill, this is the smallest of the crossbills and is best identified by its double, bold, white wing bars. This crossbill rarely strays to western Europe, but if found among Common Crossbills, the more intense red of the male and smaller size are good distinguishing features.

SEED EATER A female Two-barred Crossbill skilfully uses her curved bill and long tongue to extract seeds from a cone.

Parrot Crossbill

FAMILY Fringillidae
SPECIES *Loxia pytopsittacus*
LENGTH 17–18 cm (6¾–7 in)
HABITAT Pine forest
CLUTCH SIZE 2–4

DISTRIBUTION Resident in forests of Scots Pines in Scandinavia and northeastern Europe; rarely wanders outside this area, but has bred in Britain.

THIS IS A CONFUSINGLY SIMILAR species to the Common Crossbill, but it is slightly larger and has a very bulky head and bill – good identification features for this, the largest of the crossbill family. In good light and at close range the large crossed mandibles show pale cutting edges. The male has similar colours to other male crossbills, but the females are usually a dull greyish olive.

FOREST HOME Parrot Crossbills feed almost exclusively on Scots Pine cones, so are rarely seen away from pine forests and are less likely to mix with other crossbill species.

Scottish Crossbill

FAMILY Fringillidae
SPECIES *Loxia scotica*
LENGTH 18 cm (7 in)
HABITAT Caledonian pine forest
CLUTCH SIZE 3–4

DISTRIBUTION Resident and sedentary in the ancient Caledonian pine forests of Scotland and rarely seen outside this habitat.

INTERMEDIATE IN SIZE and structure between the Common Crossbill and Parrot Crossbill, the Scottish Crossbill is most reliably identified by its location in Scots Pine forests where it feeds almost exclusively on pine cones. The bill is not quite as stout as that of the Parrot Crossbill, but when several birds are observed, there is seen to be a range of bill sizes. The 'toop' call is rather deeper in tone than the Common Crossbill's. Nests are built high in Scots Pines early in the season.

RESTRICTED RANGE A male Scottish Crossbill perches in a Scots Pine tree, which provides its food.

FEMALE SCOTTISH CROSSBILL The Scottish Crossbill is superbly adapted to life in the ancient pine forests of Scotland. The curious hooked bill is perfectly shaped for extracting seeds from between the scales of pine cones.

Common Rosefinch

FAMILY Fringillidae

SPECIES *Carpodacus erythrinus*

LENGTH 14 cm (5¾ in)

HABITAT Woodland/scrubland

CLUTCH SIZE 5

DISTRIBUTION A summer visitor from India to woodland clearings, farmland, and scrub, often near water, in eastern and northern Europe, Turkey, and the Caucasus.

OTHER COMMON NAMES for this species are Scarlet Rosefinch and Scarlet Grosbeak, both reflecting the most obvious features of this conspicuous bird. In males, the head, breast, and rump show varying degrees of bright red, with the tail and wings being mostly brown. The strongest colours are found in the oldest males. A double pale wing bar can be seen in good light. Females and juveniles are plain brown, looking rather like plump female House Sparrows (*see* p 338) or Corn Buntings (*see* p 368), but still with the large powerful bill. This is used to feed on seeds, buds, and shoots, but in summer insects are also eaten.

HIGH PERCH Male Rosefinches will sometimes sit out in the open to sing their soft whistling song; young males, resembling females with dull plumage, will also sing from high perches.

Trumpeter Finch

FAMILY Fringillidae

SPECIES *Bucanetes githagineus*

LENGTH 13 cm (5 in)

HABITAT Arid country

CLUTCH SIZE 4–6

DISTRIBUTION Resident in arid and coastal zones in a small area of southern Spain and Portugal; more widespread in the Canaries, North Africa, and the Middle East.

THIS IS A SMALL and rather plain finch, but it is easily distinguished by its large bill. In the breeding season, the male's bill becomes bright pink and there is a variable pink tinge to the plumage. Females are pale brown with less of a pink tinge, but both have contrasting dark brown wing tips. The name derives from the loud nasal, buzzing 'cheez' calls, which have been likened to a toy trumpet. Small flocks can be found in very barren areas, but they always remain within flying distance of water.

GROUNDED Trumpeter Finches live in the most arid of habitats, where water is always an attraction. At home on the ground, they are never seen to perch in trees.

Desert Finch

FAMILY Fringillidae

SPECIES *Rhodospiza obsolete*

LENGTH 14 cm (5¾ in)

HABITAT Arid country/oases

CLUTCH SIZE 5–6

DISTRIBUTION Resident in cultivated areas and open country in Israel, north Egypt, the Caucasus, and the Middle East, occasionally straying further afield.

DESPITE ITS common name, the Desert Finch is more at home in areas where there is some cultivation and access to water, so it can be found in farmland and gardens as well as more arid areas. Although similar in many ways to the Trumpeter Finch (*see* p 357), both sexes have a large black bill, and pink patches on the hind wing; in flight the wings appear mostly black, the rump is pale buff, and the tail is white with a black central band.

PERCH Desert Finches are likely to be seen perching in trees and shrubs, where they also build their nests.

Crimson-winged Finch

FAMILY Fringillidae

SPECIES *Rhodopechys sanguinea*

LENGTH 15 cm (6 in)

HABITAT Montane areas

CLUTCH SIZE 4–5

DISTRIBUTION Resident at very high altitudes, rarely descending below 1,100 m (3,600 ft), in North Africa and the Middle East.

PINK WING PANELS, pink cheeks, and a pink rump are clear identification features of the male Crimson-winged Finch, but the females and juveniles are mostly paler versions of the male. The dark crown, almost black in the male, separates them from Trumpeter Finches. Both sexes have a large yellowish bill, which is used for seed eating. These birds are usually spotted in the most barren rocky habitats where there is little vegetation; they feed in small flocks on the ground.

WINTER FORAYS Crimson-winged Finches may leave the high mountain-tops in winter to forage on the ground for seeds at lower altitudes.

Yellow-breasted Bunting

FAMILY Emberizidae

SPECIES *Emberiza aureola*

LENGTH 14 cm (5½ in)

HABITAT Open woodland/ boggy ground

CLUTCH SIZE 4–5

DISTRIBUTION A summer visitor to a wide expanse of northeastern Europe and into Siberia. Migrates to southeast Asia for the winter.

THE MALE Yellow-breasted Bunting is a most colourful bird in breeding plumage, with bright yellow underparts, a dark band across the chest, and a dark head. The upperparts are a rich brown, and the conspicuous white wing patches show clearly in flight and at rest. The female has much paler yellow colours and a brown head with bold buff stripes. They arrive at their breeding grounds in midsummer, leaving early in the autumn for their wintering sites.

LOUD SONG The male often sings his loud, jingling song from a high perch in the spring and early summer.

Red-headed Bunting

FAMILY Emberizidae

SPECIES *Emberiza bruniceps*

LENGTH 17 cm (6½ in)

HABITAT Steppes/arid country

CLUTCH SIZE 3–5

DISTRIBUTION A summer visitor to dry steppes, high mountain grasslands, and open, dry cultivated areas to the east of the Caspian Sea, returning to India in winter.

THE BREEDING PLUMAGE of the male is mainly bright yellow with a chestnut-red head and throat and yellow rump; the female is difficult to identify. She is much paler, with a hint of yellow on the underside and grey-green streaked upperparts. This is a very similar species to the Black-headed Bunting and the songs are almost identical; hybrids between the two are known to occur and can be tricky to distinguish.

ESCAPEE Although restricted as a breeding bird to the far east of the region, this is a popular cage bird, so any individuals seen in western Europe are likely to have escaped from captivity.

Grey-necked Bunting

FAMILY Emberizidae

SPECIES *Emberiza buchanani*

LENGTH 14 cm (5¾ in)

HABITAT Mountain slopes

CLUTCH SIZE 5

DISTRIBUTION A scarce summer visitor from India to high mountain plateaux and rocky slopes above 2,000 m (6,500 ft) in eastern Turkey and the Caucasus.

THE GREY-NECKED Bunting is best recognized by its grey head and neck, white eye ring, and pale pink underparts; the latter have a slightly scaly appearance due to pale feather edges. The sexes are similar, although the females are paler, but juveniles are light brown and streaked above and much paler below. These rather quiet buntings rarely stray from their high mountain haunts and may be overlooked as they feed on the ground.

FACIAL FEATURE This bunting has a pale sub-moustachial stripe separating the grey head from the pink throat.

Cretzschmar's Bunting

FAMILY Emberizidae

SPECIES *Emberiza caesia*

LENGTH 16 cm (6¼ in)

HABITAT Arid country

CLUTCH SIZE 4–6

DISTRIBUTION A summer visitor to dry, open rocky areas of the eastern Mediterranean region, including many of the larger islands, returning south in the autumn.

MALE CRETZSCHMAR'S Buntings have a conspicuous white eye ring set in a blue-grey head; there is a blue-grey chest band, but the underparts are mostly rusty red. Females are far less brightly coloured and have a streaked crown and throat. In spring small flocks may be seen feeding on the ground in dry, cultivated areas, sometimes coming to puddles to drink and bathe. The calls and songs are rather similar to other buntings, consisting of a series of slightly rattling 'zeeou' notes.

SINGING BUNTING The male Cretzschmar's Bunting sings on arrival on his territory in spring, making a rare foray onto a shrub for a song post.

Rock Bunting

FAMILY Emberizidae
SPECIES *Emberiza cia*
LENGTH 16 cm (6¼ in)
HABITAT Rocky slopes
CLUTCH SIZE 4–6

DISTRIBUTION Resident over southern Europe, Turkey, the Middle East, and North Africa, on mountain slopes above the tree-line in summer, lower down in winter.

DESPITE ITS CONSPICUOUS head markings, the Rock Bunting can be difficult to find in its stony, mountain-slope habitat, especially when feeding quietly on the ground. Small flocks can sometimes be approached quite closely before they move off. The upperparts are mainly brown with darker streaks, providing excellent camouflage from above. In flight, the rusty-red rump and dark tail with white edges are useful identification features. Males will sometimes sit on a rock fluttering their wings while delivering their buzzing song. Although mainly a high-altitude species, in certain uninhabited areas Rock Buntings can be found almost at sea level in suitable habitats.

STRIPED The male's head has black, white, and grey stripes; the female's stripes are less defined.

Cinereous Bunting

FAMILY Emberizidae
SPECIES *Emberiza cineracea*
LENGTH 17 cm (6½ in)
HABITAT Rocky slopes
CLUTCH SIZE 3

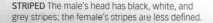

DISTRIBUTION A scarce summer visitor to locations in the eastern Mediterranean, Turkey, and the Middle East, wintering around the Red Sea.

THIS IS A RATHER PALE grey bunting with relatively long wings and tail. The male has a yellowish-grey head with a pale eye ring. Females and juveniles are browner with streaked upperparts and are very similar to other female buntings. Not common anywhere in its range, the Cinereous Bunting rarely strays far from the dry grassy slopes of the mountains in summer and can be tricky to find unless singing males are located.

ROCKY PERCH Males perch on rocks to deliver their rather brief snatch of song, which is usually made up of phrases of five short notes.

Cirl Bunting

FAMILY Emberizidae
SPECIES *Emberiza cirlus*
LENGTH 17 cm (6½ in)
HABITAT Woodland margins
CLUTCH SIZE 3–5

DISTRIBUTION Resident across south and southwest Europe, but very rare in Britain, and has declined considerably in the north of its range.

COLOURS In the breeding season the male Cirl Bunting's head markings are at their most intense; in winter the throat becomes paler.

THE MALE Cirl Bunting's black-and-yellow-striped head and greyish-green chest band are unmistakeable; the female has plainer brown-streaked plumage, resembling that of a Yellowhammer. In flight, both sexes show an olive-coloured rump, differing from the chestnut rump of the Yellowhammer. Once very widespread, the Cirl Bunting has declined, mainly due to reduced availability of winter stubble.

Yellowhammer

FAMILY Emberizidae
SPECIES *Emberiza citrinella*
LENGTH 17 cm (6½ in)
HABITAT Farmland/hedgerows
CLUTCH SIZE 3–5

DISTRIBUTION A widespread resident across most of Europe in a range of lowland habitats. Birds in the far north migrate south in winter.

THE MALE YELLOWHAMMER is one of the most strikingly yellow small birds, often seen sitting prominently in a hedgerow tree in spring singing the distinctive rattling call, described as 'a little bit of bread and NO cheese'. The females are browner than the males but still show some yellow and both have a chestnut rump. In winter, they gather in mixed flocks to feed in stubble fields.

YELLOW BIRD Although the colours of the Yellowhammer are not as bright in winter, it remains one of the most colourful of the buntings.

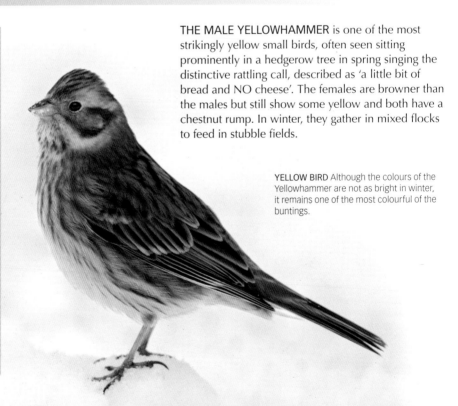

Ortolan Bunting

FAMILY Emberizidae
SPECIES *Emberiza hortulana*
LENGTH 17 cm (6½ in)
HABITAT Farmland/scrubland
CLUTCH SIZE 4–6

DISTRIBUTION A summer visitor to southern and eastern Europe; absent from Britain, Ireland, and north Scandinavia. Returns to Africa in winter.

ALTHOUGH superficially similar to the Yellowhammer, the Ortolan has an olive-grey head with a yellow eye ring and drooping moustachial stripes. The upperparts are rather dark and heavily streaked. The male has orange-brown underparts. Females are browner than the male with streaked underparts. The male's song has a mournful tone and there are some harsh call notes as well. This is rather a shy bird and it usually migrates at night.

DAMP AREAS The Ortolan often forages on the ground in wetland areas, always on the lookout and frequently flying off.

Pallas's Reed Bunting

FAMILY Emberizidae
SPECIES *Emberiza pallasi*
LENGTH 13–14 cm (5–5½ in)
HABITAT Tundra/birch woodland
CLUTCH SIZE 4–5

DISTRIBUTION A scarce summer visitor to scrubby areas beside tundra rivers and birch and larch forests in far northern Russia and Siberia, migrating to India in winter.

SMALLER THAN the more familiar Reed Bunting (*see* p 365), Pallas's has greyer plumage and a plain underside. In breeding plumage, males have black heads with a white cheek stripe, while females and juveniles are paler brown with streaking on the flanks. Close up, the small bill with a pale lower mandible can be seen. In other respects, the habits are very similar to the Reed Bunting, but the call is more like the House Sparrow.

RARE BUNTING The rather grey appearance and plain underside of Pallas's Reed Bunting help to separate this European rarity from the more common Reed Bunting.

Little Bunting

FAMILY Emberizidae
SPECIES *Emberiza pusilla*
LENGTH 13 cm (5¼ in)
HABITAT Tundra/scrubland
CLUTCH SIZE 4–5

DISTRIBUTION A scarce summer visitor to tundra, taiga, and open forest glades in northern Scandinavia and Russia, with most migrating southeast in winter.

THIS IS A VERY SMALL bunting, with plumage resembling the larger female Common Reed Bunting. In breeding plumage, males have rusty-brown cheeks and a chestnut crown stripe. Females are very similar to the males. In winter, the cheek colours are paler. Males have a short, robin-like song and a sharper alarm note. A regular but scarce visitor to western Europe in autumn with a few remaining to overwinter.

GROUND BIRD
Little Buntings spend most of their time feeding on the ground, eating seeds in autumn, but catching caterpillars in summer.

Rustic Bunting

FAMILY Emberizidae
SPECIES *Emberiza rustica*
LENGTH 14 cm (5¾ in)
HABITAT Swampy forest
CLUTCH SIZE 4–5

DISTRIBUTION A summer visitor to damp, mixed spruce and pine forests or deciduous woodland in northern Scandinavia and Russia.

THE BOLDLY MARKED black-and-white head and the chestnut blotches on the flanks are unique to the male Rustic Bunting in summer; females have a much paler version of the head pattern. In winter, the male loses the dark head markings and becomes much more like a Common Reed Bunting in appearance, but the two white wing bars and pink lower mandible are useful features for identification if the bird is seen in good light.

VARIED DIET Although they are primarily seed-eaters, Rustic Buntings collect caterpillars for their nestlings in summer to provide them with some extra protein.

Common Reed Bunting

FAMILY Emberizidae

SPECIES *Emberiza schoeniculus*

LENGTH 15 cm (6 in)

HABITAT Reedbeds/ streamsides

CLUTCH SIZE 4–5

DISTRIBUTION A widespread resident across southern and western Europe, spreading north into Scandinavia and Russia in summer; some fly to southern Europe and even further south in winter.

BOLD MARKINGS The male Reed Bunting is an easy bird to see in the breeding season when its head markings are at their most striking.

IN THE BREEDING SEASON, the male Common Reed Bunting's charcoal-black head and throat with its white moustachial stripe and white collar is easily spotted as the bird sits out in the open to sing. The upperparts are a rich dark brown, contrasting with the pale underside. Females are plainer brown with streaked flanks, buff stripes on the head, and brown cheeks. Both sexes show white edges to the dark tail when flying away. Reed Buntings are usually found at wetland sites where there are reedbeds or withies to provide some cover, but they are also found in drier habitats at times, such as young plantations. In winter they gather in mixed flocks with other buntings and finches to feed on stubble fields and will also visit garden bird feeders at this time of the year.

COMMON REED BUNTING The Reed Bunting usually conceals its nest low down in thick vegetation; the female incubates the eggs, as her plumage is less conspicuous. Both parents feed the young, mainly on insect larvae.

Corn Bunting

FAMILY Emberizidae
SPECIES *Miliaria calandra*
LENGTH 18 cm (7 in)
HABITAT Farmland
CLUTCH SIZE 4–6

DISTRIBUTION A widespread resident across western Europe, Turkey, the Middle East, and coastal North Africa, but declining in some areas, especially northwest Europe.

THE CORN BUNTING'S cheerful rattling song, rather like a jingling bunch of keys, is a characteristic sound of summer in much of the drier, open farmland of Europe in summer. They sing from low perches, often roadside fences, or sometimes in a short, fluttering flight between perches. Corn Buntings prefer arable land and dry grassland where they can feed on seeds.

The largest and plainest of the buntings is best distinguished by its bulky appearance, large bill, and habit of making short flights with its legs dangling. The sexes are alike, with grey-brown upperparts, and paler streaked flanks and chest. Perched birds sometimes show a darker patch in the centre of the breast. The lower mandible is paler than the upper one.

DECLINE Changes in land use have led to a huge decline in this chunky bunting in the north and west of its range.

Snow Bunting

FAMILY Emberizidae
SPECIES *Plectrophenax nivalis*
LENGTH 17 cm (6½ in)
HABITAT Tundra/coasts
CLUTCH SIZE 4–6

DISTRIBUTION Resident in Iceland, a summer visitor to Scandinavia and northern Russia, and migrates to North Sea coasts and the plains of Russia in winter.

IN SUMMER, THE MALE Snow Bunting's plumage is all black-and-white, but the female has more muted buff and brown colours with a pale underside to provide camouflage when nesting on the ground. Snow Buntings breed in remote, exposed tundra areas or on barren stony mountain tops, but in winter they often gather in flocks on sandy shores, feeding on seeds on the strand line.

ROCK SONG The male Snow Bunting chooses a fairly prominent rock as a perch from which to deliver his pleasant musical song during the breeding season.

Lapland Longspur

FAMILY Emberizidae
SPECIES *Calcarius lapponicus*
LENGTH 15 cm (6 in)
HABITAT Tundra/coasts
CLUTCH SIZE 5–6

DISTRIBUTION A summer visitor to areas of willow scrub and tundra in northern Scandinavia and Russia, migrating to Russian steppes and North Sea coasts in winter.

THE MALE Lapland Longspur resembles a Common Reed Bunting in summer, but the chestnut nape and white eye stripe distinguish it. The females are plainer brown but also have a chestnut nape and yellow bill. Males moult to look more like females in winter, but retain some dark spots on the upper chest. Although a bunting, the name Longspur comes from the long straight hind claw – a difficult feature to observe in the wild. This is a wary bird on its breeding grounds, flying off strongly if disturbed.

NECK COLOUR The chestnut nape of the Lapland Longspur is the best feature for identification in summer as the long hind claw is difficult to see.

USEFUL BOOKS AND REFERENCES

Alderton, David. *The Illustrated Encyclopedia of the Birds of Britain, Europe and Africa*. Lorenz Books, 2004.

Alstrom, Per; Mild, Krister; and Bill Zetterstrom. *Larks, Pipits and Wagtails: An Identification Guide*. Christopher Helm, 1995.

Aulen, G. and Johan M Stenlund. *Where to Watch Birds in Scandinavia*. Hamlyn, 1996.

Beaman, Mark; Madge, Steve; Burn, Hilary et al. *The Handbook of Bird Identification for Europe and the Western Palearctic*. Christopher Helm, 1998.

Bircham, Peter. *A History of Ornithology*. New Naturalist series. Collins, 2007.

Brewer, David. *Wrens, Dippers and Thrashers*. Christopher Helm, 2001.

Brown, Roy; Ferguson, John; Lawrence, Michael; and James Lees. *Tracks and Signs of the Birds of Britain and Europe*. Christopher Helm, 2002.

Burton, Robert. *RSPB Pocket Birdfeeder Guide*. Dorling Kindersley, 2004.

Butler, John R. *Birdwatching on Spain's Southern Coast: Costa Del Sol, Costa De La Luz, Almeria, Donana and Some Inland Sites*. Santana Books, 2004.

Cabot, David. *Irish Birds*. Collins, 2004.

Clement, Peter; Harris, Alan; and John David. *Finches and Sparrows: An Identification Guide*. Christopher Helm, 1999.

Couzens, Dominic and Peter Partington. *The Secret Lives of Garden Birds*. Christopher Helm, 2004.

Cramp, Stanley; Simmons, KEL et al. *Handbook of the Birds of Europe, the Middle East and North Africa. The Birds of the Western Palearctic, vols 1–9*. Oxford University Press, 1978–1994.

Dorst, Jean. *The Life of Birds, vols 1 & 2*. Weidenfeld & Nicolson, 1974.

Dubois, Philippe. *Where to Watch Birds in France*. Christopher Helm, 2006.

Elphick, Jonathan. *RSPB Pocket Birds*. Dorling Kindersley, 2005.

Ferguson-Lees, James and David A Christie. *Raptors of the World*. Christopher Helm, 2001.

Fry, C. Hilary; Fry, Kathie; and Alan Harris. *Kingfishers, Bee-eaters and Rollers*. Christopher Helm, 1992.

Gibbs, David; Barnes, Eustace; and John Cox. *Pigeons and Doves*. Pica Press, 2001.

Golley, Mark; Moss, Stephen; and Dave Daly. *The Complete Garden Bird Book: How To Identify and Attract Birds to Your Garden*. New Holland, 2001.

Harrap, Simon and David Quinn. *Tits, Nuthatches and Treecreepers*. Christopher Helm, 1996.

Hayman, Peter; Marchant, John; and Tony Prater. *Shorebirds*. Christopher Helm, 1986.

Hilmarsson, JO. *Icelandic Bird Guide*. Bay Foreign Language Books, 2000.

Hoyo, Josep del; Elliott, Andrew; and Jordi Sargatal (series' editors). *Handbook of Birds of the World, vols 1–12*. Lynx Edicions. 1992–2007.

Hume, Rob. *RSPB Birds of Britain and Europe*. Dorling Kindersley, 2006.

Jonsson, Lars. *Birds of Europe with North Africa and the Middle East*. Christopher Helm, 2005.

Madders, Mike. *Where to Watch Birds in Scotland*. Christopher Helm, 2002.

Madge, Steve and Hilary Burn. *Wildfowl*. Christopher Helm, 1988.

Madge, Steve and Phil McGowan. *Pheasants, Partridges and Grouse*. Christopher Helm, 2002.

Message, Stephen and Don Taylor. *Waders of Europe, Asia and North America*. Christopher Helm, 2005.

Moss, Stephen. *Collins Gem: Garden Birds*. Collins, 2004.

Ogilvie, Malcolm and Carol. *Flamingos*. Alan Sutton Publishing, 1986.

Olsen, Klaus M and Larson, H. *Gulls of Europe, Asia and North America*. Christopher Helm, 2004.

O'Shea, Brian and John Green. *In Search of Birds in Wales*. Skylark Books, 2000.

Sample, Geoff. *Garden Bird Songs and Calls*. Collins, 2000.

Sterry, Paul. *Birds of the Mediterranean: A Photographic Guide*. Christopher Helm, 2004.

Svensson, Lars; Grant, Peter J. et al. *Collins Birds Guide: The Most Complete Guide to the Birds of Britain and Europe*. Collins, 2001.

Urquhart, Ewan and Adam Bowley. *Stonechats*. Christopher Helm, 2002.

GLOSSARY

B

Breeding plumage The typically more colourful plumage acquired in the case of some species by one or both members of a pair at the start of the breeding season.

C

Carrion Dead animals eaten by some birds, such as vultures.

Cere Unfeathered area incorporating the nostrils above the bill, which is a characteristic of parrots.

Cob A male swan.

Cock Term for the male bird of a species.

Contour feathers The small feathers that cover the surface of the body.

Crown The top of the head.

Cryptic plumage Feathering that serves to disguise the outline of the bird, helping it to blend into its background.

D

Dabbling A term used for ducks that feed at the surface, rather than diving in search of food.

Distribution The typical area where a species occurs, although this may vary at different times of the year.

Diurnal A description applied to those birds of prey that are active during the day, in contrast to others, such as owls, that fly under cover of darkness.

Down The rather fluffy plumage of chicks, also present but less conspicuous in adult birds, serving primarily to insulate the body.

E

Ear coverts The feathers covering the ear orifices, behind the eyes.

Eclipse plumage The feathering that replaces the **breeding plumage**, with the result that over the winter, for example, it may not be possible to distinguish between the sexes in the case of waterfowl.

F

Flanks The sides of the body.

Flight feathers The long feathers running along the back of each wing that allow the bird to fly.

Frugivore A bird that feeds mainly on fruit.

H

Hen Term for the female bird of a species.

I

Insectivore A bird that feeds mainly on invertebrates.

L

Lek A communal display area where **cock** birds of certain species display at the start of the breeding period, in the hope of attracting a mate.

Lores The area between the bill and the eye, on each side of the face.

M

Mantle Area of the back and wings.

Melanistic A bird with darker plumage than normal, thanks to the increased presence of the dark pigment melanin.

Migration The way in which birds may fly from one area to another, depending on the season. Birds that undertake such journeys are called migrants.

Moult The process by which plumage is replaced, typically in the spring and then in the autumn.

N

Nape The back of the neck.

Nidicolous A description of chicks, such as those of passerines, that hatch in a helpless state, and are totally reliant on adult birds for their wellbeing.

Nidifugous A description of chicks of waterfowl, for example, that hatch in an advanced state of development with their eyes open, and are able to move and swim almost immediately afterward.

Nuchal Refers to the neck.

O

Orbital The area of skin around the eye.

P

Passage The route flown by birds on **migration**, along which they may be spotted when resting or feeding.

Pectoral Relating to the breast.

Pen A female swan.

Precocial Equivalent to **nidifugous**.

R

Raptor A general name to describe a bird of prey.

Rump The lower back.

S

Seabird A general description of a species that ranges out over the ocean.

Supercilium Striped area of feathering running above the eyes, as seen in many passerines.

T

Territory An area occupied by one or more birds, which may be defended against potential intruders.

Torpid Inactive, a situation usually

arising in birds from cold temperature combined with a shortage of suitable food.

U

Underparts The underside of the bird's body.

Upperparts The upper area of the bird's body.

V

Vagrant A bird that is present outside its usual area of distribution.

W

Wader A bird that frequents the shoreline.

Webbed feet The skin that links the toes of water birds, acting rather like a paddle and making it easier for them to swim.

Wing bar One or more stripe-like areas of different coloration running across the wing.

Wing coverts The feathers covering the wing.

INDEX OF COMMON NAMES

INDEX OF SCIENTIFIC NAMES

INDEX

ACKNOWLEDGEMENTS

With thanks to the whole team at Studio Cactus, and also the late Stan Bayliss-Smith, author of *Wild Wings to the Northlands* for early inspiration, both as an ornithologist and as a teacher.

Studio Cactus would like to thank Andrew Cleave, MBE, for providing text for the catalogue pages and for his invaluable contribution to the project, and Katrina Cook for additional material. In addition, thanks to Sharon Rudd and Laura Watson for design work; Sharon Cluett for original styling; Jennifer Close and Jo Weeks for editorial work; Penelope Kent for indexing; Robert Walker for picture research; Anthony Duke for range maps; Claire Moore for introductory illustrations; Sharon Rudd for Order silhouettes. Huge thanks to Tim and Joanne at NHPA, and also to those who have helped with additional picture research: Ali Safak of Ozsafak Panson (www.ozsafak.net), Mike Read, Paul and Andrea Kelly, Klaus Malling Olsen, Ole Krogh, Michael Westerbjerg Andersen, Vincent van der Spek, Tim Edelsten, Mike Danzenbaker.

PICTURE CREDITS

The publishers would like to thank the following for permission to reproduce copyright material:

Abbreviations: a = above, b = bottom, c = centre, l = left, r = right, t = top

Carlos Arranz 17 (br), 52–53; Marilyn Barbone 344–345; Nigel Bean/Nature Picture Library 305 (b); Bob Blanchard 383; Mike Danzenbaker 34 (t), 169 (b), 295 (b); easyshoot 18 (br); Tim Edelsten 203 (b); Getty Images 176; Hanne and Jens Eriksen/ Nature Picture Library 220, 281 (b); FLPA/Neil Bowman 317 (b); FLPA/Robin Chittenden 297 (b); Karel Gallas 18 (blc), 384; A Greensmith/ardea.com 358 (b); Gertjan Hooijer 156–157, 254–255; Gail Johnson 232–233; Kerioak – Christine Nichols 15 (b); Klaus Malling Olsen 293 (t), 358 (t); Markus Varesvuo/ Nature Picture Library 236 (b); Konstantin Mikhailov/Nature Picture Library 120 (t); Erin Monn 18 (brc); Christian Musat 16 (b), 371; Nature Photographers Ltd/Mark Bolton 37 (t); Nature Photographers Ltd/Michael Gore 123 (t); Nature Photographers Ltd/Paul Sterry 26 (l), 39, 143 (b), 152 (t), 240 (b), 243 (r), 256 (t), 258 (b), 265, 268 (r), 270 (t), 298 (b), 318 (b), 320 (b), 321, 322 (b), 324 (t), 359 (b), 364 (t); Nature Photographers Ltd/ Roger Tidman 222 (l), 223 (b), 363 (b); pasphotography 18 (bl); Ed Phillips 18 (bc); Photo Request 373; Photolibrary Group 171 (b), 207, 124 (b); RF Porter/ardea.com 360 (t); Mike Read (2006) www.mikeread.co.uk 318 (t); George Reszeter/ardea. com 242 (b), 293 (b); SouWest Photography 18 (crc); Peter Steyn/ardea.com 128 (l); Rick Thornton 380; Graham Tomlin 210–211; Z Tunka/ardea.com 280 (t); Joanna Van Gruisen/ ardea.com 260 (b); Jason Vandehey 18 (cc); M Watson/ardea. com 335 (t); Michael Westerbjerg Andersen 311 (t); Workmans Photo 18 (cr); Andy Z 18 (clc); Serg Zastavkin 121. All other images © NHPA
Cover images all © NHPA